Lawrence Davis

review copy

SCIENCE, FICTION, AND THE *FIN-DE-SIÈCLE* PERIODICAL PRESS

In this revisionary study, Will Tattersdill argues against the reductive 'two cultures' model of intellectual discourse by exploring the cultural interactions between literature and science embodied in late nineteenth-century periodical literature, tracing the emergence of the new genre that would become known as 'science fiction'. He examines a range of fictional and non-fictional *fin-de-siècle* writing around distinct scientific themes: Martian communication, future prediction, X-rays, and polar exploration. Each chapter explores a major work of H. G. Wells, but also presents a wealth of exciting new material drawn from a variety of late Victorian periodicals. Arguing that the publications in which they appeared, as well as the stories themselves, played a crucial part in the development of science fiction, Tattersdill uses the form of the general interest magazine as a way of understanding both the relationship between the arts and the sciences and the creation of a new literary genre.

WILL TATTERSDILL is Lecturer in Victorian Literature at the University of Birmingham.

CAMBRIDGE STUDIES IN NINETEENTH-CENTURY LITERATURE AND CULTURE

General editor
Gillian Beer, *University of Cambridge*

Editorial board
Isobel Armstrong, *Birkbeck, University of London*
Kate Flint, *University of Southern California*
Catherine Gallagher, *University of California, Berkeley*
D. A. Miller, *University of California, Berkeley*
J. Hillis Miller, *University of California, Irvine*
Daniel Pick, *Birkbeck, University of London*
Mary Poovey, *New York University*
Sally Shuttleworth, *University of Oxford*
Herbert Tucker, *University of Virginia*

Nineteenth-century British literature and culture have been rich fields for interdisciplinary studies. Since the turn of the twentieth century, scholars and critics have tracked the intersections and tensions between Victorian literature and the visual arts, politics, social organization, economic life, technical innovations, scientific thought – in short, culture in its broadest sense. In recent years, theoretical challenges and historiographical shifts have unsettled the assumptions of previous scholarly synthesis and called into question the terms of older debates. Whereas the tendency in much past literary critical interpretation was to use the metaphor of culture as 'background', feminist, Foucauldian, and other analyses have employed more dynamic models that raise questions of power and of circulation. Such developments have reanimated the field. This series aims to accommodate and promote the most interesting work being undertaken on the frontiers of the field of nineteenth-century literary studies: work which intersects fruitfully with other fields of study such as history, or literary theory, or the history of science. Comparative as well as interdisciplinary approaches are welcomed.

A complete list of titles published will be found at the end of the book.

SCIENCE, FICTION, AND THE *FIN-DE-SIÈCLE* PERIODICAL PRESS

WILL TATTERSDILL

University of Birmingham

CAMBRIDGE
UNIVERSITY PRESS

CAMBRIDGE
UNIVERSITY PRESS

University Printing House, Cambridge CB2 8BS, United Kingdom

Cambridge University Press is part of the University of Cambridge.

It furthers the University's mission by disseminating knowledge in the pursuit of
education, learning and research at the highest international levels of excellence.

www.cambridge.org
Information on this title: www.cambridge.org/9781107144651

© Will Tattersdill 2016

First published 2016

Printed in the United Kingdom by Clays, St Ives plc

A catalogue record for this publication is available from the British Library

Library of Congress Cataloguing in Publication Data
Names: Tattersdill, Will, author.
Title: Science, fiction, and the fin-de-siècle periodical press / Will Tattersdill.
Description: Cambridge ; New York : Cambridge University Press, 2016. |
Series: Cambridge studies in nineteenth-century literature and culture ; 105 |
Includes bibliographical references and index.
Identifiers: LCCN 2015042015 | ISBN 9781107144651 (Hardback)
Subjects: LCSH: English periodicals–History–19th century. | Serialized fiction–Great
Britain–History and criticism. | Wells, H. G. (Herbert George), 1866–1946–Criticism
and interpretation. | Popular culture–England–History–19th century.
Classification: LCC PN5124.P4 T38 2016 | DDC 052.09/034–dc23
LC record available at http://lccn.loc.gov/2015042015

ISBN 978-1-107-14465-1 Hardback

Contents

v

Illustrations

Acknowledgements

This book exists because of my parents, to whom it is dedicated. I don't just mean that they have been an unfailing source of emotional support without which this book could not have been written, although goodness knows that is true. I also mean that the realities of academic life in the United Kingdom practically close off the profession to anybody who does not have someone else both willing and able to pay the bills for a while. Currently, doctoral graduates are all but required to be out of paid work for at least a year while they revise, publish, and look for jobs (for many, it is much longer). In my case, I was able to move back into my teenage bedroom during this period. I was fed and kept warm and safe, and I was permitted the space and time to find work. It was embarrassing and it was stressful; it was an enormous privilege, and I am one of the very lucky few. Young scholars less fortunate in their circumstances are increasingly being pushed out of academia, their work correspondingly unlikely to find print. You will have your own opinion on the desirability of a university system staffed exclusively by those from affluent backgrounds.

This book is also indebted to the considerable feedback, support, and forbearance of Mark Turner, Jim Mussell, Roger Luckhurst, Ralph O'Connor, Clare Pettitt, Pat Palmer, Josephine McDonagh, Rebecca N. Mitchell, Valerie Rumbold, and Deborah Longworth. Thanks, too, to Natasha McEnroe and Subhadra Das at the Galton Archive (University College London); to Kate Lancaster of the Rutherford Appleton Laboratory; to Linda Bree and Anna Bond of Cambridge University Press; and to Shane McCorristine of the Scott Polar Research Institute. Mike Ashley deserves a particular mention for his encouragement and enthusiasm.

Through the Arts and Humanities Research Council's 'Theories and Methods in Literature, Science, and Medicine' programme I met an entire scholarly community – too many people to name here – whose work and conversation shaped the present volume. That programme was run by Sharon Ruston, to whom I'm forever grateful; it led me to the British

Society for Literature and Science, among whose members John Holmes, Martin Willis, Rachel Crossland, Michael Whitworth, and Charlotte Sleigh are only the most immediate of a large number of scholars who have helped and supported me in this work.

I'm also indebted to the friends I found at King's College London: Mary L. Shannon, Maria Damkjær, Megan Murray-Pepper, Camilla Mount, Brian Murray, Hannah August, Jennifer W. Lo, Susie Christensen, Tullia Giersberg, Ali Wood, Mary Henes, Chisomo Kalinga, and in particular (and of course) Jordan and Ivy Kistler. A problem I have is that I tend to go on a bit, especially when excited: these people have tolerated this weakness, were frequently the cause of it, and sometimes even joined in.

Two anonymous readers provided generous reports on the manuscript, and I hope I've done justice to their comments in the final draft. I received invaluable support and advice over a period of several years from Liz McCarthy and Ernesto Gomez at the Bodleian Library, Oxford, and have also to thank Martin Killeen and Catherine Martin (Cadbury Research Library, Birmingham), Adreinne Sharpe (Beinecke Library, Yale), and the staff of Senate House Library, University of London. A section of Chapter 2 and some of the content of the introduction have also seen print in articles published in the *Victorian Periodicals Review* (46:4, Winter 2013) and *Textual Practice* (31:3, due in 2017) – I'd like to thank Alexis Easley and Peter Boxall respectively for their kindness and help in editing that material, and for their permission to rehearse its arguments in these pages. Thanks, too, to the College of Arts and Law at the University of Birmingham, whose research fund covered part of the cost of illustrating this book.

Adam Ferner, Matt Sangster, and Jon Day provided much informal friendship, advice, and inspiration. Finally, I must mention two Sarahs: without tactical prodding from Sarah Galletly, I would never have started this work; without general support and tolerance from Sarah Crofton, I would never have finished it. Thank you to you both.

I've definitely forgotten somebody. Nobody could argue that academia lacks an abundance of warm, intelligent, generous, and above all interesting people, and it has been a privilege to be able to think with a few of them over these last years. Long may they remain.

Introduction
Material entanglements

Reading the general magazines of the *fin de siècle* is enormously good fun. There's a reason, and the reason is important: virtually anything could be over the next page, be it a report from a war artist, some photographs of cats, or the latest adventure from Arthur Conan Doyle. In the 1890s, a cohort of new monthlies had arisen to answer an increasing commercial appetite for curiosities of all kinds, taking advantage of recent developments in printing and distribution technology and depending for their success on high sales to a wide audience. These publications – Mike Ashley loosely designates them 'Standard Illustrated Popular Magazines' – created the precedents for the next century of popular fiction, and it is chiefly because of their fiction that we return to them: Sherlock Holmes, Captain Kettle, and the various creations of H. G. Wells all found their audiences through this periodical press.[1] But although their effect on fiction has been enormous and lasting, they also contained important contributions to non-fiction and journalism. They are endlessly exciting because the next item might equally be a horror or romance tale, a nautical adventure, a detective story; or it could be an interview, an opinion piece, political commentary, or popular science. This mix of genres, together with the formal framework which made them cohere in spite of their differences, was at the heart of the publishing strategy of illustrated magazines, and of their commercial success. It is also at the heart of this book.

In many respects, what follows is a glimpse at the early life of science fiction (SF), a genre whose history is closely intertwined with the illustrated magazines of the *fin de siècle* (even though its name would not be coined until decades later).[2] But the first comma in this book's title is there on purpose. Science and fiction appeared together, separately, in the pages of these magazines, and my principal argument is that their material proximity was one of the things which allowed SF to thrive and eventually gain its own dedicated publications, becoming a fully-fledged genre in its own right. In other words, I regard the magazines not only as a significant archive of early SF works, an uncontroversial position since at least Sam Moskowitz's *Science Fiction by Gaslight* (1968), but also as a physical form whose key features – temporality, repeatability, and above all breadth of authorship and subject matter – made them active agents in the rise of SF as a commercial entity.

In a study of this kind, far more than simply the history of genre-SF is in play. To recognise that SF was to some extent produced by the co-presence of discourses in Standard Illustrated Popular Magazines is to recognise that, in the right conditions, there can be a fertile dynamic between voices – "science" and "fiction" – traditionally regarded as estranged from one another. Understanding this has important implications for the wider study of the relationship between literature and science. Reading the magazines with an eye on genre, on the various discourses and types of writing which coalesced in each issue, we can therefore recover all kinds of interchanges which are lost when we isolate individual stories or articles from the vessel in which they originally reached the public. Literature and science, considered as generic voices present amidst a host of others, were everywhere materially entangled in the magazines, literally bound together.[3] These publications therefore offer those interested in what is sometimes called the "Two Culture divide" a unique lens on the history of the taxonomy of knowledge. More, though: just as they present the student of SF with more than a simply historical insight, periodicals provide an important *formal* opportunity to re-imagine the literature-science relationship in a more vivid, less divisive manner.

This reconciliation, capturing the complexity of the cultural interchanges between literature and science and resisting the straightforward binary opposition which springs so easily to most of us, is the end goal of this book. My principal methodological conceit is to treat types of popular writing (eg. thriller/adventure/SF) and types of knowledge or inquiry (eg. literature/ science) equally as genres, understanding them and the mechanisms which govern them as broadly analogous and scrutinising each through the lenses of genre theory and Bruno Latour's notion of "enrolment". Most importantly, I trace them all as strands which run through the harmonising vessel of the general magazine. The eclecticism which makes these magazines so enjoyable was the reason for their considerable success in their own time, but it also remains a formidable metaphorical apparatus for understanding the history and mechanics of genre demarcation. They are fun to read, in short, for the same reason that they challenge the habits which govern our preconceptions of writing, knowledge, and thought.

Dyadic division

> The rigid divisions between disciplines, the lack of mutual comprehension, the misplaced feelings of superiority or disdain in different professional groups – these should be seen as *problems*, not fatalistically accepted as part of the immutable order of things.[4]

Stefan Collini describes the disciplinary map of the academy as it stands today: not only sharply divided but divided into opposites, each subject incapable of bearing on any but its closest neighbours. Moreover, Collini points out that such divisions are conceived so as to appear *inherent*. There is no incentive to solve a problem which arises from a disjunction between two disciplines, since these disciplines will always inevitably be irreconcilable – to draw attention to this is simply to comment on "the way things are".

In fact, a glance through history (or a moment's abstract thought) is enough to tell us that there is little which is essential about the barriers between fields of learning at all – indeed, that what may be said to legitimately constitute "literature" or "science" (say) is constantly up for renegotiation. It is a strength of both "sides" that there is no one coherent activity called literature, no one coherent activity called science; that they are diffuse categories capable of adaptation and evolution. This book is based upon the idea that the barriers *between* disciplines are as mutable, as subject to historical forces, as the disciplines themselves. Like literary and subliterary genres, disciplines are constantly-shifting entities, born out of culture rather than imposed upon it. This is not the same as saying that they are meaningless. On the contrary, specialisation has been a crucial tool for both sciences and arts in their rapid developments over the past century. The trouble comes, I suggest, when we forget that our current taxonomy of knowledge is constructed and has a history. Such amnesia encourages not only division, but the assumption that division is inevitable; under such a conception, we no longer make an effort to understand one another.

As the go-to example of this kind of division, the opposition between literature and science has a long history, from at least F. R. Leavis's exchanges with C. P. Snow in the early 1960s to what Bruno Latour calls the 'no-man's land' across which the science wars of the 1990s were fought.[5] Conflicts like these, and the reductive language they necessitate, pass damaging stereotypes into the popular consciousness. Both the sciences and humanities in Britain currently face ministerial scepticism about relevance; both are turning increasingly to the language of "impact" to defend themselves, justifying their activities as an economic investment rather than in terms of the pursuit of understanding. This failure to convince the public of the value of education and research is partly attributable to the commonplace that both literature and science operate in ways which are somehow too abstracted from "the real world", an impression which episodes like the science wars do little to dispel: a *Times Higher* report published in April 2015, to take just one example, proposes a direct link between the perception that universities are disconnected from reality and governmental unwillingness to spend money on them.[6] This negative perception of universities, though it has damaging consequences, nevertheless constitutes a problem shared variously by the whole academy – literature, sciences, and beyond – and arguably presents an incentive for renewed cooperation between the warring tribes lamented by Snow.

How can the popular magazines of the *fin de siècle* – niche material, I am bound to admit – help us to think about this enormous and important subject? Two of their core characteristics bring them to bear in a particularly useful way. Firstly, there is the very explicit fact of their popularity. In the pages of the Standard Illustrated Popular Magazines, one reads not a dry, philosophical encounter between literature and science but rather sees them both as active agents within popular culture, within the 'public sphere' whose constant changes, Habermas tells us, are contingent on the shifting 'relations between author, work, and public'.[7] It is before the public that literature and science become most thoroughly intertwined, and, in a democracy, it is there that conversations about how they should be resourced are the most influential. Present-day exchanges on this subject are frequently articulated in the mass media, a fact which, as Ben Goldacre has powerfully observed, substantially contributes to their character.[8] It is therefore important to study not only the abstract, conceptual relationships between the disciplines but the ways in which those relationships are shaped and circulated in the press. Such an enquiry benefits hugely from an awareness that these relationships have historical roots, and this is an important contribution which Periodical Studies can make: 'causes, effects, needs, and strategies', as Richard Ohmann writes, 'show themselves more plainly in times of rapid emergence than in times of elaboration and refinement'.[9]

The second characteristic is one to which I have already alluded: general magazines were an inherently inclusive medium. To expand on this point, which is vital for all that follows, it is worth describing these publications in a little more detail. Although I draw on work from Periodical Studies which has explored the potential of many different kinds of newspaper and magazine, and although I have tried to keep wider media culture in mind throughout, for the most part my focus in this book is particularly on general magazines of between roughly 1891 and 1905 – claims I make about "the magazines", whilst hopefully carrying force in other areas of Periodical Studies, on the whole refer only to this group.[10] Ashley's term 'Standard Illustrated Popular Magazine' is too cumbersome to use fluently throughout an argument of this length, but it is nevertheless well-chosen. It describes a kind of periodical which thrived after 1891 due to both rapid technological improvements and the (far from unrelated) rise to prominence of a new species of popularist journalism. This was a period during which scientific innovations which were to have enduring and significant effects on culture appeared (or became accessible or affordable) at a dizzying rate: the light bulb, bicycle, telephone, telegraph, motor car, and aeroplane are only the most obvious examples. Standard Illustrated Popular Magazines reported on and conveyed these developments to the public, profiting from an enthusiasm for the new – but they also incorporated some of them into their fabric, taking advantage of the improved printing, reproduction, typesetting, communication, advertising, and distribution technologies which helped to characterise the encroaching modernity. The first and most successful of these monthly publications was George Newnes's *Strand* (January 1891–March 1950). Still probably the most famous magazine of its day, in large part due to the early coup it obtained in acquiring the Sherlock Holmes stories, it inspired numerous imitators and ushered in a period during which magazines were particularly influential in the development of fiction.[11] Publications which followed the *Strand*'s model included *The Idler* (February 1892–March 1911), *Pearson's Magazine* (January 1896–November 1939), *The Windsor Magazine* (January 1895–September 1939), *The Royal Magazine* (November 1898–November 1930), and the *Harmsworth Monthly Pictorial Magazine* (later *Harmsworth Magazine*, later still *Harmsworth London Magazine*, and finally *London Magazine*, July 1898–May 1933).[12] As might be expected from publications following the same leader, these magazines had numerous traits in common: David Reed observes that '[t]o open one at random among a group would be to risk difficulties of identification. Only a look at their contents demonstrates the real differences'.[13]

What they particularly shared, then, were their physical characteristics, which Ashley summarises as follows:

> The magazines in question were 'standard' in size and format – about 170mm wide by 250mm tall, with spines and fore-and-aft advertising

sections. They were copiously 'illustrated' with line drawings or engravings, and soon with photographs, and it was in order to provide space for their illustrative matter that such magazines adopted the standard format in the first place (a size somewhat larger than the various book-like octavo formats which the majority of sparsely illustrated Victorian fiction magazines had clung to). And they were 'popular' – that is to say, they were popularly priced in order to reach a mass audience, the rapid growth of which would greatly fuel advertising revenues.[14]

This last point is the most crucial for our purposes, for it was that aspiration towards enormous audiences (the *Strand*'s monthly circulation was around 300,000 throughout the mid-1890s) which placed eclecticism squarely at the heart of the New Journalism's mission.[15] That phrase, 'New Journalism' had been coined pejoratively in 1887 by Matthew Arnold. In the same breath he had derided it as *'feather-brained'*, but its magpieish tendencies concealed a publication strategy which was extremely deliberate and successful.[16] It sprang from a determination to exploit an audience of "busy" readers with new levels of disposable income who exhibited a preference for breadth over depth.[17] Standard Illustrated Popular Magazines based their appeal expressly on variety, a strategy mirrored in their adoption of the latest print technology. The super-calendered paper on which they were printed – rolled between sets of cylinders to make it smoother, thinner, and glossier than the stuff of previous periodicals – allowed an unprecedented volume and quality of illustration as well as making white space an affordable and striking extravagance. Newnes, who had pioneered some important New Journalist ideas in the pages of his scissors-and-paste review *Tit-Bits* (October 1881–July 1984), famously aimed to have an image on every page of the *Strand*, creating a visual as well as a textual cornucopia for his readers.

A quick examination of a *Strand* contents page chosen more or less at random (Fig 0.1) will testify to the diversity of content which was to make Newnes and his competitors commercially sustainable. This issue, which is from June 1898, opens with 'The Beetle-Hunter', the first in Arthur Conan Doyle's new series of tales *Round the Fire*. This adventure is neither as realistic as Walter Wood's tale of 'A North Sea Rescue', nor as fantastical as Cutcliffe Hyne's 'The Lizard', both of which are also reprinted here. The sixth instalment in L. T. Meade's continuing series *The Brotherhood of the Seven Kings*, co-written with the physician Robert Eustace, adds to the adventure element, but there is much else on offer: an illustrated interview with Jan van Beers, an article about different forms of pictorial handwriting, a fictionalised tale of Nelson's youthful indiscretions, and a short piece

THE STRAND MAGAZINE.

Contents for June, 1898.

FRONTISPIECE: "I SPRANG TO THE RESCUE."

MSS. and Drawings must be submitted at the owner's risk, and the Editor will not guarantee their safety, though when stamps are inclosed he will endeavour to return them. MSS. should be typewritten.

THE STRAND MAGAZINE, including Double Numbers, will be forwarded direct from the Offices of George Newnes, Ltd., to any part of the world, post free, for one year, on receipt of 10s. Cases for binding any volume of THE STRAND MAGAZINE may be obtained to order from Booksellers for 1s., or post free for 1s. 3d., direct from the Offices.

0.1 A contents page for *The Strand Magazine* (June 1898). Courtesy of the Bodleian Libraries, The University of Oxford.

of popular physics, F. M. Gilbert's 'What Makes a Cricket Ball Curve in the Air?'. A photographic feature shows two children modelling various stages of the 'Jack and Jill' nursery rhyme; it comes just a few pages after pictures of the new submarine boat being tested in Baltimore. All of these items, and the many others in the issue, successfully cohere in the genre of "general magazine" precisely because the other genres they evoke are so miscellaneous. As Reed succinctly puts it, publications like this were 'heavily dependent on fiction and a broad range of topics that counter-pointed one another to generate sufficient sales'.[18] Aimed at whole families, their feather-brainedness was predicated not on the scattiness of one implied reader, but on the passing, general interest of thousands.[19] Data on readership is hard to come by, and this book focusses on publications rather than readers' responses to them, but given the fifty-nine–year success story of *The Strand* and the number of imitators it immediately generated it seems fair to say that the strategy was a successful one.

The two key characteristics upon which I've alighted, then – popularity and inclusivity – are closely related to each other. General magazines had an emphasis on commercial success which required them to address readers in a range of different voices. They therefore cultivated corporate identities based precisely on multiplicity, and this is what makes them so important from a literature and science perspective. As Mark W. Turner has argued, 'Periodicals, by nature collectives of different voices, require that some notion of plurality be accepted in critical interpretation'.[20] The idea of plurality might remind us of the way in which Mikhail Bakhtin understood the novel, as a genre characterised by its dialogic function, its 'heteroglossia', its awareness that 'language, when it *means*, is somebody talking to somebody else, even when that someone else is one's own inner addressee'.[21] Bakhtin's notion of the novel is not limited to the volumes of prose with which we commonly associate the term after Defoe and Richardson. For him, the novel encompasses a thread of rebellious discur-siveness which can be traced back at least as far as Ancient Greece.[22] It is certainly legitimate to include the contents of these periodicals in this conception, for each of their constituent items is not only explicitly in dialogue with itself but implicitly in dialogue with its neighbours, a fact emphasised by the physical object which binds them together, foreground-ing their harmonies and holding their contradictions in suspension. Periodicals which contain elements of both literature and science therefore necessarily contain a discourse between them (probably more than one), and retracing these discourses can create a nuanced picture of their historical interactions.

Before going any further, it is worth pausing over a possible objection to this crucial part of my argument. Are articles in general magazines really in dialogue with each other? The processes of their composition by many authors and consumption by an enormous range of different readers (very few of whom, it can be safely supposed, read every word in order, or at all) superficially offers tumult rather than the harmonies of which I have been speaking. Indeed, "tumult" has been the classic objection to the New Journalism ever since Matthew Arnold first lamented its arrival. Copy for issues of these magazines was submitted roughly a month before the publication date and, except in especially closed circles, contributors would not be aware what pieces were to accompany theirs in print. Surely, then, they could not participate in a discussion with them either knowingly or unknowingly? In the course of his application of Bakhtinian principles to the periodicals of the 1850s and 60s, Dallas Liddle puts this point well:

> Many separate monologic discourses collected in a single issue of a period-ical cannot constitute Bakhtin's dialogized heteroglossia, but can only be a site where monologic discourse is multiplied.[23]

The important thing set aside by Liddle here is that texts need not directly reference each other in order for their *genres* to be in dialogue. Precisely because they self-consciously exist in a series-oriented commercial econ-omy of types – because they are popular rather than capital-L literary – the individual pieces in Standard Illustrated Popular Magazines are more than capable of, indeed, *inevitably must*, respond to the other discourses to which they are physically appended. 'All texts', as John Frow points out, 'are shaped by the repetition and transformation of other textual struc-tures'.[24] Individual items may not consciously react to each other, their authors may not even be aware of each other, but all are motivated by an appeal to general interest which compels a cross-genre engagement with enduring preoccupations of the day. It may be useful to think of Benedict Anderson's well-known characterisation of the act of reading a newspaper here:

> It is performed in silent privacy, in the lair of the skull. Yet each communi-cant is well aware that the ceremony he performs is being replicated simultaneously by thousands (or millions) of others of whose existence he is confident, yet of whose identity he has not the slightest notion.[25]

The imagined communities of magazine readers create and reinterpret genres just as the imagined communities of countries create and reinterpret nations. Of these two processes, the periodical is both the enabler and the archivist.

It is also worth remembering that magazine issues, however isolated their individual contents, were still mitigated by the organising power of the editor, a power which, Reed notes, 'cannot be discussed as though editors were autonomous men who conducted themselves with the freedom of authors'.[26] These magazines were commercial concerns, and their low-cost, high-sales business model incentivised editors to commission pieces of all kinds which engaged with current societal preoccupations. Four such themes, four scientific subjects much in the public eye at the *fin de siècle*, form the bases for the chapters of this book (I will outline them in a few moments). In tracing the way they move across the periodicals, I uncover exchanges and collaborations between generic structures far more frequently than direct lines of influence between individual items.[27]

It seems to me that Liddle's point would be conclusively dismissed if we could find evidence that contact between genres in the discursive format of the periodical had indeed been a factor in the emergence of new, hybrid forms of writing; if the magazine itself had a traceable effect on the transformation of the genre economy. With this in mind, and with notions of genre interrelation increasingly at the heart of our view of the relationship between science and fiction, it is time to return to SF – and to take a brief detour into the 1920s.

Enrolling science fiction

The study of contemporary writing from outside the 'élite' tradition brings us closer, perhaps, than does the study of acknowledged modern masters to the process by which a literary heritage is constituted, and to the way in which it changes.[28]

The first articulation of what would become genre science fiction was an exercise in magazine publishing, not one in fiction or criticism: the April 1926 appearance of the American monthly *Amazing Stories*. Its editor, Hugo Gernsback, was carving out a niche in the print market as much as in the world of fiction when he proposed, in the first sentences of his opening editorial, 'something that has never been done before', a magazine which was fundamentally different from 'the several hundreds now being published' and which '[t]herefore [. . .] deserves your attention and interest'.[29] Frequently quoted as Gernsback's manifesto for the genre, this editorial sets up a perimeter around a certain kind of writing, arguing for its coherence explicitly within the commercial field of the magazine. But though *Amazing Stories* was the first magazine in English to print *solely* SF, or 'scientifiction' as it was at first labelled, Gernsback's claim that it represented something 'entirely new' (p. 3) may justly be treated with incredulity. Every one of the six items in the first issue of *Amazing Stories* had been printed before. The oldest, Edgar Allan Poe's 'The Facts in the Case of Mr. Valdemar' (*American Magazine and Broadway Journal*, December 1845), was over eighty when *Amazing Stories* appeared, and even the most recent, G. Peyton Wertenbaker's 'The Man From the Atom', had been published more than two and a half years previously (*Science and Invention*, August 1923). With the exception of Jules Verne's novel *Off on a Comet* (1877), the first instalment of which Gernsback reprinted in translation as his opening item, the contents of *Amazing Stories* #1 had all made their débuts in earlier, more general periodicals.

Gernsback's innovation, then, was about arrangement rather than content. In editing his first issues, he was composing a canon for science fiction, drawing the map of his new genre not with a tightly-worded definition or by offering a platonic holotype for future writing, but by grouping a selection of pre-existing stories under one label – Patrick Parrinder has described this as a 'shrewdly commercial reprint policy'.[30] The important point is that the magazine itself provided this re-labelling capacity as well as the actual stories, to say nothing of the dialogic potential of the letters page through which Gernsback nurtured the first generation of SF fans.[31] Instinctively or otherwise, Gernsback had understood that 'magazine fiction and science fiction arose at the same time and were allowed to develop together', that there was a simpatico between form and content.[32] Ashley concludes that *Amazing Stories*'s 'appearance was neither sudden nor a surprise, but the inevitable result of years of development of science fiction in the popular magazines' (p. 44). Likewise, Sam Moskowitz argues that a 'golden age' in pre-*Amazing* science fiction was precipitated by the availability of 'mass-circulation, quality middle-class general' magazines in the 1890s and 1900s.[33] But though science fiction thrived in those general magazines, it could not be separated from them until Gernsback's periodical had shaped perceptions of the genre's independent existence. Although there were certain conventions on how they presented different types of material which could be picked up on by regular readers, no overt labelling capacity had existed within or between Standard Illustrated Popular Magazines to distinguish kinds of fiction from each other, or from factual content; even individual authors frequently wrote in several different registers. For all Gernsback's talk, then, the real novelty presented by *Amazing Stories* concerned demarcation rather than invention. By offering a periodical rather than a formal definition of science fiction, it segregated a single strand of the general magazine's inclusive contents page for literary and commercial development.

This fact goes some way towards explaining not only why it took until the late 1920s for an organised idea of "science fiction" to appear (print technology and size of potential readership being important factors in the emergence of niche periodicals), but also the ease with which we now apply that term to the work of authors writing much earlier, authors who would likely have had difficulty identifying themselves or their writing either with each other or with Gernsback's stated project. Addressing the anachronism inherent in referring to these authors and works as anything approaching a coherent group, Mark Bould and Sherryl Vint make the point that '[s]uch fiction could only retrospectively become SF once the idea of the genre was established, while the idea of the genre could only come into being because such fiction existed'.[34] Bould and Vint evoke Bruno Latour's notion of 'translation', seeing SF 'as an ongoing process rather than a fixed entity' and examining it 'in terms of shifting, rhizomatic networks of connection and the building of collectives' (pp. x, 4). Gernsback's articulation of SF perhaps bears similarities to Latour's example of Pasteur working in his laboratory, his germ theory outpacing Pouchet's spontaneous generation as an explanation of the world not because of its greater insight but because it was able to form the most numerous and convincing connections between a series of human and nonhuman actants.[35] Like Pasteur, Gernsback forms an assembly of actants sufficiently persuasive that the model is eventually held to be true even of the time before it was propounded.

Of all Latour's important work on the cultural dimensions of science, the idea I have found most useful for this book is that of 'enrolment', the term with which he describes the work done by humans and nonhumans in the composition of scientific facts. Bould and Vint argue convincingly that this notion can equally be used to understand the emergence of popular literary genres, SF in particular.[36] Gernsback's publishing enterprise depended on coercing pre-existing texts which were not necessarily similar to each other into his unitary project. His three keystone authors – Edgar Allan Poe, Jules Verne, and H. G. Wells – had little in common before Gernsback performed his enrolment work in the 1920s, as Bould and Vint make clear in the early pages of their *Concise History of Science Fiction*.[37] But important though Gernsback was in this process, Latour also stresses that it takes groups of actants working together (deliberately or otherwise) to create new assemblages. The articulation of SF required the participation of numerous human and nonhuman agents, and its further development into contemporary SF, which generally finds little in common with Gernsback's didactic vision, required the activity of still more.[38] On this list we may include other important editorial figures (such as John Campbell), the writers who rose to prominence under their stewardship (such as Isaac Asimov and Robert A. Heinlein), and the readers whose feedback shaped their discursive communities. But we may also consider the networks between them and, most importantly for my purposes, the nonhuman elements which shored them up. Such a conception of the enrolment of SF necessarily understands the magazine itself as *active* in the process, an enabling agent as well as a source of *a priori* material, one which was in turn altered and shaped by the new genres it was shepherding into existence.

Readers have, on the whole, lost the sense of the magazine's importance in SF's history.[39] There are a number of possible reasons for this, including the ephemeral status of magazines as opposed to books, SF criticism's frequent desire to disassociate itself from the demotic fiction of the pulps, and the oppositional twentieth-century construction of 'literature' which draws attention away from periodicals in general and which is Laurel Brake's topic in *Subjugated Knowledges*.[40] However, our diminished appreciation of the magazine as a format for early SF is also testimony to Gernsback's success in making the genre something now widely perceived as an *innate* category of fiction. By the very fact of its ephemerality, the periodical collaborates with enrolment by de-emphasising, after the event, the work done.[41] Geoffrey C. Bowker and Susan Leigh Star, writing that the most successful infrastructures are those which become invisible, point out that 'there is a lot of hard labor in effortless ease'.[42] To put it another way, each issue of a magazine is implicitly superseded by its successor, whereas printed volumes are designed to endure over time, carrying with them the impression of an immutable, pre-existing genre. Today, SF has its own dedicated publishers, shelves in bookshops, and academic journals. Our tendency is to think of it as essential rather than composed. When we do this, to adapt Gillian Beer's synopsis of Darwin's impact on culture, we pay Gernsback the homage of our assumptions.[43] I have found it useful to think of a large public building when trying to understand this process: more obviously a whole, discrete object with the scaffolding removed, it is nonetheless easier to investigate details of its construction (and to remember that it is, after all, constructed) if the scaffolding is still there.

Perhaps this sounds abstract. It is important to remember that the consequences are extremely tangible. Considered broadly, SF is now an industry spanning a range of media from literature to video games to fine art, incorporating subversive niche practitioners and Hollywood block-busters. It has provided livelihoods for generations of artists, writers, and directors and, of course, publishers, producers, and executives. Gollancz's *Encyclopedia of Science Fiction* is now published online, since few book-shelves (or purses) could support its 4.9 million words.[44] Like all genres, SF exists *because* we assume it does: opinions vary widely as to how it should be defined, but it would be impossible to deny that the endeavour to define it has had real-world consequences. Latour's conception of enrolment connects the esoteric to the concrete in a network of actants which collude to create reality – he is keen to distance himself from postmodernist assertions that the world is not real, that there are no facts. He has been criticised for calling science 'fabricated', but insists that those who interpret this as meaning he believes it to be detached from reality have misunderstood.[45] Science, in his argument (and this argument is easily extended to SF), is only 'fabricated' in the same way a chair is: it is the product of conscious invention, but you can still sit on it. Anderson, too, draws attention to the difference between 'fabrication' and 'imagining' as interpretations of the word 'invention' when he seeks to understand the historical processes which gave rise to nations as collectively invented entities.[46] Anderson's nations and Latour's science are discursively emergent rather than historically inevitable constructs – as is Habermas's public sphere. My contention is that we can see magazines as playing a crucial role in all three analogous processes, as well as adding a fourth to the list - genre.

Periodicals, then, not only had a crucial formal role in the emergence of SF and the enrolment of its corpus, but also conspired to subdue evidence of that process after the fact, enabling the perception that SF is a discrete and essential entity. With the periodical's help, it becomes easier to assume that SF is a genre which pre-exists its constituent texts and to which works either do or do not belong based on their adherence to certain predefined characteristics. We can and do routinely have discussions about whether a certain text is or isn't SF (and even agree on the answers) in spite of the fact that decades of acute critical exertion have entirely failed to find a robust definition of the sort whose existence such discussions imply.[47] Gary K. Wolfe's 1986 effort to pin SF down resulted not in one definition but thirty-three: 'Strictly applied, every single one of those definitions would admit to the genre works that we would prefer to exclude, or would omit works we feel belong in the genre', Paul Kincaid comments.[48] Brian W. Aldiss goes so far as to cast SF *itself* as a 'search for a definition', co-opting the genre's practitioners as well as its readers into the taxonomic endeavour which it would not be unfair to describe as a central goal of academic SF criticism.[49] Producing a definition of SF, though, is certainly not my purpose here – indeed, it is precisely the amorphous quality of SF as a term (and its success in spite of that amorphousness) which makes it the perfect object of study from my perspective. And this too is part of the legacy of that original, periodical definition, which leaves the genre open to reader feedback, to multiple authorship, to change over time. In both SF's emergence as a real entity and its evasiveness in the face of rigid definition, then, we find the magazine an active agent.

Some of the writings I discuss in this book have certainly been enrolled as SF since they were published; others now feel decidedly distant from the genre. The majority of the pieces I examine are somewhere in between and these, I suggest, are more interesting. They are more interesting because they allow us to realise with John Frow that 'texts – even the simplest and most formulaic – do not "belong" to genres but are, rather, uses of them; they refer not to "a" genre but to a field or economy of genres, and their complexity derives from the complexity of that relation'.[50] This book is an argument for this complexity, understood through notions of genre. It is now time to consider these notions in more detail.

Understandings of genre

All of the observations which Latour's ideas allow us to make about the emergence of SF also apply to the relationship between the academic discourses of literature and of science. That the ways in which we categorise literature are in some respects analogous to the ways in which we categorise academic knowledge is one of this book's foundational ideas, and it is worth taking a few pages to explain exactly where it comes from. My conceit here is that in literature and science, as in early SF, we are seeing shifting dynamics between constructed categories made real by processes of enrolment. SF begins to exist in part because of discursive actions within and between magazines; in the self-same publications, substantively similar processes were shaping the public relationship between literature and science.

Is it reasonable to think of literature and science as genres, or at least as being like genres in certain respects? "Genre" is a useful but incredibly slippery term, and its several different but closely related meanings are the first headache one encounters in trying to use it for this kind of work:

> Much of the confusion surrounding the term arises from the fact that it is used simultaneously for the most basic modes of literary art (narrative, dramatic); for the broadest categories of composition (poetry, prose fiction),

and for more specialised sub-categories, which are defined according to
several different criteria including formal structure (sonnet, picaresque
novel), length (novella, epigram), intention (satire), effect (comedy), origin
(folktale), and subject-matter (pastoral, science fiction).[51]

The *Oxford Dictionary of Literary Terms* here sums up the tangled sets of
standards that combine in our apprehension of what genre is. In fact, the
word is even more multifarious than this definition implies – the *Dictionary* has a separate entry for 'genre fiction', 'the kind of story that offers
readers more or less what they would expect upon the basis of having read
similar books before' (p. 140). 'Genre' is therefore widely used both to
describe the various modes of capital-L literature and to segregate demotic
or formulaic elements from it; there are, as John Rieder has put it, the
'classical-academic' and 'mass-cultural' genre systems, the latter rising out
of nineteenth-century efforts to secure the former on its cultural pedes-
tal.[52] These uses of "genre" are normally kept quite separate from each
other, with the result that popular fiction is seldom thought about in
terms of its many connections to and exchanges with the diffuse genres of
"high" literature.

'Genre', John Frow argues, 'is a universal dimension of textuality'.[53]
Curiously, he makes this statement precisely in the act of all but dismissing
popular fiction from his enquiry into the subject. To speak of "genre
fiction", he argues, is to circumvent the fact that all fiction (and all other
writing) participates in genre. This is very true, but not a reason to sideline
the study of popular fiction in its own right: the most formulaic mass-
cultural genres surely offer an insight into their "higher" counterparts
precisely because their constituent texts are engaged with them more
explicitly. And in any case, as we shall see in a moment, very few mass-
market texts turn out, upon close examination, to be pure uses of a single
genre in a fixed economy.

Frow follows Carolyn R. Miller in understanding 'genres as typified
rhetorical actions based in recurrent situations', and one of the consequences of this understanding is an emphasis on the multiplicity of ways
in which individual texts engage with a spectrum of discourses.[54] This is
vital because it encourages us to find multiple genres within a single text
(with greater or lesser emphases) rather than treating genre as a series of
pigeon holes which are necessarily resistant to each other; it dissuades us
from exclusive definitions. Frow also stresses that the ways in which works
participate in genres contribute to shifts in the overall genre economy.
Genres move over time, and they do so precisely because of the discursive
uses made of them by individual publications. As Bakhtin argued, 'the

growth of literature is not merely development and change within the fixed boundaries of any given definition; the boundaries themselves are constantly changing'.[55] Miller agrees: 'the set of genres is an open class, with new members evolving, old ones decaying'.[56]

Most critical works touching this subject make it clear early on whether they are talking about "genre fiction" or "genres of fiction". *I am talking about both*, acting as if emergences and shifts in boundaries within classical-academic and mass-cultural genre systems are equivalent and related. Approaching genres as dimensions of textuality rather than as the boxes into which texts are placed allows us to sense popular fiction's involvement in the complex discursive network which also includes the grander voices of "high" literature. It is important, Miller says, 'not because it might permit the creation of some kind of taxonomy, but because it emphasizes some social and historical aspects of rhetoric that other perspectives do not' (p. 151). Such an approach has the incidental (and virtuous) effect of problematising value-driven approaches to literary classification, but more importantly, it allows us to locate "literature" as a generic voice in itself, and once this is done it can be situated alongside other cultural discourses amongst which "science" looms large.

This move – my placement of "literature" and "science" on the same analogical plane as "journalism", "editorial", "adventure", "romance", "SF" – is not without precedent. Frow himself comes close to it when, in the closing chapter of his work on genre, he discusses the 'generic differences of value' which occur in the school classroom, the 'socially sanctioned division of knowledge' which characterises education.[57] Even Derrida's rather different treatment of the concept of genre carries with it the determination, despite its narrow parameters, to 'exclude nothing, at least in principle and *de jure*', turning repeatedly (as have many others) to the language of biological taxonomy (genus and species, order and family) as the quickest shorthand by which textual categorisation may be metaphorically articulated.[58]

The complexity of genre relationships on which my argument rests is best illustrated by practical example. Between January 1903 and June 1904, *Pearson's Magazine* ran six stories by Fred M. White, each imagining a different disaster for an unspecified future London: blizzards, toxic fog, plague, financial collapse, explosions in the underground, and drought.[59] These stories seem straightforward at first glance, but their relationships with each other and with the magazines in which they appear is complex and fascinating. Despite their thematic grouping, it is unlikely that they are meant to function as a sequence, describing one (extremely unlucky) city.

They share no characters, no one of them mentions any event described in the others, and there is no common lens through which the various disasters are witnessed: two fraudsters, a newspaperman, a pair of nobles, and other diffuse individuals are amongst the protagonists. Even the disasters London faces in each story are not of a kind – some are natural, some are man-made, and others blur this distinction. In short, these tales considered as a whole do not aim at internal coherence; rather, they offer a series of contingencies, one identifiable goal being to stir readers into preventative real-world action.[60]

Suppose that we took it upon ourselves to classify these stories according to genre. Where would we place them? Their often heavy-handed desire to effect social change gives them a political resemblance to utopian works such as Edward Bellamy's *Looking Backward: 2000-1887* (1888), which had a galvanising effect on socialism on both sides of the Atlantic throughout the *fin de siècle*. The series also knowingly follows numerous other magazine forecasts of the capital's destruction, such as Grant Allen's 'The Thames Valley Catastrophe' (*Strand*, December 1897) or Robert Barr's 'The Doom of London' (*Idler*, November 1892). It might seem reasonable to combine these observations with the implicit future setting of White's tales, classifying them as SF. But here we run into difficulties. For example, 'A Bubble Burst', the fourth tale in the sequence, betrays absolutely none of SF's hallmarks – it's the story of a financial meltdown. We might – just – manage to make something of the technology complicit in the crash, although this is far from the story's emphasis, but the desire to make that effort can only arise from the tale's associations with the others in the series. Once made, such connections would be obliged to ignore other links, such as those with the significant corpus of tales of financial derring-do, which could also be found in the pages of the general magazines. This kind of difficulty resonates across all the stories: if their central objective is political motivation, for instance, then they surely profit from the material associations with argumentative pieces of non-fiction which also graced the pages of the magazines (such as a sermon on 'The Problem of Inebrity' in the same issue of *Pearson's* as 'The Dust of Death'), or with the fictitious but non-SF works which leaned towards a wry didacticism (such as the New Woman romance story set in a science college, same issue), or with the incitement to political action which, especially thanks to the writings of W. T. Stead, characterised the New Journalism more generally.[61] Placing them in the SF "box" hides all of this.

Despite a plot-level superficiality which would guarantee a swift dismissal from many critics, then, these stories bulge with complexity when glanced at in the light of their genre activity, activity which of course includes interactions with many other discourses not mentioned in my thumbnail sketch.[62] Re-situating the stories in the periodical in which they first appeared necessarily highlights this complexity, since we can notice similarities and moments of exchange with adjacent genres we might be disposed to think of as disconnected. What this adds up to is an observable tendency in the magazines' structure to resist definitive classification, traceable also in surface details such as the refusal to physically demarcate their contents (there are no section divisions; visual distinctions between, for example, factual and fictional accounts tend to be extremely subtle). Just as they provided the archive and structure for Gernsback's enrolment of SF, then, magazines provide us with a formal apparatus for looking at genre barriers and seeing them for the historical entities which they are.

Due to their commercial philosophy, mass-market periodicals of the *fin de siècle* have a necessary ability to hold apparently contradictory discourses in suspension. Such discourses are not reconciled to each other by their material vessel, but its properties allow the reader to move between them without a sense of dislocation, and this naturally supports any reading seeking a more nuanced view of notional "enmities" like that which notionally obtains between literature and science. It is worth reflecting on the fact that this characteristic of the periodical finds an analogue in an important feature of SF: to be a present-day reader of the genre is to be literate in moving between imagined worlds with different rules, different histories, different relationships to reality. Many contradict each other; all cohere, in a manner that evades ultimate definition, under the genre label of SF.

Roger Luckhurst has argued that critical work on early science fiction 'has to be acutely aware of the complex, overlapping forms of popular literary culture that exist in the forty or so years before distinctive SF genre publishing begins in the 1920s'.[63] Those 'complex, overlapping forms' are my focus in this book. One of the crucial ways in which they overlapped was by appearing in the same magazines, and though Luckhurst does draw attention to the importance of the periodical for SF in the *fin de siècle*, his genre study focuses on single authors (particularly H. G. Wells in this period) rather than on the publishing environment *per se*. By focussing instead upon the genre relationships embodied in the materiality of the magazines, and hence on the fabricated nature of SF as a category, I am attempting to mollify the exclusionary discourses which arise from the assumption of rigid, *a priori* definitions.

Literature and science

At this point, it is worth recapping my argument so far. Periodicals remind us that labels have histories; they are themselves active in these histories, but they also resist them, this apparent paradox being one of many advantageously sustained by the form's ability to hold competing ideas in suspension. In the magazines of the *fin de siècle*, we find embedded locutions of literature and science meeting in a discursive space which eventually helped to produce, among many other things, SF as a discrete commercial entity. To retrace this history is to recapture the sense of the periodical's importance, to gain insight into evolving processes of genre which continue to dictate the ways in which we arrange our understanding of both literature and science. Finally, these particular magazines reveal those processes in a distinctly public space, allowing us to explore the ways in which the literature/science relationship is portrayed and shaped in the popular arena which, today, retains significant influence over the future of both disciplines.

Scholars in the humanities are becoming increasingly aware of the potential of a more nuanced view of the Two Cultures, and since the pathfinding work of scholars like Gillian Beer and George Levine in the 1980s studies on this subject have crystallised under the name "Literature and Science".[64] This label is itself the product of a gradual enrolment, and there is still (advantageously for all, in my view) no consensus on the methods or priorities of this field of enquiry.[65] On the whole, though, the main focus of Literature and Science in nineteenth century studies has remained on canonical figures, tending, in the words of one critic, 'to favour the scientific mainstream', and likewise preferring to think about well-known literary figures like Thomas Hardy and George Eliot.[66] There are of course exceptions to this rough generalisation, and their number is growing, but it remains the case that Charlotte Sleigh's important current textbook on Literature and Science feels comfortable avoiding popular literature altogether: 'science fiction is, rightly or wrongly, not taken seriously as a genre of literature with a capital "L"', it says, 'and I hope this book might be taken seriously'.[67]

This tendency towards canon-orientation is eminently defensible. As a comparatively young field of enquiry, Literature and Science vies for a scholarly legitimacy which is still more easily gained through discussing Samuel T. Coleridge than Samuel R. Delany. It is also the case that SF, along with several other strains of popular fiction, has a well-established academic community of its own: the risk of repeating work or treading on toes is very real, and participation requires engagement with a daunting range of primary and critical material. On top of these concerns, it may reasonably be argued that Literature and Science scholarship is best communicated by referring to texts with which it can be assumed that academic readers will already be familiar. And of course, there is the important point that nothing about Literature and Science obliges scholars to turn to any texts other than those which cast light on the relationship between literature and science; many such have been identified from canonical authors, and a considerable number are of interest precisely because of their influential cultural status. Nevertheless, I hope I have made the point that popular literature does have something distinct to contribute to this exciting area of study – the very fact of its popularity, the fact that it is 'not taken seriously', makes its formal history a vital example of how the attitudes of the Two Cultures were shaped and circulated in the public sphere.

The case for SF's contribution to this area has been forcefully made in an essay collection edited by Gary Westfahl and George Slusser.[68] Meanwhile, the value of magazines in studying Literature and Science has been incontrovertible since at least the SciPer project, run jointly by the Universities of Leeds and Sheffield between 1999 and 2007. Publications resulting from SciPer have explored in detail the relationship between the magazine format and the cultural work performed by (and upon) scientific discourse; James Mussell's subsequent work included analysis of science in the *Strand* magazine.[69] These studies share an important realisation – that science's impact on periodical culture cannot be fully apprehended simply by reading the non-fiction articles which engage with it directly. '[I]t is the performance of a scientific narrative, rather than the representations of scientific observation', Mussell says, 'that provides the scientific value of popularisation' (p. 66). Popular science is fertile ground for those interested in the cultural currency of scientific ideas, and has been the site of important work.[70] But science is a ubiquitous presence in Standard Illustrated Popular Magazines, stretching far beyond the articles which engaged with it deliberately. This should not surprise us, since the publications in question were themselves the products of cutting-edge developments in printing technology and sold on the basis of their newness, their high volume of illustration, and their rapid production times.

For our purposes, science is perhaps best regarded as a genre-thread within the corporate body of the mass-market magazine: a strand in the *Strand*, and one among many. Sometimes, it is hardly visible at all, although in the literal fabric of New Journalism it is always implicit. Sometimes, it requires work to recapture the scientific influence on these publications from the perspective of a society even more saturated in technological developments. Superficially, for example, nothing could seem a more ossified cliché of Victorian-ness than the *Strand*'s own regular feature of 'Portraits of Celebrities at Different Times in their Lives', but the quality and number of illustrations (including photography) which such articles were able to deploy was the direct result of a very deliberate engagement with the latest technology and a crucial part of the magazine's up-to-the-minute sales strategy. And of course, the voice of science is frequently heard in fiction – nowhere more explicitly than in Arthur Conan Doyle's 'The Voice of Science' (*Strand*, March 1891), one of many stories which explicitly features scientific content without ever verging on SF.

I opened by mentioning the sheer wealth and range of material published by Standard Illustrated Popular Magazines. But the resulting fecundity, the sense of genres participating in each other, is very easy to miss. Partly, this is because of the scale of content available. According to a contemporary estimate, 2,263 separate periodical titles were in print in Britain in 1891, and this had risen to 2,767 by 1907.[71] Since it would be impossible to do more than scratch the surface of this volume of material in one lifetime, critics have understandably focussed their attention on individual items which match their predetermined interests; the advent of the searchable digital archive for some (but by no means all) of the titles discussed here has made it easier than ever to abstract individual articles from the issues in which they appeared.[72] The almost complete demise of 'the issue' as a unit of study, even when scholars remain alert to the differences between 'titles', has meant that increasingly, we only search for things in places where we know they will be found. Dallas Liddle believes that this unfortunate fact can be circumvented with careful attention to the qualities of genre; I, on the other hand, believe that it is precisely because of the qualities of genre that we have a responsibility to the whole issue, to the material entanglement which was the original conduit for so many late-Victorian articulations of literature, science, and SF.[73]

But Liddle does have a point. Reading everything, especially to the criteria I am suggesting here, would be impossible. How, then, to proceed? In the rest of this book, I have selected four scientific topics around which public interest (or at least, the interest of New Journalist editors) seemed to cluster in the 1890s and 1900s. Each forms the thematic basis of one of the chapters which follows. This approach is drawn from a suggestion in Stephen Kern's landmark study of cultural changes in the *fin de siècle*, the outset of which includes the following claim:

The categories of time and space provide a comprehensive theoretical framework that allows not only the integration of many areas across the cultural spectrum but also integration along a theoretical vertical axis from 'high culture' to popular culture and the material aspects of everyday life.[74]

Time and space are explicitly knit together in the pages of periodicals, and periodicals addressed to general interest provide a particular insight into the high cultural and material subjects which commanded public attention at a given moment. My approach was to read through several years' worth of popular magazines, noting subjects of repeated interest to writers of both fiction and non-fiction. My four topics were chosen from a group of scientific subjects which naturally came to the fore during this process. I then widened my enquiries with targeted research: archive visits and keyword searching. I read whole issues rather than individual items wherever possible, and found some surprising things. More importantly, I found numerous moments of adjacency, collaboration, and competition between the voices of literature and science, and these are what I have sought to highlight. I make no claims to comprehensiveness: I am not attempting to write a balanced history of the entire magazine press in this period. Nor is this anything like a definitive history of early SF, although I certainly hope it will contribute to that wider project. What I do want to show is the mechanics of enrolment at work, the general magazine's usefulness as a tool for foregrounding the fact that barriers dividing spheres of apprehension are perpetually in motion. 'After all', writes Mikhail Bakhtin, 'the boundaries between fiction and non-fiction, between literature and nonliterature and so forth are not laid up in heaven'.[75] Reading the magazines with this in mind, my hope is to replace the Two Culture paradigm with something more sensitive, more nuanced, and more sympathetic to both sides. Science and literature are two of the defining discourses of our time – it is almost impossible to imagine somebody who is not somehow engaged with both on a daily basis. The vast majority of public and academic treatments of literature and of science pay little heed to this obvious fact. From a literary-critical perspective, and with the magazine as a formal and historical tool, this book is an attempt to close that gap.

We begin in Chapter 1, though, with a more focussed objective: a close reading of a single article. Francis Galton's 'Intelligible Signals between Neighbouring Worlds' (*Fortnightly Review*, November 1896) encompasses many sides of the public fascination with Mars following its favourable opposition in 1892. Its ostensible purpose is to detail a code for communicating between the Earth and Mars using a series of sun-signals reflected from giant mirrors. Galton was a renowned scientist and a Fellow of the Royal Society, and this is undoubtedly a piece of popular science, but in its efforts to communicate its own message to the general reader, it relies on some of the sensationalist tropes of fiction and the New Journalism to the point that it ends up becoming a highly imaginative work in its own right. Seemingly conflicted, the piece postulates a variety of details about a supposed Martian civilisation and implied speculation about the messages which they might want to send us. My reading of this article reveals that far from creating a text at war with itself, the combined presences of science and fiction serve to bolster each other, the fictional apparatus supporting the mathematics at the core of Galton's project.

From here, my argument widens. Chapter 2 examines a selection of fictional and non-fictional writings about the future by writers including Rudyard Kipling, Mrs. Humphry Ward, F. L. Oswald, and Alfred Arkas. Following the first chapter's focus on the space of the periodical, I now engage closely with its sense of time, understanding both SF and the format of the magazine as conceptually dependent on the idea of stability through a gradually changing, infinite future. The temporal properties of the periodical are also conducive to science itself, since periodicals incorporate the capacity for gradual revision and refinement alongside the promise of a traceable connection to past knowledge.

I then seek to complicate the case made in the first two chapters for a broadly harmonious relationship between literature and science in the magazines. Chapter 3, 'New Photography', takes in many more genres of writing than the preceding chapters, examining a wide range of responses to Wilhelm Röntgen's discovery of X-rays in November 1895 – interviews, biographies, spiritualist tracts, and satirical sketches feature in this chapter alongside fiction and popular science. What is at stake in the various presentations of this bleeding-edge technology is nothing less than the status of truth, and the discourses of authenticity to which photography, journalism, science, and fiction variously aspire. In this chapter, I show that scientific aims could be hindered as well as helped by the New Journalism's formal insistence on equality of voice, an insistence which had developed into a democratic imperative by the 1890s and which conferred authority not only on scientific speakers but on their unevidenced rivals. One of my chief examples in this chapter is the spiritualist movement, to which X-rays (a phenomenon physics was unequipped adequately to explain at the moment of their discovery) appeared a vindication.

Chapter 4 is the most expansive in the book, taking in material from across the *fin de siècle* and drawing to a climax the arguments made so far.

It scrutinises a wealth of material on polar exploration, the aim being to engage with the colonial attitudes which underscore geographical discovery and which are also implicitly evoked in discussions around genre or scholarly discipline. The guiding metaphor here is *territory*, which underpins notions of imperial and disciplinary appropriation. As one of the last unexplored places on earth in the 1890s, the Pole was a focal point for fictional and non-fictional treatments of lost civilisations, dinosaurs, and hollow-earth theory. Tracking some of the periodicals' responses to real-life voyages into the unknown, in particular Fridtjof Nansen's *Fram* voyage (1893–96), this chapter explores the relationship between fantasy and reality in the production of empire. SF, it claims, is the product of the imperialism which drove explorers towards the North Pole as well as the noble inquisitiveness which motivated scientists in the laboratory – indeed, the two are harder to separate than might at first be expected. When human categorisations of the world take on this political element, questions of genre swiftly lose their esoteric flavour.

Throughout all four chapters, I have one eye on the legacies left to us from this formative moment in the history of the modern mass media. The present-day successors of the issues I focus on here are of great interest to me, and a brief conclusion addresses them more explicitly, incorporating some thoughts on the repercussions of this work from a pedagogical perspective.

As well as a gradually developing (and widening) argument about disciplinary relationships understood as and via genres, there is another thread which connects the chapters of this book. The single dominant figure in *fin-de-siècle* SF is H. G. Wells, the breadth of whose engagement with the periodical press has been the subject of recent attention following the welcome appearance of a recent annotated bibliography.[76] As it happens, each of the themes I tackle is prominently embodied in one of Wells's major early works of SF, and this fact seems too suggestive to ignore. Each chapter, then, also spends a short time with a specific Wells text: Chapter 1 with *The War of the Worlds* (*Pearson's Magazine*, April–December 1897), Chapter 2 with *The Time Machine* (*New Review*, January–May 1895), Chapter 3 with *The Invisible Man* (*Pearson's Weekly*, June–August 1897), and Chapter 4 with *The First Men in the Moon* (*Strand*, December 1900–August 1901). There are two reasons for this recurring focus: a desire to present the reader with at least some primary material with which they will probably already be familiar, and an interest in re-situating Wells in his periodical context. The latter goal is not only important given this book's overall argument about the multiple historical contingencies of genre ("H. G. Wells" could certainly be considered a genre just as much as "SF" or "science"), but also follows on from Steven McLean's important observation that it would 'be difficult to understate the role of the periodical press in shaping the fortunes of the young Wells'.[77] Just as individual articles are frequently abstracted from their original issues, we have become used to reading Wells in book-format novels and edited collections rather than in periodical instalments – an efficiency, but not one without loss.[78] This desire to reconnect material with its original periodicals is also the motivation behind my practice, with Wells and all other authors, of quoting wherever possible from primary magazine sources even where more recent, edited, scholarly versions of a text exist.

Martian communication, future prediction, X-rays, and polar exploration: these are four of the themes which fascinated the readers of the Standard Illustrated Popular Magazines, and which have, in turn, fascinated me. To both contemporary reader and present-day scholar, their great attraction is the wide variety of texts and ideas to which they will take us. There is always a danger, in pursuing such variety, of sacrificing depth for breadth – of slipping into the feather-brainedness which so riled Matthew Arnold. I have made every effort to conduct myself responsibly, but in any case perhaps there is something to be said for a gesture towards breadth in a work seeking to understand and challenge rigid disciplinary division. I have also written this book under the assumption that there is value in deploying a handful of subjective terms ('fun', 'enjoyment', 'fascination', 'interest') as critical tools, partly because they seem to me a compelling way of resisting that same rigidity: in their nebulousness, they are useful for the same reasons that the equally ambiguous "literature and science" or "science fiction" have been. Besides, given their position in the commercial enterprise of the New Journalism and the rhetorical constitution of the wider public sphere, it seems to me that any discussion of these texts which did not centrally acknowledge fun would be missing something important.

Regardless of how convinced the reader is by that last point, my earnest hope is that my breadth of focus will make this work useful, or at least stimulating, to people in several different fields. From the perspective of SF scholars, what follows offers insight into the accretions which led to the commercial genre, casting light on the formal role of magazines in that complex process – I also identify and analyse some interesting (and occasionally hilarious) science-fictional texts which have so far garnered little critical attention. From the perspective of Periodical Studies, I draw out some of the growing coverage of science in the *fin-de-siècle* press and present an in-depth argument for the considerable formal and organising power of the magazine's heteroglot voice. Finally, from the perspective of Literature and Science, I demonstrate the cultural embeddedness of processes of disciplinary definition, the apprehension of which could scarcely be more vital at a moment when "public engagement" and "impact" are increasingly the focus of both sciences and arts. Whatever the reader's background, though, this book's argument first and foremost is for complexity and interconnectedness, for the value inherent in recognising the composed nature of our categories through which we understand ourselves, our art, and our universe.

CHAPTER I

Intrinsic intelligibility
Communications with Mars, and between disciplines, in the pages of the magazines

The Mars craze

In the autumn of 1892, the Earth and Mars were in favourable opposition. The two planets "lined up" with the Sun, and a few days later passed within 60,000,000 kilometres of each other, almost as close as they ever get. On Earth, Mars would have appeared as one of the brightest objects in the night sky, easily visible to the naked eye as a blood-red star outshining everything but the Moon and Venus. It was the best view of Mars which the Victorians had seen since Schiaparelli had observed his *canali* during the favourable opposition of 1877, and it prompted much excitement in the periodical press as professionals and amateurs gazed skywards. An article in the *Pall Mall Gazette*, written three years later, makes reference to one result of the craze:

> [T]here was a considerable amount of discussion as to the probability of [Mars] being 'inhabited'. Letters appeared in the daily papers, and nearly every one had something to say on the subject, and there was even some talk of trying to attract the attention of our Martian neighbours by heliographic signals. What language was to be used, and whether the signals were to be according to the Morse, or some other code, was apparently left for astronomers to decide, but scientists declined to undertake this interesting work, and in the meantime Mars drifted away from us on his circumscribed journey through space.[1]

P. L. Addison, the author of this piece, captures wonderfully the correspondence between the planet's fading from the night sky and its fading from reported popular consciousness. But in claiming that scientists had 'declined' to investigate the idea of communicating with the red planet, he was slightly premature. As Addison was writing, an intelligence greater than his, and yet as mortal, was hard at work on the problem.

One of the 'letters in the daily papers' which Addison mentions had been written by Francis Galton (1822–1911; Fig. 1.1), a man of whom it may

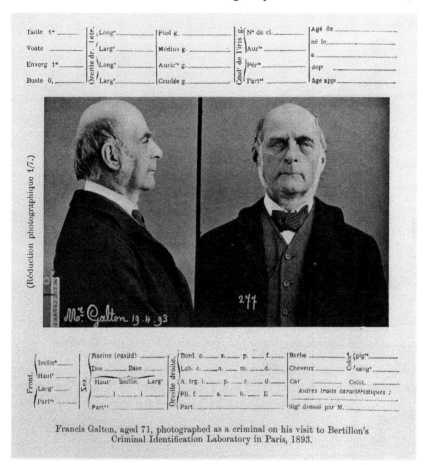

Francis Galton, aged 71, photographed as a criminal on his visit to Bertillon's Criminal Identification Laboratory in Paris, 1893.

1.1   Image of Francis Galton, from Karl Pearson's *The Life, Letters, and Labors of Francis Galton* (1924). Courtesy of the Cadbury Research Library, University of Birmingham.

be enough to say that he invented both eugenics and a primitive kind of bicycle odometer. Half-cousin of Charles Darwin, Galton was responsible for breakthroughs in fingerprinting, statistics, meteorology, and much besides.[2] As close a figure as we might hope to find to the stereotype of the polymathic Victorian inventor-scientist, he was also an enthusiastic communicator, writing prolifically for a general audience – lectures, books, and articles in periodicals. His zeal for this role was such that when he hadn't written an article, he was frequently to be found making some point or clarification on the letters page of a magazine or newspaper. His

1.2   A heliostat designed by Francis Galton. © UCL Galton Collection.

contribution to the Mars craze was a letter published in the *Times* at the height of the 1892 opposition, in which he claimed that:

> With funds and good will, there seems no insuperable difficulty in [...] sending signals that the inhabitants of Mars, if they have eyes, wits, and fairly good telescopes, would speculate on and wish to answer.[3]

Galton had invented a hand-held version of the heliostat – a signalling device which reflects sunlight in a targeted direction – whilst travelling in Africa in his youth (Fig. 1.2). He had reported his experiences in *The Art of Travel* in 1858 and delivered a paper on heliostats to the British Association for the Advancement of Science that same year. His experience gave him some authority with which to address the possibility of using similar devices to communicate with Mars, and in his letter to the *Times* he comes to the conclusion that it should be possible to produce a signal visible at that distance, although not without difficulties:

> My own method is not practicable, at least without considerable addition and modifications, as it requires the object to be visible towards which the flash is directed, but Mars is not visible to the naked eye at day.[4]

This implied call for other suggestions was left unanswered, and Galton, like Addison, was compelled to watch Mars recede from the public eye. In a passage which strikingly mirrors Addison's, he was later to remark that:

> [T]he craze about Mars died away; the planet ceased to be particularly conspicuous, people grew tired of the topic, and the heated thoughts of many writers were cooled by copious douches of astronomical common sense.[5]

Galton's interest, however, had not been completely washed away. In the draft of an unpublished letter to the *Spectator* written less than a week after his letter to the *Times*, he had proposed using algebra as the basis of a language for the heliotrope signals. '[I]t is an interesting subject and possibly worth writing a few lines about', he wrote.[6] In fact, he found the subject so interesting that it was still in his mind nearly four years later, in the summer of 1896, when a 'somewhat dreamy vacation' afforded him the opportunity of enlarging upon his ideas.[7] The eventual result of this was the publication of a short article called 'Intelligible Signals between Neighbouring Stars', which appeared in the *Fortnightly Review* for November of that year.

Although it is by no means an important work, even within the comparatively restricted scope of Galton's own output, 'Intelligible Signals' (as I shall refer to it from now on) is a fascinating piece of writing, offering a rich microcosm of the issues surrounding the periodical format's engagement with science. Fusing together locutions of several notionally distinct modes of writing, often apparently in spite of itself, the article is an excellent case study for approaching the material entanglement of genres of literature and science. This entire chapter is devoted to an analysis of Galton's piece, the aim being to explore the way in which he confounds rigorous categorisation, showing not only exchange between the supposed opposites 'science' and 'fiction' but also that each provides essential components without which the article would be incomplete; fiction and the periodical format are not merely window-dressings for a scientific idea, but reinforce the argument and subtly alter it. I will also contend that the image of two worlds hanging in an isolating vacuum is an appropriate analogy for later twentieth-century understandings of the 'Two Cultures', and that Galton's idea for a communication system between them (based on intrinsic, shared qualities) disrupts it most usefully. It does so, I will argue, not only in its own right but because of the mix of genres in the article advancing it and the mix of interests represented by its author. In this respect, 'Intelligible Signals' is an excellent ambassador for the *fin-de-siècle* periodical.

Medium and message are identical in Galton's algebraic scheme for interplanetary signalling, which makes it significant that they are also closely allied in the article which proposes it. The idea of universal communication can therefore be enrolled to do some powerful metaphorical work in the consideration of the genre and disciplinary relationships, and it is to this end that the following close and contextual readings are ultimately directed.

Reading 'Intelligible Signals Between Neighbouring Stars' for science, fiction, and the popular press

'Intelligible Signals' is much more the successor to Galton's unpublished *Spectator* letter than it is to the letter which appeared in the *Times*, for it focuses purely on linguistic difficulties, disregarding almost entirely the technical side of how the signals to Mars might be sent. Addison had observed in the *Pall Mall Gazette* that Morse code would be useless for an enterprise like this, since it translates only back into the language from which it was encoded (and even then, only with a key). 'Signals have to be devised', remarks Galton, at the outset of his *Fortnightly Review* article,

> . . .that are *intrinsically* intelligible, so that the messages may be deciphered by any intelligent man, or other creature, who has made nearly as much advance in pure and applied science as ourselves.[8]

The puzzle which the article sets out to solve, in other words, is that any message sent to Mars must be capable of translating itself – into any language. Galton's solution rests in mathematics and geometry. Signalling numerical rudiments via a series of flashes, his code slowly increases in complexity until it is transmitting quite sophisticated maths and conveying along the way a series of characters (sets of flashes) such as 'π', which could eventually form the basis of pictorial communication. Galton claims that 'the reader will probably feel surprised at the unexpected simplicity' of his solution (p. 657), but a present-day observer, even one with no training in linguistics or mathematics, will almost certainly feel dubious from the start. There are a number of assumptive leaps in Galton's plan, not least the supposition that any intelligence looking at a certain set of dots, dashes, and lines will be able to infer an equals sign:

Every line begins with one or more dots; then follows a dash; and then a word of two letters. There is one dot at the beginning of the first line, two at that of the next, and so on regularly up to the seventh. The symbols at the end of successive lines are those of the successive combinations of *dot, dash,* and *line,* taken in order up to the seventh; the eighth which is — –, and the ninth which is — —, are not used. The arrangement suggests that the dash means 'is equal to', and that the symbols are those of numerals. . .[9]

A century of SF has made us good at quickly noticing some other objections. The Martians would already have to have a concept of letters, words, and line breaks before they got to something as delicate as the equals sign, for example, which is a lot to assume of a completely alien civilisation.

Criticising the scientific assumptions underpinning Galton's proposal, though, is not my primary purpose here; I am more interested in what the article tells us about disciplinary and generic relationships in the periodical press than in what it tells us about how we might communicate with Mars. In order to definitively argue that the piece can provide insight into the relationships between literature, science, and popular culture, it is first necessary to establish that Galton was participating in all three. The work of this section is therefore to argue that 'Intelligible Signals' constitutes a piece of imaginative writing; that it not only exhibits the tropes of popular fiction but that they are materially entangled with (and arise in consequence of) its scientific arguments. The necessary first step here is to establish that Galton, a Fellow of the Royal Society, considered his own idea a genuine scientific proposition, regardless of how idly he formulated it and how feasible it may look to us today.

The following passage comes from later in 'Intelligible Signals', a point at which the signalling system has been developed to the extent that messages are being used to draw pictures as if on graph paper:

> [B]oth the length of the stitch and its inclination may be specified more delicately by the help of decimals. Thus let j be the symbol for a stitch in any given direction, then $0.5 \times j$ means a half-length stitch in the direction j. A series of 4 triangles were signalled to explain this, in which the angles corresponded exactly with certain of the rhumbs, while the sides had to be expressed with decimals.[10]

The tone Galton uses here is dry and measured, the voice of the lecturer. The 'let x equal y' model of sentence construction remains an archetype of scientific language, and the word 'expressed' in this context would appear at home in a present-day maths textbook. This passage is taken from a far longer section, pretty much any of which could have been excerpted to make my point: Galton's language and bearing throughout the piece indicate a seriousness of purpose, and he is often at pains to underline the fact that he has thought thoroughly about his subject and is speaking with good authority. Complementing this language is his choice of the *Fortnightly Review* as the venue for the article's publication. The *Fortnightly* had been in print since 1865 with a mandate to promote independent, intelligent thought. By 1896, its relatively advanced years carried almost as much weight as the names of its contributors, and it was the first magazine to adopt signature – George Eliot, Walter Bagehot, and George Meredith had all contributed to the first volume.[11] Whilst it was not an avowedly science-oriented publication, the *Fortnightly* had committed itself to science in its opening manifesto, listing it as one of the six key areas in which it intended to intervene (the other five were literature, art, philosophy, finance, and politics) and it had strongly supported the evolutionists, publishing articles by T. H. Huxley and Herbert Spencer among others. Its type was set in one column across the page and carried no illustrations, printing diagrams and tables only when the subject matter strictly demanded it. A synopsis of nineteenth-century literature published in the same year as Galton's article mentions the *Fortnightly* as a publication which, despite printing some fiction, 'busied [itself] with more or less serious subjects', and the magazine typically featured a large amount of social and political commentary, with articles on 'The Cyprus Convention', 'Lord Rosebery's Resignation', and 'The Struggle Before Us' all appearing in the same issue as 'Intelligible Signals'.[12] Galton shared space with literary criticism too, in the form of 'Emile Verhaeren: The Belgian Poet' and 'William Morris: A Eulogy'. In short, then, the *Fortnightly* was *not* one of the Standard Illustrated Popular magazines I proposed to focus on in the introduction; Galton's choice of it suggests that he wished rather for 'cultivated and thoughtful readers' than for the fickle implied consumer of the New Journalism.[13] This fact, combined with the time he spends on the mathematical nuances of the idea, the tone in which he expresses it, and his own reputation as a scientist, all strongly indicate that he was far from frivolous in putting his idea forward.

The fact that Galton was making a serious suggestion, however, has not prevented the final document from incorporating into its very heart elements of imaginative writing which align it distinctly with early works of science fiction, and with the tone of the illustrated magazines with which the *Fortnightly* initially seems to contrast. Galton sets up the imaginative conceit of the piece on its second page in a revealing and rather wonderful sentence:

The simplest way of explaining my method is to suppose that Mars began to signal, to the wonderment of our astronomers, who sent descriptive letters to the newspapers from day to day, out of which the following imaginary extracts are taken:[14]

The eleven fake newspaper extracts which these words introduce constitute almost the entirety of the piece: written from the perspectives of several unnamed personae, at least one of them a scientist, they are distinguished from the brief introduction and conclusion (and the text of the other articles in that issue of the *Fortnightly*) only by the fact that they appear in slightly smaller print. Apart from a few headlines in small caps, there is no attempt to re-create the visual style of a newspaper (Fig. 1.3), but the excerpts, notionally gleaned from successive days' reporting on an actual Martian communication attempt, take the reader through the decipherment of Galton's code as if they were witness to the gradual unfolding of a current event rather than to the solution of a scientific problem.

It is immediately and inescapably obvious that this method of exposition is very far indeed from the 'simplest way' of explaining anything. There are certainly advantages to the format, since it provides a way of gently introducing the non-specialist audience to a fairly complex idea, but it seems a cumbersome imposition on the mathematical side of the discussion which is purportedly Galton's primary focus. It forces numerous descriptive tangents, of which more presently, as well as breaks and lacunae which feel increasingly superfluous as the piece moves on. But though it appears to be an artificial medium for scientific discourse, the 'newspaper extracts' format – specifically, the sequencing of the solution around a developing event – are an excellent source of *narrative*, which the "pure" idea of communicating with Mars using algebra notably lacks. The newspaper, despite its notionally objective tone, implicitly generates sensation as well as narrative: Matthew Rubery has argued that it is *because* of their neutral tone that nineteenth-century novelists were able to use newspapers as such ample sources of drama and suspense.[15] This is a dimension of the media which the New Journalism brought to prominence, and Galton's adoption of the sensationalist tone of the newspaper within the generally sombre pages of the *Fortnightly* is revealing. It is difficult to imagine a reason other than suspense, for instance, for the entry among Galton's series of fake extracts which simply reads 'COMPLETE DECIPHERMENT OF THE FIRST PART OF THE MESSAGE FROM MARS. Full particulars tomorrow'.[16] Redundant as either exposition or explanation, this short passage can only have been included as a dramatic device, Galton's 'use of the methods of the press [...] to strike

·INTELLIGIBLE SIGNALS BETWEEN NEIGHBOURING STARS.   659

long strip of telegraph paper is slowly drawn by clockwork under a hinged pencil
on which the observer rests his finger.   When a flash is on, he presses with his
finger and the pencil leaves a mark ; when the flash is off, he ceases to press, a
spring lifts the pencil, and a blank is left on the travelling slip of paper.

4. The signals have improved considerably in regularity and power, and
occasional sequences of them have been gone through in a masterly way.   So the
drilling of the operators appears to be nearly complete, and we may expect soon to
see what the system is intended to show.   The phenomenon is most extraordinary.
If it be effected through the money of a mad millionaire, he must have had the
sense to subsidise an uncommonly intelligent director of works.

5. A most eventful night has been passed at the X. observatory.   At first the
sky was hazy and partly clouded, so Mars was, at the best, but imperfectly seen,
and was often quite invisible ; then, at half-past nine, all cloudiness disappeared,
and the flashes were observed to be proceeding from Mars with greater power and
precision than ever before.   The whole assemblage of their heliographs must have
been simultaneously at work, and the drill was excellent.   The signalling continued off and on for more than three hours.   The recorder being kept at work
the whole time, every signal then made is preserved in a permanent form, of
course including occasional mistakes.   The records are as yet totally unintel-
ligible, possibly owing to the loss of the first part of the communication, which
may have contained the key to what followed.   It is noticeable that during the
last two hours the signals consisted almost wholly of three-letter words ; in the
earlier part there was a preponderance of two-letter words, some of four and of
five letters, but none of three.

6. A large typed telegraphic dispatch appeared in all the evening newspapers—
COMPLETE DECIPHERMENT OF THE FIRST PART OF THE MESSAGE FROM
MARS.   Full particulars to-morrow.
(Signed) Director of the X. Observatory.

7. The evening was serene, and the whole of the night continued to be beauti-
fully clear.   The experiences of previous days enabled every preparation to be
made for the expected event.   And it came.   First there was a succession of
" lines" with intervening pauses, evidently as a note of preparation, and then
after a longer pause the message began with the accompanying sentence, which

No. of dots.		Is equal to.	Symbols for Numerals.
(1)	.	—	. .
(2)	. .	—	. —
(3)	. . .	—	. — .
(4)	. . . .	—	— .
(5)	. . . . .	—	— —
(6)	. . . . . .	—	— — .
(7)	. . . .	—	— — .
(8)	. . . .	—	. . — — —
(9)	. . . .	—	. . —
(10)	. . . .	—	. . . —
(&c.)	. . . . .	—	. . . . .

occupied less than six minutes in transmission.   The headings and the column

1.3   A page from Galton's 'Intelligible Signals' piece in the *Fortnightly Review* (November
1896). Courtesy of the Cadbury Research Library, University of Birmingham.

the reader right between the eyes'.[17] Galton's deployment of this technique places him – if only in one small respect – in the footsteps of the most established fiction writers and sensation journalists of the Victorian age.

The use of the feigned newspaper extracts brings an even greater depth to Galton's imaginative work, however. Since they were never published individually, the suspense generated by this headline comes not directly from the temporal gaps between them, but rather through an implied empathic connection with the imagined reader in Galton's world who must wait until the next day for 'full particulars'. The real-world readers of the article need only flit their eyes to the next line in order to find out what happens next, but to experience the story as a developing event (which is what the narrative demands) they must at some level imagine the sequence of extracts as being separated chronologically as well as physically. The extracts therefore evoke a periodical temporality, imposing upon an article concentrated in one time and place the imaginative and narrative dimensions of an unfolding news event. The reader comes to the extracts as an historical artefact, the suspense being generated retrospectively. This two line diversion, then – 'full particulars tomorrow' – doesn't just give reign to narrative, it also breathes life into an entire fantasy universe. This universe, the one in which the Martians are signalling, is materially demarcated from ours on the page by the smaller font size in which the extracts appear. It functions, complete with novum, in exactly the same way as an SF universe created without the agenda of real-world scientific explanation might.[18]

Not only is the newspaper format sensational in and of itself, the practice of quoting from it for the purposes of narrative exposition also aligns 'Intelligible Signals' with part of the tradition of popular fiction. The device echoes, for instance, Edgar Allan Poe's decision to use a newspaper to lay out the facts in his famous tale 'The Murders in the Rue Morgue' (*Graham's Magazine*, April 1841). In this story, a review of nearly all the evidence put before the detective M. Dupin is first encountered by the reader in pages of quotation from 'an evening edition of the *Gazette des Tribunaux*'.[19] The narrator's voice returns only to link quotations from the newspaper together ('The next day's paper had these additional particulars', p. 100), performing a similarly retrospective suspense function to Galton's 'full particulars tomorrow'. Newspapers in the nineteenth century, says Rubery, were 'just one of the ways in which novelists played upon audience expectations by introducing competing layers of verisimilitude into the fictional narrative'.[20]

On first glance, Galton's deployment of this same strategy seems indicative of an important break with the scientific style in which he couches much of his essay. But it is worth mentioning here that Poe also depends on the scientific style, using it not only during the newspaper description already quoted (detailed, lengthy, and dry despite its disturbing content) but also for the weighty essay on inductive reasoning which opens the story and which is anything other than sensational in tone. Since 'The Murders in the Rue Morgue' is often regarded as a highly influential early work of detective fiction, it is perhaps no surprise that the genre has connections with popular science, a point which H. G. Wells was keen not only to draw attention to, but to applaud:

> The fundamental principles of construction that underlie such stories as Poe's 'Murders in the Rue Morgue,' or Conan Doyle's 'Sherlock Holmes' series, are precisely those that should guide a scientific writer. These stories show that the public delights in the ingenious unravelling of evidence [. . .]. First the problem, then the gradual piecing together of the solution. They cannot get enough of such matter.[21]

Already, science and sensation begin to look far from mutually exclusive as forms of writing. Wells's comment suggests that the scientific method could itself be considered a form of entertainment, and it is to this suggestion that Galton plays when he presents his scientific idea in the form of an imaginary universe: first the problem, and then, step by step, the solution.

Galton brushes against fiction again when, not wishing either to commit himself to a definite physical location or to fall back on a potentially jarring fabrication, he substitutes 'the X. observatory' for the name of the institution where the signals are being recorded. On the one hand, this looks like a scientific gesture: it makes explicit the hypothetical nature of the account, and doesn't draw a particular institution (such as the Lick Observatory, which Galton names in his initial, narrative-free letter to the *Times*) into collusion with Galton's theorising. At the same time, though, the 'X' also encourages the reader to fill in the blank, just as the narrator does in 'The Murders in the Rue Morgue' (for instance) to evoke a sense of mystery and innuendo around the identity of '–of Chantilly' or the location of 'the Rue C–'. The em dashes in place of these proper names will be familiar to anybody who has read fiction of the nineteenth century or earlier, as will the fact that each draws attention to the text's own fictionality while at the same time wryly sidestepping it.

This inviting absence is present beyond the simple omission of proper nouns in Galton's writing. Precisely because he wishes to stay on-topic, he leaves undiscussed or undescribed nearly all of the most tantalising questions arising from communication with extraterrestrials. The narrative stops just at the moment when the Martian signals have been fully decoded, and when they are finally on the verge of transmitting content beyond the mathematical rudiments which are required, under Galton's system, to establish communications. This reluctance to talk about the Martian society, although almost certainly a product of wishing to stay focussed on the communication system, imbues that society with a compelling mystique. At times, Galton himself has trouble resisting it. For instance, when the algebraic signals reported in extract seven reveal that the Martians seem to have a base-eight (octal) rather than a base-ten (decimal) counting system, the director of the X. observatory offers a perfectly sensible-sounding mathematical solution (the numbers 1 to 7 and 0 'exactly use up the nine words of two letters each' available when using only the three different types of flash which Galton has limited himself to) before adding, arrestingly:

> A clever little girl who has helped us much by her quick guesses, intreats me to add her own peculiar view, which is that the Mars-folk are nothing more than highly developed ants, who count up to 8 by their 6 limbs and 2 antennæ, as our forefathers counted up to 10 on their fingers. But enough of this.[22]

That last, short sentence is highly revealing. It suggests not just the director of the observatory resisting the urge to slip into idle theorising but also Galton resisting the urge to slip into idle fantasising. Narrative eddies like this, bursts of character which pull the narrative in the direction of the fantastic apparently against Galton's better judgement, crop up throughout the article; Galton, it seems, has great difficulty living up to his declaration, in the first newspaper extract, that 'it is well not to indulge too freely in wild speculation' (p. 658). It is important that the speculation in which Galton goes on to indulge arises directly *because* of his urge to be restrained and scientific, rather than in isolation from it: there is, in other words, a causal link between these supposedly contradictory tendencies.

The clever little girl's 'ants' theory is not the only example of Galton being carried off by the force of his narrative. I have quoted more extensively here in order to emphasise the rapidity with which the article's tone changes:

> Also the average times occupied in signalling these words, including the 3 seconds' pause at the end of each, are 6, 10, 15, 20 and 24 seconds respectively. Whatever the Mars-folk may have to say must be briefly expressed, and it seems incredible under these conditions that anything could be communicated by them to us which shall be intelligible and of value. Some persons are disposed to ascribe this immense undertaking to the caprice of a mad millionaire in Mars, or rather to a mad billionaire. There have been instances in the past history of our earth of many gigantic follies, without counting the traditional Tower of Babel.[23]

Without even a paragraph break, a discussion about the brevity of the interplanetary signals lapses into a huge set of assumptions about the Martians: they apparently have an individualist society structured around a capitalist economy, and they are also capable of mental eccentricities and madness. Madness carrying the concept of sanity along with it, this sentence also gives us the existence of Martian status quo, one which looks suspiciously similar to our own. And before any of this, we have numerous other assumptions implicitly to accept: that the Martians have eyes, that those eyes are sensitive to the same wavelengths of light as ours, that the Martians share our curiosity for the heavens, that they would regard flashes from a nearby planet as strange or interesting, that they would strive to communicate with their neighbours even if they thought it possible, and so on. Galton's reluctance to think outside the framework of what he calls 'the civilised nations of the earth at the present time' is not merely a narrative flaw, for, as mentioned earlier, his assumptions pervade the actual communication system, not just the manner in which 'Intelligible Signals' advances it (p. 664). That the scientific substance and compositional style of this piece both, for all their superficial disconnectedness, exhibit this flaw is a compelling argument against reading the narrative eddies as purely decorative.

The mystery surrounding the Martians is heightened by Galton's decision to cast Mars, rather than Earth, as the sender of the messages. This was a decision made relatively late in the article's composition. A draft of a lecture which contains an early form of Galton's scheme entirely lacks narrative elements, not even mentioning interplanetary signalling until the sixteenth of its twenty-four pages. When it does finally come on to it, the Earth is the *source* of the hypothetical messages – indeed, Mars is not named (although a reference to 'speculation last summer of the possibility of inter planetary communication' makes it unlikely that Galton is referring to anywhere else). There is even some suggestion that in the very early stages of composition, Galton was thinking too abstractly even to name Earth: the phrase 'so let us suppose then two detached planets having absolutely no other knowledge of one another' has been amended in the draft to say 'the inhabitants of another, some imaginary celestial body, having absolutely no other knowledge of us or we of them...'.[24] This draft, which I discuss further below, shows that the little girl, giant ants, newspaper format, and orientation of Earth-as-receiver were all added later, when the idea was rewritten for publication in the periodical press. We know, then, that the shift from an active (transmitting) Earth to a passive (receiving) one took place at the moment in the idea's history when Galton was re-framing it for a large audience in the language of a mass media format which cast its readers as witnesses to developing current events, receivers of notionally unprejudiced information transmitted to them unaltered via the new communication technologies of the late-Victorian press.

At first, this seems at odds with Galton's agenda as a scientific educator. If the objective were the mathematical explication of a hypothesis, making Earth the source of the signals would eliminate the temptation to stray into speculation about the Martian civilisation. But whilst it might be argued that the change explains the scheme more effectively by showing the signals being decoded, walking the reader through the inductive processes which constitute the scientific idea, the decision to cast Mars as the sender also has the undeniably useful effect of eliding a number of the scheme's flaws, principally the fact that Galton did not know (as he admits in his 1892 *Times* letter) how such signals might actually be sent. All need to discuss the mechanical side of how to transmit these signals is wiped away by this narrative decision. Galton can now focus on the scientific problem he finds really interesting – the code – without being encumbered by technical pitfalls. Put another way, asking an audience to believe in an apparently untenable signalling apparatus is easier if you already have them imagining an entire civilisation on a different planet. Galton's science, as well as his story, is therefore to some extent dependant on the existence of a fantasy universe. In his world, unlike the real one, his brilliant idea can work, and does.

A rather more basic observation makes the narrative eddies seem less like afterthoughts on Galton's part: they recur, their apparently throwaway characters and speculations popping up again after a few pages' absence.

> The phenomenon is most extraordinary. If it be effected through the money of a mad millionaire, he must have had the sense to subsidise an uncommonly intelligent director of works.[25]

The clever little girl also makes a reappearance:

> There was some delay in puzzling out the above interpretation ; it was first discovered by the young lady mentioned above, who is more successful than most of her companions in guessing charades and at such like games.[26]

Though the nameless little girl's time on the page is brief – I have now quoted every sentence which mentions her – it is more than enough to create through implication an entire new subplot to Galton's story. The trope of the young, perspicacious heroine had been prominent in popular literature since at least the publication of *Alice's Adventures in Wonderland* (1865), and Galton's passing evocation of it here is not all that different, mechanically, from the 'X' in 'X. Observatory'. In both instances, the reader understands a signal (I use this word quite deliberately) to draw on a range of other texts and deploy their generic literacy in order to fill in the blank. On the one hand, Galton declines to give details about the little girl in order that he may be seen to be focussing on the maths; on the other, the pre-existence of a set of tropes surrounding precocious young ladies in extraordinary situations mean that he does not have to describe the character in order to imaginatively evoke her in some detail. Genre, in short, is what allows Galton to have his cake and eat it.

There are other moments in 'Intelligible Signals' where Galton turns away from efficient scientific communication to indulge fictional or assumptive idiosyncrasies, but hopefully sufficient evidence has been amassed here for me to make two main points. The first is that these idiosyncrasies arise inevitably from Galton's choice of narrative architecture. A piece of purely scientific writing, a treatise of the kind sometimes published by the *Fortnightly*, might not have required the giant ants or the little girl. But the New Journalism had made the newspaper form, even in the assessment of its enemy Matthew Arnold, inherently 'full of [. . .] novelty, variety, [and] sensation'.[27] Galton could not assume that form, even briefly, without bringing traces of those characteristics along with it. Adopting the voice of journalism, his article could not entirely avoid *becoming* it, becoming a piece 'whose appeal derived from a subjective interest in the evolving human drama'.[28] The failure of Galton's system to appear before the public several times prior to its eventual publication in the *Fortnightly* can be at least partly attributed to the fact that its various draft versions lacked the fictional apparatus, and were in some sense incomplete or unsatisfactory without it, either to Galton or to his editors.

The most obvious objection to my reading of this article would be to point out that the disruptive eddies in Galton's narrative represent an attempt on his part to sugar the pill, to ameliorate the complexity of his ideas and make them palatable to a general audience. It is quite probable that they were intended for this purpose, but I am arguing here that it cannot be *all* they are for. Gillian Beer has demonstrated with her famous reading of the *Origin of the Species* 'the degree to which narrative and argument share methods'. 'Intelligible Signals' and the *Origin* are very different pieces of work, but they were both written by eminent scientists (Galton was also Darwin's half-cousin) who thought carefully enough about how to lay their ideas before the public that the methods they eventually chose should not be dismissed as superfluous. The eddies in 'Intelligible Signals', to use Beer's words, 'cannot be skimmed off without a loss'.[29] This brings me to my second main point, which is that as well as being the consequence of Galton's narrative choices, the idiosyncrasies in this text are so closely related to the serious scientific content that it is not necessarily useful to think of them, as I have so far for rhetorical purposes, as separable elements of a conflicted text. 'Intelligible Signals' is not conflicted at all – it has, in fact, a remarkable singularity of purpose, one which is masked only when the text is approached with the preconception that science and fiction are fundamentally incommensurate. The blanks which the reader is implicitly invited to fill in are not only part-rooted in a desire to be more dispassionately scientific, but also, combined with the suspense mechanisms inherent in the newspaper extracts, constitute an encouragement to speculate, to approach the problem actively rather than passively.

It is on this point, with reader activity placed at the heart of the article's message, that 'Intelligible Signals' itself begins to resemble the communication scheme which it proposes. The (real) people reading the newspaper extracts in the *Fortnightly* have something in common with the (fictitious) readers finding them in their dailies as Mars sends its signals: both audiences are being slowly educated in a complex mathematical idea by having it introduced to them piecemeal, from basic principles up to sophisticated geometry. The signalling system is designed this way so that it can be universally decoded; the article is designed this way so that every reader can understand Galton's thinking. At both levels, that of interplanetary communication and that of popular science communication, the idea of intrinsic intelligibility is key. At both levels, it is through a combination of empirical understanding and an appeal to fill in the blanks for oneself which drive the communications forward. Galton's appeal is to the scientific imagination, and it is with this in mind, with 'science' and 'fiction' drawn on together rather than as opposites, that his article is best read.

When Galton sent the article to the *Fortnightly*, its editor, W. L. Courtney, wrote back to ask if its introduction could be removed: 'Would you mind if I omitted the opening sentences & made the paper read like a genuine account, only disclosing at the end that it was imaginary[?]'.[30] Galton's refusal to accede to this request demonstrates even better than his imaginative restraint against the odds, even better than his predominately dry tone, how crucial it was to him that this piece not be misconstrued as fantasy or a hoax.[31] Had "science fiction" been a term in 1896, he would presumably have baulked at its being applied to 'Intelligible Signals'. Even today, the piece could not be so labelled without some contention, and although I have demonstrated that the case could be made, what is important here is not ultimately whether or not this piece of writing by a famous scientist "is SF". SF or not, 'Intelligible Signals' shows that an idea from a serious scientist is not in conflict with a fantastical framework. Far from it, it seems to its author that an alliance of the two is 'the simplest way' to explain his thinking.

In an essay on 'Late Victorian Science and Science Fiction', Paul Fayter draws attention to the complexity of the relationship between these two supposed opposites:

> Professional scientists not only helped shape science fiction, in many cases their work was shaped by it. In a time of rapid industrialization, professionalization, and specialization, this late Victorian literature played a role in maintaining a common popular scientific culture.[32]

In Galton's article we see an illustration of Fayter's point: Galton both draws on and, in somewhat smaller measure, contributes to the development of both science and popular fiction. 'Intelligible Signals' evinces cooperation between the form of journalism and the content of a scientific thesis, and the two demonstrate a remarkable synergy precisely thanks to their shared relationship with narrative, not in spite of it. Galton wrote in a draft of the idea that the laws of arithmetic were the best way of achieving intrinsic intelligibility because they 'have the property of expressing much of their meaning by their *form*'.[33] The whole point of his signalling system, in other words, is that its form and content are synonymous. As with the code, so, more subtly, with the article advancing it.

'Intelligible Signals' *in situ*: H. G. Wells and W. T. Stead

'Intelligible Signals' appeared in November 1896. The previous month, the *Fortnightly Review* had published an essay on evolution by H. G. Wells, forty-four years younger than Galton and just at the beginning of his literary career. Wells had already made a name for himself with a number of short stories and, of course, the serialised publication of *The Time Machine* (*New Review*, January–May 1895), a book now regarded by many as a watershed moment in the emergence of SF.[34] Though it is because of his imaginative writings that Wells remains popularly known, much critical attention has been paid to his own scientific education (under T. H. Huxley) and his considerable body of writing on non-fictional scientific themes. In this section, I place Wells and Galton alongside each other in order to problematise the easy juxtaposition of them as 'novelist' and 'scientist'. I will then introduce the figure of W. T. Stead, a journalist reporting on supposed psychic communications from Mars, arguing that although the three writers approach the relationship between fact and fantasy in considerably divergent ways, focussing on their similarities might lead us to a more nuanced appreciation of the relationship between nineteenth-century literature and science.

Wells's article in the *Fortnightly*, called 'Human Evolution, an Artificial Process', sets out to explain why, if evolution is indeed a reliable theory, humans have not changed biologically since the Palaeolithic period. It includes sentences like this one:.

> Holding the generally-accepted views of variation, we must suppose as many human beings are born below the average in any particular as above it, and that, therefore, until our civilisation changes fundamentally, the intrinsic average man will remain the same.[35]

Focussing on the tone rather than the content of this sentence, we can see a marked similarity to the introduction which Galton refused to let W. L. Courtney cut from 'Intelligible Signals' – the dry, persuasive patter of the inductive reasoner. But the similarities between Wells and Galton are not just stylistic: both men are arguing a distinct scientific theory before the public; both attempt to convince on the basis of logical reasoning rather than experimental evidence. Their pieces are fairly light on statistics, emphasising (and, perhaps, attempting to encourage in others) the thought processes that drive scientific advancement rather than showcasing new data or research. Nowhere in 'Human Evolution' does Wells seem hindered by the fact that his principal qualification in discussing the subject is his own interest; similarly, Galton was a well-known scientist, but astronomy and linguistics were hardly his areas of special expertise. The underlying implication is that science can be expected to interest anybody of intelligence, and that this applies to those who write it as much as those who read it. As Wells had said elsewhere:

> It should also go far to reconcile even the youngest and most promising of specialists to the serious consideration of popular science, to reflect that the acknowledged leaders of the great generation that is now passing away, Darwin notably, addressed themselves in many cases to the general reader, rather than to their colleagues.[36]

The two men have subject areas in common as well. The issues which Wells is discussing in 'Human Evolution' interested Galton deeply, and he did some of his most famous work on them. Though the two differed in their conclusions, Wells closing with a view which 'reconciles a scientific faith in evolution with optimism', their shared subject matter, along with their shared language and choice of publication in the *Fortnightly*, testifies to a proximity which might at first be surprising given that one was the author of famous scientific romances and the other a Fellow of the Royal Society.[37] Where there are differences between the two, they are not always the ones which might be expected. For instance, Wells would not have enjoyed Galton's light-hearted asides about Martian ants – at least, not if his article on 'Popularising Science', published two years earlier in the science journal *Nature*, is to be believed. An explicit discussion of the value of communicating science to the public and the best ways of approaching that task, this essay begins by asserting that the contempt in which popular science is held by many scientists may be 'not altogether undeserved', and continues:

> . . .one may even go so far as to object altogether to the facetious adornment of popular scientific statements. Writing as one of the reading public, I may testify that to the common man who opens a book or attends a lecture, this clowning is either very irritating or very depressing.[38]

Wells here identifies himself as a consumer rather than a producer of popular science. His authority is that of the educated layman, and it is on behalf of the general readership that he is aggrieved by what he interprets as condescending gimmickry. His message is straightforward: 'scientific exponents who wish to be taken seriously should not only be precise and explicit, but also absolutely serious in their style'.[39]

Wells is writing several years before Galton published 'Intelligible Signals', but it remains intriguing that of the two of them it is the author of *The Invisible Man* who is calling for science to present itself seriously and the author of *On the Anthropometric Laboratory at the late International Health Exhibition* who is throwing around the idea of alien ants.

Nowhere in his 'Human Evolution' article does Wells lapse into fiction in the way in which I have argued Galton does. But of course, Wells had the considerable luxury of being able to do that elsewhere. His 'Human Evolution' article may make reference to 'Professor Weissmann's destructive criticisms of the evidence for the inheritance of acquired characters', but it also deploys Wells's own fictional writing in support of its case:

> . . .in this view, what we call Morality becomes the padding of suggested emotional habits necessary to keep the round Palæolithic savage in the square hole of the civilised state. And sin is the conflict of the two factors – as I have tried to convey in my *Island of Dr. Moreau*.[40]

I have already mentioned that the *Fortnightly* had been the first periodical to adopt a policy of signature. At the end of this article, though, its author is credited not only by name, but as 'H. G. Wells. (author of *The Time Machine*, *The Wonderful Visit*, &c., &c.)' (p. 595). Listing an author's other works in this fashion below the signature was unusual for the *Fortnightly*, and no other authors in that issue were signed with anything more than their names. It seems likely that Wells, or at least W. L. Courtney, believed that the essay would derive real credibility by association with the famous scientific romances.

Wells's reputation as a fiction-writer, in other words, bought him a certain latitude to enter real scientific debates. The converse was equally true: Wells's series of 'Stories from the Stone Age', which began publication in the *Idler* seven months after 'Human Evolution' appeared, are adventure tales (not considered SF by Everett F. Bleiler's index of the early genre) which, despite their very different tone and publication venue, are closely linked to the *Fortnightly* piece, their imaginative world powered by the scientific ideas which Wells had soberly laid out in 'Human Evolution'.[41] The opening paragraph of the first tale, with its description of an alien landscape (the geological past) which is also known intimately to the implied reader (the English countryside), is also a textbook example of the kind of cognitive estrangement which was, for Darko Suvin, one of SF's defining features:[42]

> In that remote age the valley which runs along the foot of the Downs did not exist, and the South of Surrey was a range of hills, fir-clad on the middle slopes, and snow-capped for the better part of the year.[43]

Once again, the point is not to quibble about whether or not this tale can be defined as SF, but rather to demonstrate that, much like Galton, Wells is using popular science and popular fiction to support each other. The difference is that he insists on dividing them into separate pieces of writing in order to do so, whilst Galton amalgamates the two in one article.

As for Wells's engagement with the favourable opposition of Mars, we need look no further than one of his most famous works, which began its run in *Pearson's Magazine* five months after 'Intelligible Signals' was published and whilst the 'Stories from the Stone Age' were still appearing in the *Idler*. *The War of the Worlds* is so indebted for its inspiration to the 1894 (unfavourable) opposition of Mars that it references a real article which had appeared in *Nature* in August of that year on its second page – again, non-fictional scientific writing appears directly to stimulate and power a fantastical narrative.[44] Whether or not Wells had read Galton's piece at this point (he had certainly read it by 1900[45]), it remains interesting that the book which he wrote in response to the Mars craze was fundamentally a story about humanity being on the receiving end of transmissions from the red planet. Aaron Worth, in the course of showing how willing the human characters in the book are to mistake the Martians' invasion for an attempt at communication, has drawn attention to the fact that the newspaper describes the first space capsule which lands on Horsell Common as 'A Message Received from Mars' rather than as an object or craft.[46] The similarity of this headline to Galton's 'Complete Decipherment of the First Part of the Message from Mars' is striking, and the resemblance between the two texts increases when, in *The War of the Worlds*, a deputation approaches the capsule, it having been 'resolved to show [the Martians] that we too were intelligent by approaching them with signals'.[47] Fluttering a white flag, another supposedly universal gesture (as flawed in that respect as any of Galton's), the deputation is vaporised by the Martian heat-ray, a technology which, as Worth observes, is a deadly counterpart to the heliographs which the British soldiers on the common use to communicate with each other.[48] Those devices are very similar to the heliostats which Galton had a role in inventing (Fig. 1.2), the sun-reflecting technology which formed the notional basis for his interplanetary communication system. Pointing out that they were seldom deployed by the British in anything but a colonial context, Worth argues that an implied association between signalling devices and weapons technology is part of how *The War of the Worlds* undertakes its critique of the British imperial project (p. 70). Galton's heliostat, invented for use in Africa in the 1850s, is certainly not innocent of this association.

Though it is tempting to draw links between Wells and Galton in the light of these similarities, any direct lines of influence between them are less important to my argument than the fact that they demonstrate the authors' joint involvement with wider popular culture. Both were subject to (or, it might be better phrased, successful because of their engagement with) themes which were "in the air", focal points of public interest in science such as the favourable opposition of Mars. But they also fell in with other discourses which were at large in general print culture, evidence of which can be traced by scrutinising the genres in which each participates and the extent of their engagement. The popular science writer, the career journalist, and the career scientist are categories which run into each other in the 1890s, in part because each was performing in the same theatre: the periodical press. This is a snapshot of one of component of material entanglement.

The diversity of science writing, Peter Broks argues, 'makes a nonsense of any attempt to construct a single "type"'.[49] His study of popular science attempts to stress this miasma rather than delineating a more hierarchical model of influence, arguing that:

> We should no longer see the media as a means of communication with popular science as its end product, but rather as a system of representations encompassing what was both popular and scientific.[50]

Galton and Wells represent opposite sides of Broks's cautious division of writers of popular science into 'those who were brought to science writing through their scientific activities [...] and those who came to it through their literary activities' (p. 30). The correspondences between them, despite the fact that they represent these apparently opposite camps, seem to confirm Bernard Lightman's declaration that:

> ...we cannot adopt the positivist diffusion model as a heuristic guide to research because it uncritically assumes the existence of two independent, homogenous cultures, elite and popular, and forces the latter into a purely passive role.[51]

Arguing that the key role of popularisers was 'to present the huge mass of scientific fact in the form of compelling stories', Lightman too shows that fiction need not necessarily be read as opposed to science when the two appear alongside each other (p. 188).

A rather different article about communicating with Mars illuminates this relationship from another angle. Whilst *The War of the Worlds* was appearing in *Pearson's Magazine*, W. T. Stead's quarterly journal of psychical research, *Borderland*, published a four-page item called 'News from Mars'. Written, like much of the magazine, by Stead himself, this piece offers a summary of the experiences of a medium called Mr Starling, who claims to have been receiving telepathic communications from a resident spirit of Mars named Silver Pearl. Starling's was very far from the only account which linked parapsychology to Mars around the turn of the century, and, as Robert Crossley has shown, many mediums and their interlocutors were drawn to the blend of fact and fantasy which Mars represented.[52] Stead's article, though, makes its relationship with fictional ideas of Mars particularly explicit: though Mr Starling provides spirit photographs of some Martians, their disappointingly human appearance on *Borderland*'s page is overshadowed by a large reproduction of one of Warwick Goble's famous illustrations of the terrifying Martian tripods from *The War of the Worlds* which Stead has set opposite them (Fig. 1.4). Stead's piece begins with a summary of Mars in literary culture, moving from a mention of George Du Maurier's recently published novel *The Martian* via a discussion of Wells straight into a report 'to the effect that Mrs. Burbank, one of the most noted of the Australian psychics, has been told by her invisible friends that the fauna of Mars include such creatures of the imagination as winged horses'.[53] The transition from literature to Stead's pet subject, the spirit world, comes without so much as a paragraph break. Together with phrases like 'creatures of the imagination' and the equality of footing which the layout gives to fictional illustrations and 'real' spirit photographs, this suggests that, like the editors of the *Fortnightly*, Stead had no problem with using fiction as a source of scientific authority – indeed, that he struggled to draw a distinction. This is unsurprising, given that occultism owes more to literature and the imagination than it does to the scientific method, but it remains arresting that when the article distorts an expert's views on the promise of spectroscopy into an endorsement of the spiritualist project, the expert is Tennyson rather than, say, Lord Kelvin.[54]

One possible explanation for the reliance on literary sources is that Stead proposes the existence of a larger, more intuitive and, crucially, more *narrative* truth, one which science denies. In an especially revealing sentence, seeking to distance himself from fully endorsing Starling's claims, Stead says:

> The fact that communications have been received cannot even be doubted by the greatest sceptic, but when we ask as to the truth of their origin we are confronted only with a blank wall.[55]

The distinction between *fact* and *truth* implied by this passage hints at a rather different interpretation of the distinctions between literature and

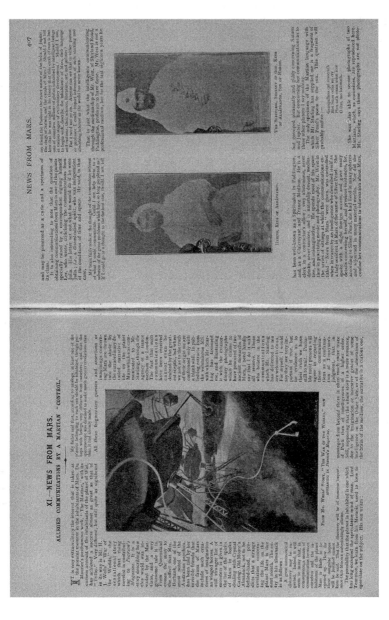

XI.—NEWS FROM MARS.

ALLEGED COMMUNICATIONS BY A MARTIAN "CONTROL."

407

1.4   Stead's *Borderland* prints illustrations from *The War of the Worlds* alongside Martian spirit photography (October 1897). Courtesy of Cambridge University Library.

science from that to which we have become accustomed. Provable reality is now a mere fact, with the unbridled power of 'the speculative mind of man' (Tennyson's, in this case) easily able to transcend it (p. 406). This explains why Stead may want to keep his distance from explicit Martian testimony offered by Starling: science may one day prove that Mars is uninhabited (or inhabited by creatures dissimilar to those reported by Silver Pearl), and the wider "truth" of spiritualism needs to be safeguarded from the possibility of this empirical disavowal. General, rather than specific truth, is the sand on which Stead needs to build.

Refusing to separate novels from spiritualist escapades (referring to both as 'stories'), Stead implies that this general, non-specific truth obtains equally in the work of Wells, du Maurier, and Starling. Later in the article Stead finally mentions a scientist when he relates that, according to Starling:

> Almost everything is done by electricity in Mars, and Silver Pearl stoutly declares that all Mr. Edison's discoveries are the result of impressions communicated to his brain by emissaries from Mars.[56]

Here, indeed, is an alternative explanation for the endurance of Mars in the public imagination. All the interest in the red planet could itself be the consequence not of Schiaparelli, or of the favourable oppositions, or of writing and speculation in the periodical press, but itself a form of psychical communication from outside: a wordless, intrinsically intelligible message from another world. This makes *Borderland*, in Stead's rather individual assessment, perform the same work as Galton's imaginary newspaper; whilst Galton theorises about interplanetary communication in the popular press, Stead fantasises that it is already taking place.

Despite their very different approaches to the question of evidence, 'Intelligible Signals' and 'News from Mars' have significant correspondences. Narrative is, in both, a kind of authority source, and both are, rather despite themselves, equally indebted to the trends *around* science in the popular culture from which they emerged. The important difference is that 'News from Mars' believes itself to be a report of literal truth, whilst 'Intelligible Signals' is up-front, at Galton's insistence, about its fantastical side. Both, though, are ultimately pieces of writing which capitalise upon fiction in order to advance a specific view about the location of truth – they are alike in their engagement with the imaginative work of popular culture in the attempt to persuade their readers.

Fiction is routinely conceived of as the opposite of fact. In Stead's 'News from Mars' we see this opposition in its most worrying form, fiction called upon as an authority source in declaring a highly dubious vision of the world literally true. But Galton and his contemporaries show us that fiction in its various forms was also a key component not only in the communication of scientific ideas but in their production and development as they moved across the various discourses of the periodical press. Wells and Galton share the tacit understanding that their audiences live in, and relate themselves to, a narrative world. Stead fantasises that reality is synonymous with narrative, Wells takes reality as the cue for his speculative writings, and Galton sees in narrative the opportunity to further his thinking about the real world. For none of the three are fact and fiction straightforwardly antithetical to each other.

The work of this chapter until now has all been necessary in order to definitively pronounce on this very basic point: fact and fiction need not necessarily be at odds. We imagine them as opposed to each other because, like literature and science (and a number of other cultural voices which I discussed in my introduction) it suits us to suppose that they precede history, that they shape culture rather than being shaped by it. Habermas points out, though, that the history of the public sphere is the history of fiction's emergence as a legitimate genre for the handling of rational debate: in the act of being defined, fiction 'shed the character of the merely fictitious'.[57] I have so far handled fact and fiction rhetorically as if they do represent mutually exclusive opposites, but that rigid conception of the exclusive territories of science and fiction quickly collapses under detailed scrutiny. Everywhere, if we go looking for them, the two are co-extant. It is the different inflections of the dynamic between them, rather than a simple question of their presence or absence, which can lead to such varied truth-effects as the scientific hypotheses of Galton or the occultist fantasies of Stead. The relationship between literature and science is significantly more complicated than the 'Two Cultures' image gives us reflexively to imagine, and with this understood it becomes possible to take a step further. Reading Galton's article with an appreciation of interplay between fact and fiction as a starting rather than an ending premise, we can now ask questions about the levels and nature of that interplay, the conditions which allowed it to flourish, and the political imperatives which extensive engagement with it suggests. It is to this more nuanced activity that I now turn.

Wide-ranging enthusiasm

Reading over the documents leading up to the publication of 'Intelligible Signals' leaves two lasting impressions in particular. The first is of the considerable verve and persistence with which Galton approached his subject. As well as the letters to the *Times* and the *Spectator* (1892), the idea also appears, as I mentioned earlier, in a version of a lecture – called 'The Just-Perceptible Difference', it was given at the Royal Institution on 27 January 1893. Galton drafted (but never delivered) a section for this lecture which contains an early form of his 'Intelligible Signals' system and which therefore gives us insight into how the communication system looked four years prior to its publication.

One of the striking consistencies across the various documents through which the evolution of the idea can be traced is Galton's tendency to characterise the idea as a caprice, even to himself. In 1893, it was 'the idle moment of a summer ramble' he took advantage of in order to devise geometric problems for his communication system; his renewed interest in 1896 was the consequence of 'being unable to occupy myself otherwise than in a desultory way' whilst vacationing at the hot baths of Wildbad.[58] Something of this holiday spirit perhaps survives in the restrained glee detectable behind some of the narrative eddies of 'Intelligible Signals'. The sense that Galton is enjoying himself is an important aspect of his writing, for the communication of that sense to a wider audience remains, for many, a defining feature of good popular science.

The other most immediately striking characteristic of the essay is the audacious breadth of Galton's thinking: the signalling project alone touches on mathematics, linguistics, astronomy, and physics, and I have argued here that fiction can be added to the list; his discussions of heliographs were dependant on his experiences in Africa and his book on *The Art of Travel*; today, he is remembered for his contributions to statistics, anthropology, and meteorology, and above all else his foundational role in the field of eugenics. These areas by no means form an exhaustive list of his interests. Though the acuity of his thinking in any one of them may be questionable, the fact that he immersed himself in so many different forms of knowledge is much more important to my argument here than how successful he was in doing so. Galton's evident enjoyment of his subject and the diversity of fields through which he was prepared to pursue it come together in the slightly hackneyed phrase 'wide-ranging enthusiasm', which I here apply (somewhat rebelliously) as a technical term: it is this combination of characteristics which makes Galton himself, as well as the article in the *Fortnightly*, a useful conceptual model for exploring the relationships between different fields of knowledge.

As I noted earlier, 'Intelligible Signals' represents only a footnote to its author's enormous and varied career. This chapter's close focus on one short article is not the product of an assumption that it represents a paradigmatic example of popular science (it doesn't even represent a paradigmatic example of the work of Francis Galton). Rather, I have concentrated on 'Intelligible Signals' because it provides such a useful crucible of the issues which arise when a scientist writes for a general audience, a point which has been made on broader ground than that of my very specific example by, for instance, Robert Crossley's book-length literary history of Mars. Crossley demonstrates that for much of human history, and especially since 1877, the red planet has repeatedly seemed to blur the lines between fiction and fantasy.[59] This blurring, says Crossley, is partly the consequence of the pull Mars exerts on the imagination, and it was this pull which was the ultimate cause of the 'Mars craze' which provoked Galton's article and so much besides (pp. 7–8). I now want to suggest that Galton's appeal to the imagination not only implicitly unites science and fiction but also uses the sphere of popular consciousness to invite a sympathetic understanding of the relationships between a host of academic disciplines, including literature and science. Seen this way, the Martian communication scheme starts to look like an emergent consequence of Galton's far broader enthusiasm for the bringing together of disparate fields of intellectual enquiry before the eyes of the public.

Underpinning many of Galton's efforts to popularise science, both in articles and in public lectures, is an implied argument about what today's university administrators would describe as "impact". This is expressed superficially in the 'practical bearings' of his less outrageous schemes, which he is at pains to emphasise;[60] we see it as an animating influence behind the decision to express most of 'Intelligible Signals' as fake newspaper extracts, couching the mathematical and linguistic concepts of Galton's signalling mechanism in a medium with which many of his readers might have been more familiar (and doing much besides, as I have been arguing). But the use of Mars itself, at a time shortly after the craze provoked by its favourable opposition, hints at another way in which Galton presents science to the public in terms of day-to-day relevancy: his continuous referencing of contemporary events. If Galton was, as the evolution of his signalling idea testifies, subject to the ebb and flow of public interest, he also sought to capitalise upon it, introducing audiences to his new concepts by showing them at work in familiar situations.

A recurring theme in all of Galton's writing quoted so far, telegraphy demonstrates this point nicely. Though it has dwindled as a source of imaginative inspiration in the intervening years (compared at least to

Mars), Peter Broks points out that in the *fin-de-siècle* '[a]chievements in
telegraphy [...] were as exciting and as promising as those in flight'.[61]
Richard Menke has drawn attention to the dramatic effect of the telegraphic revolution on fiction at large:

> ...these instruments offered figures for the connections of interest and
> intersubjectivity that linked the members of a society, and for the multi-
> farious networks of relation often postulated by Victorian literary
> realisms.[62]

The periodical press in particular was full of telegraphy, whether it was the
idea of wireless signals between ships at sea ('...no longer the dream of the
scientist. It is an accomplished fact', wrote Herbert C. Fyfe in *Pearson's
Magazine*) or the dramatic new possibilities opened up by vast cables
connecting continents.[63] 'The most interesting of all maps', wrote
J. Henniker Heaton in the *Fortnightly*,

> is a cable chart of the world. It is like a dissection of the nervous system in the
> body. From the brain, England, the cables branch out into every country
> [...]. The human race is, as it were, in a vast whispering gallery.[64]

As well as being full of telegraphy, the periodical press was in a sense made
of it: the 'vast whispering gallery' had had dramatic effects on the production of newspapers and magazines. These effects were both material,
allowing articles to be cabled from vast distances almost instantly, and
metaphorical, as W. T. Stead reveals in this piece of wisdom offered to a
young copy-editor:

> I had advised him as a remedy against the besetting sin of all young
> journalists, verbosity, never to send any copy into a newspaper until he
> had imagined he had to telegraph it to Australia at a dollar a word, and had
> struck out every superfluous word to save his dollars.[65]

By being "promising" as well as "exciting", the telegraph invited optimistic
speculation about the future of both applied science and empire. The 'vast
whispering gallery' is a utopian vision of a unified earth. Future societies
envisaged in the periodical press are seldom without something like a
telegraph; the spread of telegraphy was provoking popular imagination in
many of the same ways as SF. It was also enabling the transmission of
stories – both physically, and by providing authors with a new metaphor on
which to draw. In short, the very notion of 'signalling' when Galton was
writing was as hot a topic as Mars itself; the pictorial component of the sun
signals idea had its origin in his 'Just-Perceptible Difference' scheme to send
pictures over the telegraph.[66] 'Intelligible Signals', seen in this context,

doesn't so much envisage a communications breakthrough as it does the possibility of extending the pre-existing telegraph system further, into outer space.[67]

Galton's engagement with contemporary enthusiasms can also be observed in a remark at the end of 'Intelligible Signals' that the decipherment of his code would require 'a small fraction of the care and thought bestowed, say, on the decipherment of hieroglyphics'.[68] This is the same conclusion which he reaches in the last sentence of the 'Just-Perceptible Difference' lecture draft (the solution would take 'an amount of effort that would be trifling to that which has, for instance, been spent on hieroglyphics').[69] That Galton preserves this concluding rhetoric across nearly four years (and that it survived the numerous other changes which the idea underwent in the meantime) is a telling indication of his eagerness to capitalise on the very current fame of the 'decoding' of the ancient Egyptian language. Like hieroglyphics, the sun signals to Mars occupy the grey area between language and code, but the comparison, on Galton's part, also forms another quite deliberate engagement with a popular trend.

In the final version of 'The Just-Perceptible Difference', there is a moment where Galton uses an even more ubiquitous practice – reading itself – to link the worlds of matter and feeling:

> It happens that although most persons train themselves from childhood upwards to distinguish imagination from fact, there is at least one instance in which we do the exact reverse. Namely, in respect to the auditory presentation of the words that are perused by the eye. It would be otherwise impossible to realise the sonorous flow of the passages, whether in prose or poetry, that are read only with the eyes...[70]

Galton understands silent reading as an essentially imaginative act, and his insistence that this applies equally to 'prose or poetry' implies a connection not just between imagination and perception (the principal argument of the lecture) but also between the various subcategories of writing. It's crucial that Galton regards this connection as situated primarily in the mind of the reader, and specifically in their imagination. Mars, the telegraph, hieroglyphics: it was the *imagination* to which all of these things really appealed, and via writing that this appeal could be accessed. Mars in particular demanded imaginative attention precisely because so little was known about it. It was attractive because its malleability to personal interpretation excited the reader's imagination, as Stead's ghosts and Galton's ants so forcibly remind us. In evoking Mars, Galton is doing more than demonstrating the impact of science; he connects science intrinsically to the everyday not just via material association but by an appeal to imaginative curiosity, an instinct which he perceives as underpinning both science and fiction. This is an idea which present-day popular science continues to draw on. Television physicist Professor Brian Cox said of Carl Sagan in a 2010 radio interview that:

> That sense of, sense of wonder – it's a cliché in a way, but you hear it, you know, it suffuses everything Sagan did. And it's important, and I think it knows no boundaries when you're a kid. I mean I couldn't separate, I didn't care to separate science fiction from science fact. For me it was, it was my imagination, just reaching out to other worlds.[71]

It is significant that the 'cliché' of *wonder* is the key to Cox's early involvement with science, and that the concept is given such prominence in the titles of his programmes *Wonders of the Solar System*, *Wonders of the Universe*, and *Wonders of Life*. The term is perhaps widely considered unscientific now, but in her introduction to the collection *Literature and Science*, Sharon Ruston points out that 'wonder' and popular science have long been closely connected:

> Often stemming from Darwin's final passage of *Origin of Species*, where he declares upon contemplating the entangled bank, "there is a grandeur in this view of life," popular science writers have made it their career to enthuse the public with a sense of wonder at the natural world.[72]

In his popular history of early nineteenth-century science, Richard Holmes emphasises the unitary power of this idea:

> Romanticism as a cultural force is generally regarded as intensely hostile to science, its ideal of subjectivity eternally opposed to that of scientific objectivity. But I do not believe this was always the case, or that the terms are so mutually exclusive. The notion of *wonder* seems to be something that once united them, and can still do so.[73]

The book is called *The Age of Wonder*.

It seems appropriate, then, that one index of Victorian periodicals lists an editorial goal of *Pearson's Magazine* as being 'to create wonder about the ordinary and tell a good story'.[74] C. A. Pearson was a staunch populist, and his magazine had little in common with the intellectual *Fortnightly Review*,[75] but with Suvin's concept of cognitive estrangement, it is not hard to locate the rationale behind Galton's article, and science fiction generally, in the two halves of that proposition: 'wonder about the ordinary' and 'a good story'. It also serves to connect all of the other superficially disparate modes of writing which were materially entangled in a physical issue of *Pearson's*:

reviews, interviews, other kinds of fiction, opinion pieces and, of course, popular science. Galton uses the idea of 'wonder' himself in that passage so crucial to this chapter's arguments – Mars begins to signal 'to the wonderment of our astronomers' – but, more importantly, his wide-ranging enthusiasm, methods of narration and subjects of discussion seem to indicate that he too believes not only that all these different things can be linked, but that the imagination, aided by a 'good story', is the 'simplest way' to link them.[76]

This idea of unifying intellect provides one possible explanation for Galton's wildly tangential reference to the 'gigantic folly' of the Tower of Babel. It also makes 'Intelligible Signals' seem more suited than ever to the *Fortnightly Review*, a publication with a founding mandate to 'encourage, rather than repress, diversity of opinion, satisfied if we can secure the higher uniformity which results from the constant presence of sincerity and talent'.[77] Mark W. Turner has stressed this magazine's emphasis on this diversity, writing that:

> The *Fortnightly* – by blending the discourses of 'high' and 'low' culture, by placing a philosophical review article alongside an instalment of a serial novel – would have sent conflicting signals to the periodical-reading public: two shillings fortnightly instead of one shilling monthly, fiction alongside serious review-like articles. Where was the *Fortnightly* to be read: in the club, the drawing room, or the study?[78]

Just as the *Fortnightly* appears to Turner stuck between social and domestic space, Galton's article exists somewhere between popular science, science fiction, and journalism. My contention, however, is that both magazine and article occupy their liminal spaces to great effect, using them to empower the coexistence of apparently opposed areas of culture and politics. 'Intelligible Signals' participation in a spread of genres, then, is not only a mechanical advantage but also a political imperative.

'The perceived need from within the literary sphere to distinguish between factual and fictional writing', Matthew Rubery argues, 'arose in part from the mutual dependence on narrative in its most fundamental sense as a way of telling a story'.[79] Narrative is a language which we all speak – the closest we ever really get, perhaps, to intrinsic intelligibility. I have already quoted Peter Broks' argument that the media should be examined less 'as a means of communication' and more 'as a system of representations', an argument which could also be usefully applied to Galton's sun signals. These, too, may better be described as 'a system of representations' than as a language in themselves.[80] Mathematical, algebraic, and, in their most sophisticated incarnation, pictorial, the signals are supposed to be building blocks of intelligible communication rather than a 'means of communication', but this is ultimately an impossible goal according to Friedrich Kittler, who, in the assessment of James Mussell, urges us 'to resist reducing text to information and instead recognise its roots in the media that permit it to exist in the world'.[81]

Galton's idealised code transcends language by becoming coextensive with its form: the medium not only shapes the message, it *is* the message. The article which conveys this idea is no more inert or passive than the signals themselves. Its tone, structure, and situation in and across the periodical press – which it inhabits a relatively elite corner of whilst gesturing outward at the sensationalist New Journalist newspaper – all reflect a complex engagement with popular culture, one which produces meaning as well as conveying it. Narrative, and the spread of genres which it can articulate, might from this perspective be considered just as legitim-ate a building block for a sign-system as algebra: Dallas Liddle reminds us, via Bakhtin, that 'genre is a necessary component of meaning as well as a medium for it'.[82] Actively inviting the work of many imaginations, not just Galton's, for its effect, 'Intelligible Signals' leads by example, showing the genres of written science and fiction unified by wonder about the ordinary and a good story. It is convenient for this argument that Turner uses the phrase 'conflicting signals' in the passage quoted earlier: all writing gives off signals, usually less explicitly than Galton's, but here we see that 'conflicting signals', issuing from the body of a general magazine, need not necessarily be contradictory ones. By its appeal to the imagination as an experimental space, Galton's wide-ranging enthusiasm hints at the science-fictional possibility of bringing genres, as well as worlds, into contact. It provides a powerful metaphor for present-day interdisciplinary communications.

The situation as it stands is summarized by George Levine:

> The disciplinary divisions are almost absolute. Scientists don't talk to philosophers of science; philosophers of science don't talk to literary theor-ists; literary theorists – while implying their right through the study of language and discourse to tread on everyone's turf – seem not to talk to anybody but like minded theorists.[83]

For better or worse, debates like 'The Two Cultures' have, in the 120-odd years since Galton published his proposal, made his particular brand of wide-ranging enthusiasm a thing of the past. The tale of Habermas's public sphere, too, as Craig Calhoun has noted, is the tale of 'the loss of a notion of general interest' in the course of which 'the members of the public sphere lose their common ground'.[84] Diversification leads to isolation, and isolation to insularity. Both Calhoun and Habermas are clear that a return to the eighteenth-century bourgeois establishment would be undesirable, and I am certainly not arguing for an attempt to recapture an idealised Victorian intellectual discourse. I would like to end this chapter, though, with a pitch for wide-ranging enthusiasm as a methodological paradigm – both for research and for life more broadly. As Levine remarks, a century of specialisation has not made people themselves any less multi-faceted, any less capable of general interest, than Galton was:

> Think [. . .] about the multiple ways in which we think of ourselves from moment to moment – say, white, Jewish, professional, lover, father, liberal, cynic, unbeliever, cheese-lover, adulterer, friend, teacher, liar, good guy, writer, critic, coward, bird-lover, duck-eater, failure, success. . . And yet with all the variations and all the contradictions, every morning we wake up being us. The 'self' affirms itself in the very continuity and ordinariness of our lives.[85]

People, in other words, are as multiple and conflicted as periodicals, whilst somehow remaining coherent. Wide-ranging enthusiasm, not disciplinary myopia, is our default state. It is touching, therefore, to read in the closing sentences of Galton's essay the most telling indication of his desire for intrinsic intelligibility: the assertion that communication between two civilisations would be possible only 'if they were both as far advanced in science and arts'.[86] The unification of the human race is one of SF's major themes, and Galton's prescription remains very relevant today. Before we try to talk to the aliens, it is still necessary to think about how we talk to each other.

CHAPTER 2

Distance over time
Using periodicals to predict the future

On the absence of the future in early SF

My first chapter outlined some of the ways in which periodical space enabled connections between the genres of science and fiction. But there is another important dimension to the way in which the periodical embodies these connections – the particular way in which it engages with *time*. This chapter focusses on the magazines' temporal characteristics, demonstrating conceptual formations which made periodicals such an important home of early genre SF.

To best pursue this subject, we might begin with an observation made by Sam Moskowitz in the preface to his anthology of *fin-de-siècle* SF: 'The intriguing thing about these stories', he notes, 'is that, with few exceptions, the action occurs in the times in which the stories were written'.[1] The contemporary setting of the majority of early SF might be a surprise to readers who expect the genre to be necessarily engaged with futurity, but my argument here is that far from being oriented towards prediction, SF in this period is closely engaged with its present day. This fact, as we shall see, is closely related to the physical, periodical location of the majority of this writing.

Moskowitz's assessment holds true of a far broader spectrum of 'gaslight' literature than the twenty-six tales (all originally printed in magazines) which it introduces. The vast majority of enrolled SF from this period is set within a few years of the date it was written or, alternatively, at an unspecified date in a society which very closely resembled the author's. Naturally, there were exceptions to this – much of what is often called 'utopian literature', for example, is distinguished by its future setting. Even these works, though, draw their abiding concerns from a very specific sense of the here and now. Utopian literature, as Matthew Beaumont has demonstrated, 'dreams that the diffusion of its ideas in the present will create the conditions necessary for instituting its ideal society in the future' – in other words, it exists not to predict the future but to influence the politics of the present.[2] This impulse aside, utopian literature also generally displays a marked reluctance to imagine the kind of technological change which is so often the concern of the SF which retained a contemporary setting. Edward Bellamy's *Looking Backward: 2000–1887* (1888), for instance, imagines a very differently organised Boston at the turn of the millennium, but restricts scientific innovation to a few incidental details and is keen to stress continuities between the two epochs in order to make Bellamy's utopian society appear achievable.[3] By contrast, the *Voyages Extraordinaires* of Jules Verne, which thrive on technological novelty, are for the most part set in the present, the novum typically possessed by a single person or organisation in an otherwise recognisable nineteenth century.

With the notable exception of *The Time Machine*, of which more later, all of H. G. Wells's major scientific romances of the 1890s have near-contemporary settings; his attempt to visualise the year 2000, *Anticipations of the Reactions of Mechanical and Scientific Progress upon Human Life and Thought*, on the other hand, appeared as a non-fictional 'series of papers' in the *Fortnightly Review* (which, as we learnt in the last chapter, had a line in speculative scientific non-fiction).[4] *Anticipations* based its vision of the future on developments in transport infrastructure, and constitutes a far more rigorous attempt to imagine a technologically distinct future than Bellamy's novel. Unlike *Looking Backward*, however, it entirely lacks central characters, dramatic tension, and plot. Considered attempts to *predict* the future seem, on the whole, to be more the province of non-fiction in this period.

On the first page of *Anticipations*, Wells takes the opportunity to rebuke what he calls 'Fiction of the Future', which, he says, 'pretty frankly abandons the prophetic altogether, and becomes polemical, cautionary, or idealistic, and a mere footnote and commentary to our present discontents' (p. 747). With the important exception of the word 'mere', this is a sentiment with which I set out an agreement in what follows. I do so by reading two *fin-de-siècle* examples of that rarer strain of SF from this period which *does* portray a comprehensively imagined, definite future: Wells's *The Time Machine* and Rudyard Kipling's short story 'With the Night Mail'. Like utopian fiction, these works manifestly draw their impetus from the present, but I will also show that it is a present specifically determined by the physical properties of the magazines in which they made their initial appearances; their periodical location significantly bears on the ways in which they approach time and temporality. This is an argument which I shall make both by analysing internal language, in particular the deployment of tense, and by reading other items which appeared in the same issues, showing the stories' external connections with their material context.

My treatments of Kipling and Wells form two parts of this chapter. In between them, I examine a selection of *non*-fictional future-prediction pieces from the magazines, showing that these speculative writings also depend on their periodical surroundings for the substance of their approach to time as well as for their form and appearance. The argument I am progressing towards is that both fictional and non-fictional writings about the future drew on a periodical conception of time which was particularly useful because it was rooted in ambiguity. Magazines, by materially entangling a variety of present tenses, perform a kind of world-building which resembles that of much SF. It is natural, then, to find early examples of this world-building technique in magazines, and it becomes worth scrutinising their material contexts in more detail. Having made this argument, I propose in the final section that it also has a political dimension. Science, fiction, and the periodical press in this period all share a distrust of the authoritarian voice which their joint approach to time provides them with a meaningful way of circumventing.

Time, the periodical, and Rudyard Kipling's world-building

Laurel Brake has drawn attention to the fact that most of the Victorian works which we are now accustomed to encountering as discrete volumes made their first appearances in the pages of periodicals, the process of transition between the two constituting 'a principal model of authorship in nineteenth-century Britain'.[5] Mike Ashley points out that the popular magazine was not only 'the vehicle for the latest stories by the latest authors' but also 'the medium through which written tales passed on their way towards becoming books'.[6] These quotations emphasise two essential characteristics of periodical literature – novelty and ephemerality – and cast the periodical as a medium fundamentally embedded in the present tense. Distanced from the past by its highly contemporary associations, the magazine fades into obscurity as time passes and some of its constituents make their way into more durable volume editions.

Specific issues (and their contents) may be necessarily ephemeral, but *titles* can (if successful) be far less so. As James Mussell has pointed out, we seldom imagine titles as collections of issues, but rather as corporate identities whose characteristics are not necessarily well reflected in the contents of any given instalment.[7] Periodicals are literally and metaphorically bound into a continuum whose identity may be contributed towards by each individual issue, but which is not necessarily paradigmatically embodied by any. In other words, a magazine "title" describes not just the string of objects whose rhythmic publication constitutes a periodical's corpus, but also the metaphor underlying them, the metaphor which orders a potentially infinite succession of present tenses with their regular, serial appearance. Mark W. Turner comments on this when he points out that 'the periodical stretches back in time whilst simultaneously projecting the future'.[8] Turner describes periodical time as complex, multi-layered, chaotic, and, above all, fundamental: 'The media has always both defined and been defined by temporal division'.[9] In other words, as its form runs implicitly into both without ever fixing itself in either, the periodical speaks to eternity in the present tense. This relationship to time – and specifically to tense, I shall argue here – is part of what makes the magazine such fecund ground for SF.

Tenses play an important role at a textual level in Rudyard Kipling's 'With the Night Mail', a short story which first appeared in America in the November 1905 issue of *McClure's* and made its British début in the following month's *Windsor Magazine*. The piece describes a voyage across the Atlantic in a future where the invention of extremely efficient airships has not only revolutionised transport but also, by extension, ushered in a benign world government (the Aerial Board of Control, or A.B.C.) and an end to warfare. With its plethora of intricately described inventions and its willingness to show them at work in various situations, the story is arguably a watershed moment for the emergent SF: though it is understudied, Andy Sawyer notes, it is 'particularly important in science fiction because it does a number of things that many SF readers think such a story should do, it does them particularly well, and yet it reads with a particular strangeness to modern eyes'.[10]

Some of this strangeness originates from an abrupt shift which the tale makes from the past into the present tense, which Sawyer says enhances the tale's 'narrative immediacy' (p. 119). This it certainly does, but I believe that there is much more to be said about Kipling's use of tense in this story, which demonstrates profound connections to the periodical press. These connections can also be traced in the piece's paratextual elements, its textual history, and its resonances with other pieces published in the December 1905 *Windsor*. This section explores all of these aspects in detail.

'With the Night Mail' begins in an unobtrusive narrative past tense, to which any reader of fiction will be well accustomed:

> At 9:30 p.m. of a windy winter's night I stood on the lower stages of the
> G.P.O. Outward Mail Tower. My purpose was a run to Quebec in 'postal
> packet 162, or such other as may be appointed'. . .[11]

During the second paragraph, however, the transition noted by Sawyer
takes place:

> From the Despatching-caisson I was conducted by a courteous and won-
> derfully learned official – Mr L. L. Geary, Second Despatcher of the
> Western Route – to the Captain's Room (this wakes an echo of old
> romance), where the Mail captains come on their turn of duty. He intro-
> duces me to the captain of 162. . .[12]

By the end of this passage, the narrative has shifted smoothly to the present
tense. There it remains for the bulk of the story, not just for present-simple
exposition work, where it might be expected ('Practically, the A.B.C.
confirms or annuls most international arrangements, and, to judge by its
last report, finds our tolerant, humourous, lazy little planet only too ready to
lay the whole burden of private administration on its shoulder', p. 63) but
also when relating specific moments of action ('Our bow clothes itself in
blue flame and falls like a sword. No human skill can keep pace with the
changing tensions', p. 60). On the story's final page, the narrative tense
shifts back into the past simple with the same lack of ceremony as the first-
page shift to present continuous, the change almost hidden amidst dialogue:

> 'Thirty years,' *says* George, with a twinkle in his eye. 'Are you going to
> spend 'em all up here, Tim? Our letters'll be a trifle discharged.'
>
> 'Flap along, then. Flap along. Who's hindering?' The senior captain *laughed*,
> as we *went* in.[13]

The fact that the tale is book-ended by the more traditional past-tense
narrative, together with the inconspicuousness of the moments at which it
shifts and its tendency to drop back into the past at certain points (at one
point for nearly a whole page), all support the conceit that the present
tense narration emerges, on one level at least, with a degree of inadver-
tence; the story's unusual narrative, perhaps even in spite of itself, crystal-
lises out of the more standard past-tense mode in which it opens. Though
set in the future, the story has a superficially apparent need to function in
the present tense.

The present continuous is the tense of repetition; of a happening before,
during, and after now. It is also, as we have seen, the tense of Turner's
periodical, which stretches both forwards and back from the current
moment. 'With the Night Mail', then, evokes not only the present, but

a specifically *periodical* present. We can see this in the content of the story as well as its grammar, for example in Kipling's condescending backwards-references to the 'old romance' of the past, which is Kipling's reader's present.[14] In the parenthetical 'echo of an old romance' in the first passage quoted earlier, then – at the *exact* moment of the story's shift into the present tense – there is a retrospective glance at the present day of 1905, evoking the imagery of the naval empire to which Kipling's aerial one is constantly addressed.

Another clue that the story is anchored to the present is the date at which it is set. This is October 2147 in the *Windsor* publication, but in the American version in *McClure's Magazine,* the story is dated June 2025 – 122 years earlier. When the story made the transition to book form in 1909, the date was changed again, this time to the more iconic year 2000. The considerable variance in the story's date between published versions can be read as the macrocosmic parallel to the confused shifts of tense which take place on the narrative level, drawing attention back, like all those asides about the romantic, ancient past, to the far more stable timeframe of the story's composition, Kipling's present tense. Whatever the motivation for these changes – authorial or editorial – the fact that they were made when the three versions are otherwise virtually identical suggests, significantly, that the *specific* futurity of this thoroughly constructed world is not its abiding concern.[15]

The date of 'With the Night Mail' is mentioned only in the paratexts of each version of the story, passing unmentioned in the texts themselves. In its magazine appearances, the information appears in a dateline which was part of the story's header, just below the author's name and just above the actual text of the story (Fig. 2.1). 'Dateline', of course, is a word normally associated with print news – and in fact, this is exactly the sort of association which Kipling is hoping to make. In full, the line in the London version reads *'From "The Windsor Magazine", October, A.D. 2147'.*[16] By this rhetorical turn, it is not just Kipling who looks forwards, but the magazine itself; the story is an explicit manifestation of the anticipation every issue of a periodical implicitly holds for its successors. The dateline is a small but crucial detail, since it uses the formal apparatus of the magazine to initialise Kipling's fictive universe – it is part of the story, but *looks* like part of the periodical. It alone tells us that the story is meant to be read internally as a magazine piece, that it is a simulated magazine article (October 2147) as well as a real one (December 1905). The dateline articulates the connection between the two by stressing that the publication – the *Windsor* – is the same in both cases: Kipling links himself

WITH THE NIGHT MAIL.

By RUDYARD KIPLING.

From " The Windsor Magazine," October, A.D. 2147.

AT 9.30 p.m. of a windy winter's night I stood on the lower stages of the G.P.O. Outward Mail Tower. My purpose was a run to Quebec in " postal packet 162, or such other as may be appointed "; and the Postmaster - General himself countersigned the order. This talisman opened all doors, even those in the Despatching-caisson at the foot of the Tower, where they were

Captain Purnall, and we are shot up by the passenger-lift to the top of the Despatch-towers. Our "coach" will lock on when it is filled, and the clerks are aboard . . . .

Number 162 waits for us in Slip E of the topmost stage. The great curve of her back shines frostily under the lights, and some minute alteration of trim makes her rack a little in her holding-down clips.

Captain Purnall frowns and dives inside. Hissing softly, 162 comes to rest level as a rule. From her North Atlantic Winter nose-cap (worn bright as diamond with boring through uncounted leagues of hail, snow, and

2.1   Detail from first page of Kipling's 'With the Night Mail' – showing that dateline that is both story and paratext (December 1905). Courtesy of Cambridge University Library.

not to a generic, invented, far-future publication, but to a projection of the one in which his story is actually appearing. In its American appearance, the fictitious future-article's venue is also synchronous with the real article's venue, *McClure's*, the variance between the two versions ensuring the preservation of this sense of periodical continuity for readers on both sides of the Atlantic.[17]

Paratext and text complement each other so well that when the story appeared as a discrete book in 1909, it was evidently felt necessary to preserve a sense of the periodical. The full title of the book version is *With the Night Mail: a story of 2000AD (together with extracts from the contemporary magazine in which it appeared).*[18] This version lacks the dateline, but both elements from it on which I have focused – the date itself and its testimony to the supposed magazine appearance – have moved into the subtitle ('2000AD'; 'contemporary magazine'), a subtitle which the story retained when it was collected in later editions of Kipling's work.[19] The reader of the book version is therefore immediately confronted with the fact that the text is supposed to be imagined as part of a magazine, now an unnamed title since there is no specific current periodical with which to establish a link. This is emphasised by the presence of what the title refers to as '*extracts*' – an appendix of "magazine sections" prepared by Kipling to replicate a serial context for his tale. These include: the 'A.B.C. Bulletin' (air traffic news, including a mention of one of the incidents in the main story); notes and correspondence sections; a book review; and a diverting advertising supplement. The appendix is certainly a mechanism by which Kipling can allow 'the history and political superstructure of this world to be deduced' – an empowering device for constructing a fictitious world – but it is also a way of re-creating the "feel" of a periodical in the reader of the book version, one which might remind us of the way Galton mimics the New Journalist newspaper in the pages of the Fortnightly Review (see Chapter 1).[20] The supplement appears in neither of the story's original periodical publications: fake magazine paraphernalia are redundant when the real things abound (Fig. 2.2).

And the "real things" of the *Windsor*, although not set in the same world as Kipling's story, turn out still to have a great deal in common with it. The first instalment of B. Fletcher Robinson's 'Chronicles in Cartoon: A Record of Our Own Times' was the item before Kipling's story in the December 1905 issue of the *Windsor*. Robinson was the editor of *Vanity Fair*, and in this series of articles he reflects on that magazine's history and reprints a selection of its most eye-catching satirical artwork. His tone is highly reminiscent of Kipling's repeated references to the past when he says of the year in which *Vanity Fair* was founded, 1868:

> At that period Society still preserved its inexorable barriers. Agriculture, if depressed, was a source of fair rentals to owners of land; the Kaffir market had not successfully bombarded the citadels of the British aristocracy. The Smart Set were mercifully wrapped in the mists that surrounded alike Mr. Sutro and the future.[21]

Like the sections of 'With the Night Mail' which evoke the 'ancientest traditions' of steamships, this is a passage which takes advantage of the past's ignorance of the present. The difference is that the *Windsor* reader is in the present of Robinson's piece rather than the past of Kipling's. Mimicking not only the tone of pieces like Robinson's but also their rhetorical assumption that the reader is in on the joke (that they know, for example, who 'Mr. Sutro' is), is part of the technique by which Kipling makes his world so convincing.

Robinson seems aware of this as he discusses the history of one magazine in the pages of another. He stresses that *Vanity Fair* has provided a continuous documentation of the changes which have taken place since 1868; that it is the 'Record of Our Own Times', the emphasis on the plural, a series of documentary present tenses in perpetuity. In printing the article, the *Windsor* provides the same reassurance: the article ends (unusually)

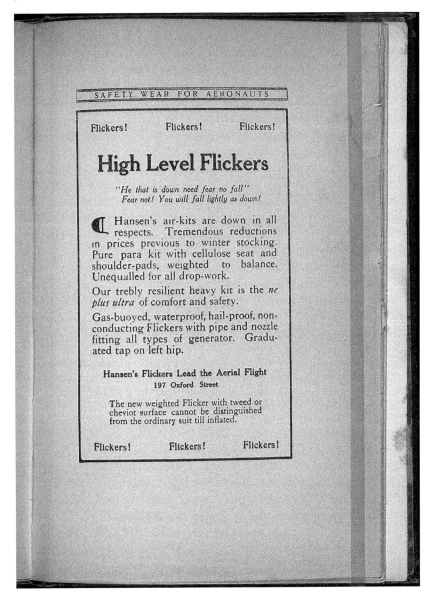

2.2   An "advert" accompanying the book version of *With the Night Mail* (1909).
Simulating the periodical? Courtesy of the General Collection, Beinecke Rare
Book & Manuscript Library, Yale University.

with a short advertisement for forthcoming instalments: 'The foregoing article is the first of AN IMPORTANT SERIES'.[22] This piece, then, looks forwards to its own looks backwards, nicely encapsulating the periodical's ordering of time. 'With the Night Mail' does not just exist within the verbal structures of the periodical but actually depends on them for a significant portion of its affect. The mechanism which gives conviction to Kipling's future world is drawn from the periodical's approach to time, actuated by the material conditions of its circulation as part of a monthly instalment.

Also published in the December 1905 *Windsor* was Charles Livingston Bull's 'An Artist in Bermuda', a glance at which can reveal further links between Kipling's fiction and the magazine's journalism. Of the sea-bed in Bermuda, Bull writes:

> . . .garden it is, if any man-made word may be applied, for the great purple sea-fans sway backward and forward, waving their branches to the rhythm of the swell just as the pine boughs sway to the breeze. Huge sprays of coral are there, too; some of it star-shaped, some like the great antlers of a forest monster, and some as finely wrought as the most delicate lace. . .[23]

Compare this with Kipling's description of riding an airship above the clouds:

> At this level the lower clouds are laid out all neatly combed by the dry fingers of the East. Below that there is a strong westerly blow. Overhead, a film of southerly drifting mist draws a theatrical gauze across the firmament.[24]

Here we have a tourist's description of ocean life in Bermuda and a tale of a future in which airships rule the skies, and the two have more in common than merely tone and tense. Both attempt to describe to their London audiences wonders which they might struggle to imagine, and of the two it is Bull, not Kipling, who says of his subject that 'there seems to be nothing within the knowledge of man' comparable.[25] Moreover, both attempt to ameliorate their fantastical subjects by describing them as the travelogue of a first-person narrator, a narrator who gazes from above the world in order to comprehend it, looking down either through the water (in Bull's case) or through the air (in Kipling's).

'With the Night Mail' is a work of fiction, but the presence of the dateline reminds us that it is also supposed to resemble a non-fictional piece of magazine reporting. Once we realise this and place the story back alongside some of the journalism with which it appeared, we can explain the initially confusing tonal eccentricity of the piece and recognise how essential the tale's periodical format and appearance are to its SF world-building strategy.

Kipling, who had begun his own career a journalist, was well positioned to understand the power of the article format as a tool for exposition.[26] The "infodump" problem, with which SF authors still struggle – that is, the fact that no précis of the history of a future society would ever be needed by one of its members – is neatly sidestepped by Kipling's invocation of a format which, at its heart, seeks only ever to describe the present to itself.[27]

Reading 'With the Night Mail' as an article also helps us understand its tendency to sacrifice plot in order to dwell on the technology in the airship and the histories of those who invented it. The story, first of all, is (although a number of exciting things happen) very little of a story': the mail ship rescues a vessel in distress, survives being buffeted by a storm, and interacts with other ships of various kinds, but the main thing it does is provide a vantage point from which the narrator can describe the ship and the world over which it sails.[28] The failure of any specific aspect of the narrative – biographies of the various inventors of airship technology, a burgeoning romance between one character's daughter and the captain of another ship, the political ramifications of a benign, technocratic world government – to rise to a position of prominence suggests that this is primarily an exercise in world-building rather than storytelling. Critics have tended to alight on the totalitarian world state as the focus of this story,[29] perhaps because Kipling dwelt on it at length in his sequel, 'As Easy as A.B.C.' (*London Magazine*, March–April 1912), but in fact the A.B.C. passes unmentioned until the twelfth of the original story's fifteen pages. Taken alone, what really characterises this story is not Kipling's social concern so much as the miscellaneousness of detail which makes the world-building so convincing, a miscellaneousness which derives specifically from the tale's periodical associations.

'With the Night Mail' is not just a breakthrough science fiction story which appeared in a magazine; it is a breakthrough science fiction story *because* it appeared in a magazine. Its wholesale adoption of the periodical's textual and paratextual architecture, which persists into (and is arguably re-emphasised in) the book version, is the mechanism by which it presents its vision of a future world. At the same time, it enables the magazine title itself – *Windsor* or *McClure's* – to draw attention to its own hybridity; to shore up its own future, its indefinite, periodical continuum. SF and the magazine's non-fiction style are more than co-present here, they are actively co-operative.

Having noted this co-operation, it is worth devoting a moment's thought to science itself. Another of the articles published in the December 1905 *Windsor* was Walter George Bell's 'A Journey Through Space', a popular astronomy piece which discusses the area of the sky towards which the Sun (and with it the Earth) is travelling. Bell spends some time explaining the history of how the astronomical calculation about the Sun's direction of movement was made and reproduces some large, quality photographs of nebulas. Once again, there are some remarkable textual resonances with Kipling's fiction, for example in its descriptions of subjective speed – Bell speaks of the solar system, including our own planet, as

> ...moving among the stars, at a speed which may sound enormous to our ears, yet is insignificant in the vast theatre in which the celestial motions take place, where space and time are infinite...[30]

Kipling's airships travel so smoothly, for all their speed, that they, like Earth in Bell's account, feel stationary:

> The hum of the turbines and the boom of the air on our skin is no more than a cotton-wool wrapping to the universal stillness. And we are running an eighteen second mile.[31]

Bell's conception of the Earth as a vessel, 'some magic chariot' journeying more or less towards the constellation of Hercules, recalls not only the airship on which Kipling's narrator finds himself, but also of the way in which the periodical, issue by issue, journeys through time. Start and end points for this ship's journey are almost irrelevant – the Earth is moving in one direction, though its passengers can look in any. Most crucially, Bell points out that to any one generation the stars appear fixed; the vessel seems to its passengers, like packet 162, to be stationary. Earth's journey, like that of the periodical or Kipling's airship, is a constant succession of present tenses.

1905 was the year Einstein published 'On the Electrodynamics of Moving Bodies', the paper which proposed the special theory of relativity. Its repercussions for our experience of time are not ones which Bell could have prepared for, and, partly thanks to it, there is perhaps no branch of science to which grammatical tenses bring more anxiety than astronomy, one of whose roles, thanks to the speed of light, is to predict things which have already happened, often many millions of years ago. Einstein showed that there is no objective rate for the passage of time; time, although progressing always in one direction, can be bent and fluctuated by local phenomena, experienced differently by observers in different situations. It need hardly be added that Einstein's theory first appeared in a periodical, the *Annalen der Physik*: since at least the establishment of the Royal Society's *Philosophical Transactions* in 1665, the periodical has been the primary venue of scientific progress, and so it remains.[32] One reason for this, beyond the pragmatic, might be that the constantly self-revising present tense of the periodical matches a core ideology of science, which views itself as being only ever the best *current* explanation of the world, an always-completing process of understanding rather than a pre-existing body of knowledge:

> In science, there are no universal truths, just views of the world that have yet to be shown to be false. All we can say for certain is that, *for now*, Einstein's theory works.[33]

In this sense, science is also something written perpetually in the present tense: it is, in the words of George Levine, 'always in the process of becoming'.[34]

On the eve of his article's appearance, Bell's understanding of time was about to be swept away by science's process of self-revision, giving way to an incrementally more accurate understanding of the universe. It is perhaps appropriate, then, that his 'Journey through Space' turns out to be, in its final paragraphs, ultimately a journey through time. Bell speculates about the future, imagining a time 'when, owing to the Sun's journey, we shall not see all the stars dotted over the sky in their present perspective'. He then looks back, reminding the reader that the constellations we find so familiar at the moment would be unrecognisable to our distant ancestors: 'As in the future', he says, 'so in the past'.[35] 'Funny how the new things are the old things', says Kipling, in the same issue of the same magazine.[36]

Predicting the future

Although an especially illuminating one, Kipling is an exception: the majority of the *fin de siècle*'s visions of the future, as I mentioned at the start of this chapter, took the less contorted route of *being* present-tense non-fiction rather than elaborately mimicking it. As might be expected, these pieces came from a range of different perspectives, adopting numerous approaches to imagining the future. Few of them would ever themselves be enrolled as SF, but their tonal and physical similarities to material which would makes them intriguing. In this section, I briefly discuss a few of these non-fictional pieces, drawn from a selection of magazines, in order to demonstrate that their various considerations of the future were equal to Kipling's in their dependency on the form of the periodicals in which they appeared.

What is immediately striking about many of the magazines' predictions is their modesty. In a piece which ran in the January 1896 *Idler*, 'Mrs. Humphry'

(Mary Augusta Ward) set out to imagine the London of thirty-four years into the future. This passage is a representative extract:

> The florists of 1930 will not dream of using such a crude and hideous blue as that of the paper in which the flower dealers of to-day envelop the blossoms they sell. Look how the glorious tone-music of the fruiterers' windows is defaced and mutilated by the frightful brick-dust pink of the paper wrappings. Even oranges are encircled with it, the effect on the colourist being so discordantly clamorous that, if translated into sound, it would go far to deafen.[37]

Among Ward's other predictions are superior window draperies, prize-giving for well-decorated houses, and more agreeably coloured omnibus tickets. Her most ambitious idea (and the only one which requires any measure of technological innovation) is that the 'complexity of disagreeable noises' which currently abound in the city might be made more agreeable by being harmonised:

> Why should not tram-rails be so constructed as to emit a deep and musical note to which itinerant vendors, newsboys, and omnibus conductors could attune their various cries?[38]

As the oratorical tone here suggests, Ward's piece does not really constitute a prediction of the future at all. Rather, it is an ambition for the present, a semi-satirical way of showing what could be if only people had taste. Like Bellamy's *Looking Backward*, this article's conception of the future is of a more "sensible" civilisation rather than a more technologically advanced one. Both assume that scientific development will be the servant of change rather than its cause. The difference between Ward and Bellamy is that Ward's piece exclusively concerns aesthetic differences, and even then, only ones associated with city living. Her first sentence:

> The next few decades may be expected to be prolific in improvements, and as many of them will deal with the details of daily life, we may, for our cold comfort, be permitted to indulge occasionally in a small day-dream of the wonders that will be. . .[39]

The key phrase here is 'daily life': as in 'With the Night Mail' ('[t]he physical form of its dominant technology has not changed its daily life'), it is the *repeated* continuum of the present which is at issue here.[40] This is materially emphasised by the fact that Ward's article is the last in a series of six which appeared in the *Idler* from August 1895 to January 1896 – subjects ranged from female bicyclists to the "problem" of educated servants. The other five articles are more straightforwardly about the present day.

This interest in the present is precisely what makes Ward's article (and, indeed, Bellamy's novel) so intriguing from the perspective of the study of SF. The idea that SF is meant to predict the future, according to *The Science Fiction Encyclopedia*, is '[t]he most widespread false belief about sf among the general public'.[41] It may be fair to say that, like SF, Ward is more interested in possibilities than predictions, and on the final page of 'London in 1930', which is also the final page of her run of articles in the *Idler*, it is to the romance of possibility that she appeals:

> If this immense improvement has taken place in the London of 1895 as compared with that of 1800, what may be expected of the London of 1930 [. . .]?[42]

Despite the conservatism of her predictions, this last passage reveals Ward to be motivated by the ideal of human progress, an ideal which she draws from the present's futuristic position relative to the past. Without being couched as SF, this piece evinces a characteristic series of temporal interests – also, of course, the interests so fully embodied by the present-tense continuum of the periodical.

Different in agenda to Ward's article, but no less comprehensively engaged with the present, are those pieces (especially common in the Harmsworth press) which discuss some technological aspect of futurity. Alfred Arkas's 'A Twentieth Century Dinner: Foods of the Future' (*Harmsworth Monthly Pictorial*, May 1899) might be presumed from its title to be a prediction of how eating will change over the coming decades. In fact, it is far more interested in what is already possible, focussing exclusively on food concentration methods which have already been developed. If it predicts anything, this article predicts only the eventual normalisation into "daily life" of currently existing technology: it is about the futurity of the present, not about the future itself. This is emphasised in its periodical context by the pictures: *Harmsworth*, like many of the illustrated monthlies, had a predilection for articles which used retooled photographs to convey statistical data. Concentrated foods are displayed beside their unconcentrated equivalents (to exactly one-quarter scale, Arkas is at pains to emphasise), but the most eye-catching images are the photographs stretched and distorted to represent the different quantities needed for sustenance by the average male (Fig. 2.3). These pictures break up the text in ways which would have been unfamiliar to readers of the previous decade, broadcasting the futurity of the magazine as much as the futurity of concentrated food. Both, of course, exist in the present tense: 'Nowadays, if you are not an epicure, you may carry a month's food in a Gladstone bag'.[43]

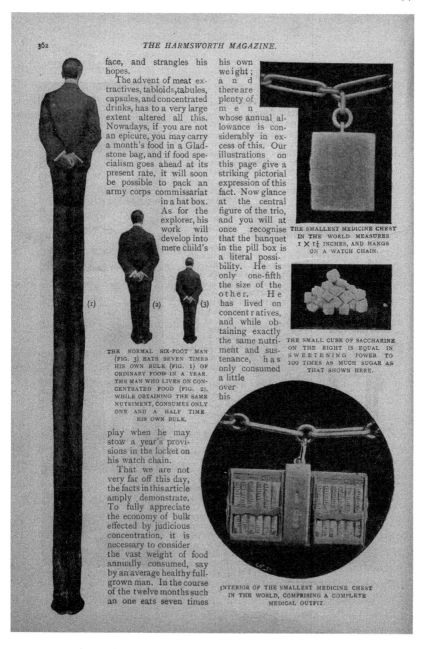

face, and strangles his hopes.

The advent of meat extractives, tabloids, tabules, capsules, and concentrated drinks, has to a very large extent altered all this. Nowadays, if you are not an epicure, you may carry a month's food in a Gladstone bag, and if food specialism goes ahead at its present rate, it will soon be possible to pack an army corps commissariat in a hat box. As for the explorer, his work will develop into mere child's

his own weight; and there are plenty of men whose annual allowance is considerably in excess of this. Our illustrations on this page give a striking pictorial expression of this fact. Now glance at the central figure of the trio, and you will at once recognise that the banquet in the pill box is a literal possibility. He is only one-fifth the size of the other. He has lived on concentratives, and while obtaining exactly the same nutriment and sustenance, has only consumed a little over his

THE SMALLEST MEDICINE CHEST IN THE WORLD MEASURES I × I¼ INCHES, AND HANGS ON A WATCH CHAIN.

THE SMALL CUBE OF SACCHARINE ON THE RIGHT IS EQUAL IN SWEETENING POWER TO 100 TIMES AS MUCH SUGAR AS THAT SHOWN HERE.

THE NORMAL SIX-FOOT MAN (FIG. 3) EATS SEVEN TIMES HIS OWN BULK (FIG. 1) OF ORDINARY FOOD IN A YEAR. THE MAN WHO LIVES ON CONCENTRATED FOOD (FIG. 2), WHILE OBTAINING THE SAME NUTRIMENT, CONSUMES ONLY ONE AND A HALF TIME HIS OWN BULK.

play when he may stow a year's provisions in the locket on his watch chain.

That we are not very far off this day, the facts in this article amply demonstrate. To fully appreciate the economy of bulk effected by judicious concentration, it is necessary to consider the vast weight of food annually consumed, say by an average healthy full-grown man. In the course of the twelve months such an one eats seven times

INTERIOR OF THE SMALLEST MEDICINE CHEST IN THE WORLD, COMPRISING A COMPLETE MEDICAL OUTFIT.

2.3   A page from Arkas's 'A Twentieth Century Dinner' in *Harmsworth* (May 1899). Courtesy of the Cadbury Research Library, University of Birmingham.

'The Horseless Future', by G. B. Burgin (*Idler*, May 1896) has an equally misleading title. Rather than an attempt to visualise a world without horse-drawn carriages, this piece is an interview with Henry J. Lawson, the engineer who credited himself with the invention of the motorbike and held the patent rights to the first motor cars in London. As in Arkas's piece, the article is entirely about what is already possible – what has been achieved in France and America, how Lawson's inventions work, and how they compare financially to current modes of transportation. The important point here is that if Burgin looks forward at all, it is only to the universal adoption of a technology which is already at large rather than to any improvements in the technology itself. These thoughts are always secondary to his reporting on Lawson's personality and his assessment of the current technological situation. The title implies that Lawson is a representative of the horseless future: that it already exists and will soon widen to prominence (rather like the revolutionary New Journalist article format, the interview). In fact, though, it is only in his last paragraph that Burgin gives way to any kind of outright consideration of the future:

> The horse is a noble animal and useful to man; but man, with his customary ingratitude, is trying to do without him – in cities at least. This is distinctly a move in the right direction [...]. It is to be hoped that the horseless carriages will mitigate much animal suffering; there is not the slightest doubt that they will effect a social revolution in England in the next few years, and do away with a great deal of the nervous strain produced by our everyday, noisy traffic.[44]

Like Ward, Burgin situates his real future reflections at the very end of his piece, allowing the periodical to stretch forwards. But, again like Ward, Burgin also looks to the past – the history of man's use of the horse – and the present – current standards of animal welfare in London. Human welfare too is under consideration, the emphasis being on the constancy of urban experience; the everyday. Through Arkas, Ward, and Burgin's very different articles, then, an insistence on "daily life", the rhythm of which is so determined by the periodical press, can be clearly discerned.

Another concern about the everyday world which Burgin shares with Ward is 'noisy traffic', also the preoccupation of yet another *Idler* piece, F. L. Oswald's 'Cities of the Future' (April 1896). Oswald argues that '[e]ven our indifference to smoke and dust will not astonish the citizens of the twentieth century as much as our tolerance of ear-splitting noises'.[45] Unlike the other pieces discussed in this section, Oswald's is a sincere attempt to imagine a technology-empowered future society; his future cities have air conditioning, skyscrapers, airships, fast railways and steamers, and more besides. Most interesting for our purposes, though, is the method by which Oswald arrives at his predictions. He opens:

> The main secret of weather prophecies is the plan to ascertain the drift of clouds and winds, and then calculate the probable result of their movements in a given time. It has often occurred to me that the same method might be applied to all sorts of other predictions.[46]

Here, Oswald seems to draw on the concept of the science experiment, in which predictions are compared to data; the future is notionally extrapolated from the past and present. A 'property that sets the genuine sciences apart', wrote Peter Medawar, 'is their predictive capability'.[47] But extrapolating the future from past data is also, as we have seen, an inherent characteristic of the periodical, which is always using the present to look forwards to its next issue – prediction, then, is not just a key feature of science, but also of the magazine. We can read the co-existence of social and scientific prediction in Oswald's work from the fact that his opening sentence contains both the word 'prophecies' and the phrase 'calculate the probable result of their movements in a given time'.

The non-fictional realm of weather forecasting is perhaps the place where science and the periodical are most obviously in concert to attempt a serious prediction of the future.[48] It is appropriate, therefore, that the subtitle of Ward's piece is 'A Forecast'; appropriate, too, that the weather is Oswald's starting point. Weather patterns recur throughout 'Cities of the Future', one of whose more minor predictions is improved meteorology: 'at the first alarm-signal of an approaching storm, [airships] will dodge for shelter like a flock of frightened birds'.[49] Many of Oswald's other predictions have a minor attachment to weather, from his opening discussion about keeping houses at an agreeable temperature to his idea that businesses will project advertisements onto the clouds. The cloud-advertising, though, is also suggestive of the links with periodical culture. News and especially advertising are the basis of several of Oswald's predictions, including the one which turned out to be his most accurate:

> [t]he time is near when metropolitan papers, full of good illustrations, entertaining stories, and news from all parts of the civilised world, will be distributed *free*, merely on the chance of attracting the reader's attention to the advertisement columns.[50]

Oswald's future is lousy with advertisements, news, and newspapers. It makes explicit the implied promise of Kipling's dateline, assuring us that the periodical press will flourish. Kipling, whose Night Mail airship rides out a severe storm over the Atlantic, also engages with the fluctuating, unpredictable present tense represented by weather. And the correspondences with Kipling do not end there, for whilst Kipling's is a work of fiction which makes several empowering formal and textual moves in the direction of non-fiction, Oswald's first-person essay occasionally finds it convenient to express itself with fictive devices. The best example of this occurs when Oswald provides the exposition for his cloud-advertising notion by reporting a conversation between two passengers on a transatlantic steamer, not tonally dissimilar from much of the Kipling story, which begins as follows:

> 'What would you call that light over yonder?' a Spanish passenger will ask his Yankee travelling companion, as their steamer approaches the coast of the American continent, in the evening twilight of a November day. 'Can that be a thunderstorm at this time of the year?'
>
> 'That flickering on those low clouds? No, that's the light of an electric reflector,' says the Yankee. 'Our enterprising business men use that method to advertise their bargains in the neighbourhood of a large city.'
>
> 'What city can that be?'
>
> 'Savannah, I think,' says the American, after consulting his watch.[51]

Here, Oswald has decided that the best way for his audience to visualise his changes is for them to be introduced to it as the foreign tourist of the future, the "infodumpee", the protagonist of SF. Crucially, as well, his speculations have given rise to characters and even a limited amount of plot in addition to a vision of the future; the cumbersome 'will ask' of the first speech gives way to the present tense 'says' of the second and fourth.

Many of the characteristics of these non-fictional pieces, from their tendencies towards narrative to their temporal conservatism in the midst of even their most extravagant hypotheses, are a part-consequence of their need to remain materially attached to the present via the ongoing continuum of the periodical. This attachment is also demonstrated by the proximity of notionally scientific approaches to more fictive speculation, a proximity of which the weather forecast is an analogue. In all of these pieces, the periodical seems to have an effect on the content as well as the appearance of the author's predictions. For the supreme example of this, though, we must return to fiction – and to one of the *fin de siècle*'s most famous pieces of SF.

Periodicity and narrative truth in *The Time Machine*

W. E. Henley began his controversial editorship of the *New Review* in 1895 by serialising H. G. Wells's *The Time Machine*. The story, which ran in instalments from January to May of that year, was the first in English to feature deliberate travel through time with a machine especially designed for the purpose.[52] Previous visions of the future, such as Bellamy's *Looking Backward*, had relied on dreams, unexplained cryostasis, or mystical teleportation in order to move people, typically somewhat to their surprise, between time periods. One of *The Time Machine*'s innovations, then, was that it bestowed temporal agency on its voyaging protagonist, a character who, appropriately in a book which has become so representative of a genre of writing, is never referred to as anything other than 'The Time Traveller'.

The Time Traveller's Thursday night gatherings echo more than just the structure of the periodical. The audience to which he addresses himself includes a poet, a psychologist, a doctor, a rector, an editor, and a journalist; a mixed crowd whose members are also, when the Time Traveller is not speaking, contributors to a mixed discussion. 'At first the conversation was mere fragmentary chatter, with some local *lacunae* of digestive silence', says the narrator, describing a typical occasion, 'but towards nine or half-past nine, if the God was favourable, some particular topic would triumph by a kind of natural selection, and would become the common interest'.[53] This harmonisation of polyphonic discourse is something that the narrator always looks forwards to: 'the arrival of that moment of fusion, when our several conversations were suddenly merged into a general discussion, was a great relief to me' (p. 99). It is easy to read this crowd as representatives of the *New Review*'s target audience: respectable and learned individuals, all male, meeting in the service of general intellectual discussion. That discussion echoes the intended mix of discourses in a periodical which 'aimed to be a critical journal on "Politics, Science, and Art"'.[54] Providing the venue for this unification of diverse specialities into a harmonious event, just as the space of the magazine does, the Time Traveller is described on the first page of the serial as a capable editor-figure, a 'vivid and variegated talker' whose 'fantastic, often paradoxical, conceptions came so close as to form one continuous discourse'.[55] Part of his intent as a host is simply bringing his various guests into contact with each other, as the contents page of a magazine brought together writers on a host of diverse subjects, including, in the month *The Time Machine* started its run, 'The Navy', 'The New Ibsen', 'An Eulogy of Charles the Second', and 'India: Impressions'.[56]

The Time Traveller's weekly meetings, then, blend the discursive possibilities of the magazine with its serial reappearance. The particularity of this effect to the periodical is underscored by the fact that in the book version of *The Time Machine*, this aspect of the narrative is significantly de-emphasised: the book begins promptly with the Time Traveller's pronouncement of his theories about space and time, and the prefatory description of their discursive context, some of which I have just quoted, is now almost entirely absent.[57] However, something of the periodical has lingered into the book form as well, for the Time Traveller's theories themselves, the science fiction principles which underpin the entire story, betray a link between the novel's original format and its content. The Time Traveller's arguments about the possibility of travel through time conceived as the fourth dimension are something with which modern readers, even those not versed in SF, will probably feel comfortable: the dinner party guest/reader is invited to consider an imaginary omniscient observer, outside the flow of time, who would regard both past and future as directions and who would therefore need to conceptualise physical objects as having an extra dimension of existence:

> An ordinary man, being asked to describe this box, would say, among other things, that it was in such a position, and that it measured ten inches in depth, say, three in breadth, and four in length. From the absolute point of view it would also be necessary to say that it began at such a moment, lasted so long, measured so much in time, and was moved here and there meanwhile.[58]

In order to be comprehensively understood, the Time Traveller suggests, an object must have both its physical and temporal dimensions recorded. This idea, too, resonates with the material existence of the periodical, which is always tracked in four dimensions – while bibliographers might be interested in the physical dimensions of an issue, most indexes are more interested in the title's duration, changes of publisher, and so on, exactly in keeping with Wells's stipulations. With the digitisation of periodicals, the more traditional first three dimensions are increasingly diminished in stature: the *New Review*'s page on ProQuest's *British Periodicals*, for example, exclusively contains temporal information (Fig. 2.4).

The fact that fourth-dimensionality is built into the format of the periodical is one of the main conceptual properties separating it from the book.[59] It is therefore unsurprising that *The Time Machine*, originally written for periodical publication, takes Oswald's non-fictional future prediction strategy to a hypothetical extreme and embeds it in its science as well as its format: '[I]f you grasped the whole of the present, knew all its

2.4 Screenshot from ProQuest's *British Periodicals* database, showing the holdings information for *The New Review*.

tendencies and laws', says the Time Traveller, 'you would clearly see all the future'.[60] Another contemporary engagement with this metaphor emerges in a review of Wells's novel written by Israel Zangwill which appeared in *Pall Mall Magazine* four months after *The Time Machine* concluded. In the review, Zangwill conceives of time as 'a vast *continuum* holding all that has happened and all that will happen, an eternal Present', adding that '[t]here is really more difficulty in understanding the Present than the Past or the Future into which it is always slipping'.[61] In the course of his speculations, Zangwill suggests another kind of time machine, based on the slow speed of light: 'we could travel to any given year by travelling actually through space to the point at which the rays of that year would first strike upon our consciousness' (p. 154). This "time machine" also recasts time as space, but unlike Wells's, does not permit the traveller 'the fallacy of mingling personally in the panorama' (p. 154). A user of Zangwill's machine can only ever be an observer, travelling forwards and backwards by moving physically closer to or further away from the object of study. On the library shelf, periodical time is stratified by distance in the same way, although it is only possible to travel backwards from the present.

The Time Traveller, of course, travels forwards. If *The Time Machine*'s science is empowered by the form and substance of Victorian periodicity, then its nightmare is a world in which that periodicity has ceased to exist. One of the defining features of Wells's 802,701AD is its lack of material culture, which includes a disturbing absence of newspapers and magazines, and, more an absence of the structured time which they both reflect and reinforce. The Eloi's life patterns are governed by the moon, the waning and waxing of which increases and decreases the likelihood of a Morlock attack. Feeling isolated in the blank time of this uncomfortable future, the

Time Traveller reassures himself by contemplating the natural periodicity of the stars: 'I thought of their unfathomable distance, and the slow inevitable drift of their movements out of the unknown past into the unknown future'.[62] This passage is similar in many respects to George Bell's 'A Journey Through Space' from the December 1905 *Windsor*, and both resonate with the periodical format as well as with astronomical reality. In the same passage, the Time Traveller also finds reassurance in the unimaginably slow (from a human perspective) revolution of the Earth's magnetic field: 'I thought of the great processional cycle that the pole of the earth describes. Only forty times had that silent revolution occurred during all the years that I had traversed' (p. 456).

Consolation, then, comes by reaching towards nature for some evidence of consistent rhythms over time. However, this consolation fades when the Time Traveller voyages farther still into the future after his adventures with the Morlocks and Eloi and even natural periodicity comes to an end:

> The alterations of day and night grew slower and slower, and so did the passage of the sun across the sky, until they seemed to stretch through centuries. At last a steady twilight brooded over the earth...[63]

This nightmarish far-future, in which the Earth's rotation has ceased and the sun has become stationary, is the end of periodicity – and implicitly, given entropy, the end of time itself, for how does one measure time if nothing changes? It is therefore unsurprising that when the Time Traveller returns to 1895 a few pages later, he instinctively looks to periodicity to reassure himself that he is home:

> I saw *The Pall Mall Gazette* on the table by the door. I found the date was indeed today, and looking at the timepiece, saw the hour was almost eight o'clock.[64]

Coming upon the clock and the copy of the *Pall Mall Gazette* is disjointing even for a twenty-first century reader who, just paragraphs earlier, has been witnessing the fixed sun over a dying Earth. This effect is, of course, deliberate. The clock and the copy of *The Pall Mall Gazette* are important not just for the specific information of time and date which they convey but for the very fact of their existence: coming so soon after the never-setting sun of the impossibly distant far-future, they provide an elemental reassurance that the Time Traveller has returned to a structured, comprehensible age. This is literally home territory for Wells, since the *Pall Mall Gazette* was an important outlet for his early publishing career.[65]

Further evidence of how deeply enmeshed 1895 society is in the rhythms of print culture can be seen in the narrator's description of his thoughts and activities as he waits – in vain, as it will turn out – for the Time Traveller to emerge from his laboratory. The scientist has embarked on another voyage, promising, after failing to convince his guests, that he will return with definite evidence that his machine works:

> I heard the door of the laboratory slam, seated myself in a chair, and took up a daily paper. What was he going to do before lunch time? Then suddenly I was reminded by an advertisement that I had promised to meet Richardson, the publisher, at two. I looked at my watch, and saw that I could barely save that engagement.[66]

This passage is saturated with words – 'daily paper', 'lunch time', 'advertisement', 'publisher', 'two', 'watch', 'engagement' – which, especially in contrast with the unregulated time of the barren landscape from which the Time Traveller has recently returned, emphasise and re-emphasise the dependency of the present, of human civilisation versus blank meaninglessness, on regulated time. 'Daily paper', first and foremost of these, engulfs the reader in a serial society: they are now reading about someone reading a periodical in a periodical. The imagined community here gains another, temporal element.

The Time Machine idealises the regulated time which magazines like the *New Review* so well embodied, contributing to what Mussell has called 'a cacophony that is built upon a shared emphasis of the present'.[67] There is yet another sense, though, also closely linked to temporality, in which the Time Traveller has an affinity with the periodical: the fact that he is, above all else, at heart a scientist. I make this point not in reference to his actual credentials, which are masked by the narrator in a rather hollow gesture towards anonymity, nor even to emphasise that the Time Traveller himself devises the machine which will project him into the future: rather, I mean to highlight a particular mindset, the attitude which the Time Traveller brings to the situations in which he finds himself. Whilst he sometimes resembles Allan Quatermain, intrepid, honourable, and tenacious, Wells's hero is much more researcher than adventurer. However, when considering late-Victorian tales of derring-do, it is extremely unwise to draw a firm distinction between the two (a point to which I shall return in Chapter 4). His cerebral reactions to dangerous situations and problems, his ability to fend for himself in the hostile environment of the far future, and his lengthy disquisitions on and hypotheses of the world in which he finds himself are all attempts at (if not textbook examples of) Victorian empiricism, a fact best attested to by his willingness to admit his own mistakes and come to new conclusions in the light of fresh evidence. I have already drawn attention to the fact that Wells's was the first narrative in which the time machine was a deliberate invention, created from a hypothetically reasoned theory about the world and verified by experiment: it is also worth dwelling on the fact that unlike many of the inventions in the "mad scientist" tales which would continue to gain popularity in the 1890s, the time machine actually works. In fact, it never stops working except by its inventor's own design. This is not a Frankenstein story, and the hubris of scientific progress, now identified as a common theme in science fiction (in part thanks to the prominence of tales like Wells's own later *The Island of Doctor Moreau*), is not something which this novel is interested in exploring.

Given Wells's scientific training and interests, a certain degree of optimism about empirical science is unsurprising. The Time Traveller's scientific qualifications and activities, though, gesture at a temporally dependant quality which the periodical incorporates into its very structure: suspense. It almost goes without saying that one of the differences between encountering *The Time Machine* in its original run in the *New Review* and reading it today in Penguin paperback is that in the former, the reader is temporally obstructed from the ending; that the speed at which the reader experiences the story depends on the publication interval of the magazine running it (monthly, in the case of the *New Review*). This returns us to the point from Laurel Brake discussed earlier in this chapter: combined with a lack of cultural pre-awareness of where the story was going, or the personality and interests of its author, the periodical format would have made that early encounter with H. G. Wells a very distant experience from the that of the novel's twenty-first century readers.[68] It is significant that the two things that function to distance it are time and the periodical format.

What has any of this, though, to do with a scientific mindset? Caroline Levine answers this question in her critical work *The Serious Pleasures of Suspense* (2003). Identifying suspense as the crucial characteristic of literary realism, Levine argues that rather than purporting precisely to depict the real world, as has since been assumed, Victorian realism invited readers to get a sense of the world's otherness by distancing themselves from their assumptions, a method drawn, she says, from post-Enlightenment science. 'In order to grasp the fundamental alterity of the world', Levine says, 'it was necessary to put aside one's own intellectual habits and presumptions. [...] Realism came to mean the suspending of assumption and belief, and narrative suspense emerged as the realist strategy par excellence'.[69]

For Levine, the suspenseful pause is a place of earnest contemplation and reflection in which the reader, like the protagonist of a novel, or a scientist, is introduced 'to the activity of hypothesizing and testing in order to come to knowledge' (p. 8). This is certainly what the Time Traveller does, as he uses his first days among the Eloi to speculate as to the origins of the society he witnesses, carefully laying out his own false assumptions and the processes by which he came to revise them. It is also the activity of the reader approaching the tale in instalments, piecing together the elements of the narrative they have in order to speculate about the whole and, in the process, to speculate about the more abstract scientific ideas which Wells is setting forth.[70] Despite suggesting that many critics of Victorian realism 'have been inclined to forget what it is like to read Victorian novels *for the first time*', losing sight of their suspenseful qualities because the plots of canon novels are now common knowledge, Levine barely mentions periodicals at all.[71] This is unfortunate, since the suspenseful pause on which so much of her argument is based is literally enacted by the periodical as a temporal function. With her focus on realism, and particularly canonical writings from Ruskin to Wilde, Levine also bypasses science fiction. Though more understandable, this omission is still a shame given the crossover between her idea that suspense encourages active readerly hypothesis and contemplation and Darko Suvin's famous identification of SF as the literature of 'cognitive estrangement', in which the very distance of SF's imagined worlds is seen as a way of inviting consideration of ours.[72] Understood this way, SF's imaginative objectives look very similar to those of Levine's realism.

I am suggesting here, then, that Levine's ideas can be readily extended to accommodate works from outside the tradition of Victorian realism on which she focuses and the book format which is her first point of contact with it. Science and suspense are continuously bedfellows in *The Time Machine*: the Time Traveller's first experiment, conducted in front of a group which is not only, as I have already argued, a model periodical demographic, but also a mixed group of sceptical peers, involves a small working model of the finished time machine; from this the group proceeds in a suitably methodical escalation of scale to the full-size machine only after the model has been shown in action. 'And now I must be explicit', begins the narrator, prefacing his long description of the machine itself, 'for this that follows – unless his explanation is to be accepted – is an absolutely unaccountable thing'.[73] He understands that his account is not just a story but witness testimony to an experiment, and his thoroughness therefore satisfies the twin requirements of science (by its exhaustive descriptions) and suspense (through the delay in narrative action which those descriptions occasion).

Science and the realist narrative are, for Levine, united by the fact that in each 'as we wait, suspended, to see whether or not the future will bear out our suppositions and desires, we experience a vital, vibrant *pleasure*'.[74] And like science-fictional futures, realist experiments are about possibilities rather than prophecies: 'Art might not itself tell truths, but it has always already shaped our capacity to imagine what might be true' (p. 41). The real world, Levine suggests (via Ruskin), takes place not in art or life but in the speculative gap between them – the suspenseful gap caused by not knowing. This, of course, is also the dynamic drawn upon by the Galton article discussed in Chapter 1, a piece which evoked the newspaper's sense of passing time as well as the space for hypothesis created by its own narrative lacunae to encourage the reader into an active engagement with its mathematical ideas.

'[V]aluable knowledge', says Levine, 'is itself narrative in form'. Truth is contingent on the passage of time; 'static visual clues necessarily fail to reveal the unsettled nature of emergent selfhood' (p. 148). This, like the Time Traveller's reflections, looks good alongside Walter George Bell's image of the solar system travelling towards a (specific, if currently obscure) point, apparently stationary in any given moment. But Levine's comment about the temporal vector of meaningful truth is also significant because it suggests that any discussion of suspense, narrative doubt, science, realism, and future prediction – and, I would add, SF and the periodical – eventually comes round to being, finally, about truth.

Specifically, it is about *ambiguous* truth. The story in which we are simply told everything, says Levine, leaves no space for us to suspend judgement, to think creatively about what we are reading. Perhaps this is why *The Time Machine* is repeatedly at pains to cast doubt on some of its own facts. It is the Time Traveller himself who leads the way on this, closing the story of his adventures in the future by insisting that it is fabricated:

> Take it as a lie – or a prophecy. Say I dreamed it in the workshop. Consider I have been speculating upon the destinies of our race, until I have hatched this fiction. Treat my assertion of the truth as a mere stroke of art to enhance its interest.[75]

Cannily, Wells speaks directly to the *New Review*'s readers in this passage, inviting them with this realist gesture (for the narrative *is* fictitious and everyone knows that) into active, Levine-like, and perhaps even scientific speculation about the intellectual implications of his story. Yet the disavowal's position in the narrative, the level of detail in the story we have just heard, and the narrator's own reassurances – 'you cannot see the speaker's white, sincere face in the bright circle of the little lamp, nor hear the intonation of his voice' – coupled with the fact that it is the Time Traveller himself who asks us to disbelieve, serve to make this passage do the opposite of what the Time Traveller says he wants it to do.[76] In real life, the story would seem wildly unlikely. From an interior perspective, though, no seasoned reader can be in doubt. The very fact of the narrative's ambiguity is proof positive of its internal authenticity.

Wells keeps the Time Traveller's account at arm's length by leaving the character unnamed and bringing all his testimony to us via the intermediary figure of the (also unnamed) narrator. In fact, *The Time Machine* is the archetypal 'club story' and one of the novels named by John Clute in his definition of the term. Clute describes a club story as 'a witness against any stable understanding of a darkening world', and indeed the provenance of Wells's novel seems to waver constantly.[77] On the one hand, there is the narrative dominance of the Time Traveller and his tale; on the other, the paucity of his evidence and the creeping elements of doubt interposed both by him and by some of his audience. Kipling's and Wells's stories have this much in common: both are empowered by the act of muddying the truth-status of their narratives. 'With the Night Mail', after all, is fiction which reads like an article and appears in a magazine alongside non-fiction pieces it is crafted to resemble. Kipling's ambiguity is drawn from its structural relationship with the periodical; Wells's is drawn from the genre traditions of the club story which the periodical's mixed discursive space so empowers.

The *New Review* for the most part printed political opinion pieces, diplomatic and historical articles, and travel writing. Throughout *The Time Machine*'s run there was never more than one other fictional piece per issue. It goes without saying that nobody is expected to actually find either *The Time Machine* or 'With the Night Mail' literally convincing, but since both pieces are so obviously fantastical, it becomes worth asking why their authors go to such lengths to render their apparent truth-status so ambiguous. In the closing section of this chapter, I want to argue that the club story, future prophecy, SF, and science itself all make profitable use of the ambiguity generated by the periodical's relationship with time, and suggest that this ambiguity is one of the most important characteristics we can retrieve from these magazines today.

Present-tense ambiguity

Bakhtin understood that science and the novel were fundamentally inter-related, locating an origin of both in the Socratic dialogues. 'When the novel becomes the dominant genre', he writes, 'epistemology became the dominant discipline'.[78] Bakhtin's novel, the main feature of which he describes as 'an indeterminacy, a certain semantic openendedness, a living contact with unfinished, still-evolving contemporary reality (the open-ended present)', is unique amongst the genres precisely because of its relationship with the present (p. 7). The Bakhtinian understanding of the genre-novel as a heteroglot form, able to admit of multiple voices and perspectives, depends on the ambiguity which is the result of the way in which it engages with time:

> The present, in its so-called 'wholeness' (although it is, of course, never whole) is in essence and in principle inconclusive; by its very nature it demands continuation, it moves into the future, and the more actively and consciously it moves into the future the more tangible and indispensable its inconclusiveness becomes.[79]

So crucial was time to Bakhtin's interpretation of the novel that he coined the term 'chronotope' to refer to 'the intrinsic connectedness of temporal and spatial relationships' that abide in it.[80] The chronotope, he claims, provides 'the basis for distinguishing generic types'; a text's relationship with time is essential to its generic status (pp. 250–51). Given this, it becomes clear that the general periodical (although not necessarily any given piece of writing within one) fits with ease into Bakhtin's category of 'novel'.[81] The scattered future-speculations of Wells and Kipling, of Arkas, Oswald, Ward, and Burgin, all have different levels of association with the idea of final truth, but each co-exists with numerous other registers of truth in the heteroglot space of the periodical press. By collecting all of these competing voices in one place and allowing none to take charge, general magazines allowed authors access to a knowing ambiguity strongly rooted in the present tense. 'The novelist', Bakhtin wrote, 'is drawn to everything that is not yet completed'.[82] This allowed for a particular kind of appeal to readers' imaginations, a particular chronotope out of which a new genre of popular writing would eventually develop.

Like Caroline Levine, Bakhtin sees the science experiment as an important model for the novel's work in subjecting an assumed reality to interrogation:

> As it draws an object to itself and makes it familiar, laughter delivers the object into the fearless hands of investigative experiment – both scientific and artistic – and into the hands of free experimental fantasy.[83]

Science and the novel are drawn together precisely by their resistance to an eternally fixed, authority-driven explanation of the world (a resistance which, for Bakhtin, pivots on laughter). This resistance manifests as a function of the way that both engage with time, their insistence on engaging with an ever-developing present tense. Levine and Bakhtin's ideas can therefore easily be brought to bear specifically on the periodical, a format which complements these structural concerns by materially and temporally allying the range of genres of fiction and non-fiction in its covers. Mussell has drawn attention to the fact that the periodical's cultivated air of work-in-progress is something which is easy for historical researchers to overlook:

> Although from our perspective newspapers and periodicals appear as finished works, neatly lined up on the shelf, what they model is a process predicated upon not finishing, where the latest issue is not the last.[84]

In fact, since they necessarily incorporate heteroglossia into their temporal and spacial characteristics, periodicals are not only authored, edited, and published by a wide range of actants but also amalgamate types of content which vary over time as well as within individual issues. No one genre, no one valency of truth, rules over any of the others.

This returns us to Wells's distrust of utopian fiction at the outset of his *Anticipations*. He dismisses utopia as a kind of writing 'necessarily concrete and definite; it permits of no open alternatives; its aim of illusion prevents a proper amplitude of demonstration'.[85] In the other pieces I have mentioned here, it is precisely the moments which seem most authoritarian – seem to exclude other genres, other voices – which now seem most dated, most uncomfortable ('What a splendid achievement it will be', says Ward, 'to harmonize the strident discords that disfigure the simple melody of life!').[86] Bakhtin is always ultimately interested in the rejection of authority, a concept in the light of which all the texts read in this chapter – Kipling's especially, with its incidental world empire hovering at the edges – perform intriguingly.

Ambiguousness as a response to authority offers a way of answering the surprising observation with which I began this chapter: that most *fin-de-siècle* SF seems more interested in present and near-present settings than in the activity of future-prophecy. It may not shock us to see SF engaged in an interrogation of social orthodoxies – that has long been one of the things the genre is known for – but I have been arguing here that the periodical's inclusive temporality brings this political dimension a kind of urgency.

These pieces demonstrate another kind of temporal ambiguity as well: an ambiguity imposed upon them by our reading their periodical present tenses from a point of retrospective hindsight. Sam Moskowitz, for example, treats the temporal specificity of these stories not as a curiosity of the genre but as a marker of its period authenticity:

> ...the events you will read about here include the destruction of the great cities of London and New York; the thrilling tale of a tube under the ocean; the implementation of weather control; systems for walking through walls; the discovery of fantastic monsters on land, sea, and in the air [...]. All have *taken place* in a familiar yet bewildering 'world of if' that once we knew, but not like this![87]

As the title *Science Fiction by Gaslight* implies, Moskowitz's emphasis is as much on the vintage of his chosen stories as their novelty. In other words, the present-ness of these stories has become, for us, a past-ness – one with commercial value, for the continuing appeal of many of these texts lies in the retro feel of their aesthetic. The success of steampunk, the SF subgenre as much an aesthetic movement as a literary one which has arisen in the years since the mid-1980s, testifies to this.[88] For the twenty-first-century reader, these stories are compelling because their imaginative worlds are simultaneously both quaint and futuristic: 'it is', as Andy Sawyer has said, 'as if we suffer from a nostalgia for the future of the past'.[89] This characteristic is enhanced by the magazines, which surround each of their articles with the markers of contemporaneity. The present tense gives us a different kind of access to the past, as well as to the future; the rate of change, to use an analogy from physics, equals distance over time.

Bruno Latour draws time's arrow on two axes, adding a scale of comprehension and reinterpretation to the straightforward temporality of the one-dimensional model. 1895 is a very different idea in 1868 and 1900, and in 2016 it is different again. Or as Latour writes, 'there is also a portion of what happened in 1864 that is produced *after* 1864 and then made retrospectively a part of the ensemble that forms, from then on, the sum of what happened in the year 1864'.[90] Reading SF – reading the period's magazines in general – is a way of trying to get at some of the other 1895s which have fallen by the wayside, the more literal "other presents". In his essay on 'With the Night Mail', Sawyer puts it another way:

> We can, if necessary, read science fiction as alternate history. But even more, we can read it as emblems of futures long passed and superseded, stories of pasts that might have been futures, creative designs made to test their plausibility and capacity for illusion.[91]

This particular kind of historicism is almost an analogue of future-prediction, for it engages in the same doomed struggle against the ineluctability of time's arrow, the unchangeable rate at which present becomes past.

The periodical is part of the wider, technologically powered project, which also incorporates clocks, calendars, and meridians, by which humans have attempted to order time's arrow into something comprehensible, something which can be controlled. Stephen Kern draws attention to the fact that this project was in the process of dramatically re-ordering cultural conceptions of space and time at the very moment that all of the material covered in this chapter was first published:

> ...the procession of days, seasons, and years, and quite simple common sense tell us that time is irreversible and moves forward at a steady rate. Yet these features of traditional time were also challenged [...]. In the *fin de siècle*, time's arrow did not always fly straight and true.[92]

Future-prediction, steampunk, and historicism are all in different ways, perhaps, the yearning which remains after the fact of the transition which is Kern's subject. Like the Time Traveller, they fantasise about escaping the gradual accumulation of the ages.

In these first two chapters, I have tried to show how the space and time of the general periodical contributed, via an insistence on miscellaneousness, to the creation of a climate of interchange between the genre discourses of many kinds of writing, including literature and science. We might even, if we were feeling spry, describe this hybrid simultaneity as the chronotope of writing in the general magazine. I have argued that early SF is inextricably bound up in this network of exchanges, and that a profitable view of disciplinary relationships and of SF's own history emerges once fact and fiction are approached other than as straightforward opposites. My focus has been on moments of collaboration in an attempt to disavow the binary model of literature/science exchange, and this has allowed me to articulate a more complex alternative picture, one based on diversity and heteroglossia. But none of this is to argue that the relationship between science and fiction in the periodicals was necessarily harmonious, any more than it was necessarily oppositional. In the next chapter, I focus on a theme which, whilst continuing to reveal a dialogue between literature and science in the periodicals, also throws some of their inherent tensions into sharper relief.

CHAPTER 3

New photography
X-rays and the images of the New Journalism

A sense of possibilities

> We are on the eve of the Fourth Dimension; that is what it is! But what is
> the Fourth Dimension, and what are we on the eve of? That will naturally
> be the question of the reader who is not familiar with the speculations of the
> scientific imagination.[1]

With these majestic sentences, W. T. Stead launches into one of his many
disquisitions on the occult in the pages of his influential *Review of
Reviews*.[2] The piece, which bears a heavy (and unacknowledged) debt to
Edwin A. Abbott's novella *Flatland* (1884), invites the reader to consider a
one-dimensional space populated by self-aware atoms who can move only
forwards and backwards. Add the concept of breadth to such a length-only
universe, Stead says, and imagine the outpouring of scepticism and
recrimination amongst its population for those who first experienced it.
Introduce height, and 'no recollection of first dimensional space, from
which they had gradually risen, would deter them from denouncing as
crazy visionaries those who ventured to talk nonsense about above and
below'.[3] Just so, argues Stead, are we three-dimensional beings on the eve
of having our eyes opened to the fourth.

Indications of the existence of the Fourth Dimension, which Stead
charmingly calls 'Throughth' ('...if I may venture to give it a name...')
apparently include clairvoyance, telepathy, crystal vision, psychometry,
and automatic writing, and Stead devotes the bulk of this article to
discussing the latter (p. 426). However, it is his general opening remarks
which make such a fitting start point for this chapter. The words quoted
earlier encapsulate an attitude towards progress which Stead surely shared
with many of his contemporaries: the defiant and excited proclamation of
the first sentence; the immediacy and awkwardness of the second; the
implied link between science and the imagination in the third. Above all,
the word 'eve' is significant: the suggestion is that we are on the verge of

achieving some great new understanding about the universe, only previously hinted at.

With the occult phenomena he yearned for thoroughly discredited by modern (and in some cases contemporary) science, it is easy to forget that Stead's optimism in this regard was actually entirely justified. Less than three years after the publication of 'Throughth', news reached England that a new kind of light had been discovered beyond the perceptive ability of the human eye, a light which passed through apparently solid objects as if they were not there, a light which could be used to photograph living bones: the X-rays.

Wilhelm Röntgen's discovery, made at Würzburg in November 1895, reached the English press in the pages of *Nature* on 23 January, 1896. The medical applications of the discovery were recognised instantly, and the speed with which they were taken up by the periodicals was equally remarkable: the first piece of fiction about X-rays which I have found appeared in *Pearson's Magazine* less than three months after *Nature*'s initial publication. The speed of this appearance, and that of the other X-ray fictions which soon followed, might partly be explained by the fact that although Röntgen had described a method of reproducing this strange new radiation in controlled conditions, the scientific community had yet to offer a convincing explanation for it. 'No crucial experiment has yet been made' uncovering the nature of the X-rays, Alfred Porter declared at the end of an eleven-page article in the *Strand* – one which, science being thus unavailable, devotes the bulk of its length to the photographic spectacle of the X-rays instead.[4] When H. J. W. Dam travelled to Würzburg to interview Röntgen for *Pearson's Magazine*, the following exchange took place:

'Is it light?'

'No.'

'Is it electricity?'

'Not in any known form.'

'What is it?'

'I don't know.'[5]

Working prior to the discovery of the electron, Röntgen's own theory was that the X-rays represented longitudinal waves in the luminiferous ether, an all-permeating medium in which the whole of creation was suspended posited to explain the behaviour of light. The ether was an established theory, but one which was losing ground in the 1890s having failed to appear in any experimental results (Einstein's special relativity finally put paid to it in 1905). Röntgen is cautious about the ether theory even in his original paper in *Nature*, which ends, guardedly, with the disclaimer:

> I must confess that I have in the course of this research made myself more and more familiar with this thought, and venture to put the opinion forward, while I am quite conscious that the hypothesis advanced still requires a more solid foundation.[6]

This paragraph, which follows the only piece of supposition in an otherwise straightforward account of the facts, emphasises a key characteristic of X-rays in the early days following their discovery: to the public, at least, they were as well explained by the spiritualists as by the scientists.

In practice, the two world-views seldom appeared in such a straightforward binary. William Crookes, noted physicist, discoverer of Thallium and inventor of a part of the apparatus with which Röntgen made his discovery, the Crookes Tube, was an avowed spiritualist and, later, president of the Society for Psychical Research (SPR). To those who had been discussing spirit photography, invisible light, and worlds beyond human perception for years, the discovery would have seemed a valorisation rather than a surprise: 'the [SPR's] belief that the photographic plate could detect ghostly rays invisible to the human eye appeared prophetic in light of Röntgen's discovery', notes Allen W. Grove.[7] This comment suggests the way in which I propose to understand X-rays here, as part of a spectrum of equally unbelievable and even laughable ideas, *some of which were true*. They can be interrogated in the light of Roger Luckhurst's comment (on the historiography of the Victorian supernatural more generally) that science and the occult:

> ...are now conceived less in monolithic oppositional structures than as complexly interwoven *networks*, looping together social, institutional, epistemological, and representational resources in ways which problematize secure disciplinary demarcations.[8]

If science and the occult are 'complexly interwoven networks', then examining a phenomenon which promised to contain elements of both might usefully illuminate some other 'loopings together'. Psychic communication with the dead; photographs to which living flesh is transparent as air: both have their place in Stead's Fourth Dimension, and in the press over which he had such a profound influence.

In this chapter, I use the example of X-rays to scrutinise the ways that a host of different New Journalist genres approached the issue of objective truth. The central point, that the magazines' insistence on diversity of both textual and visual content inherently de-emphasised objective truth and therefore helps to explain the inconsistent regard they display for scientific facts, is made via examinations of advertising, satire pieces, spiritualist writing, the interview (or "chat"), and finally fiction. After studying the conflicted attitudes towards X-ray technology documented in these various kinds of periodical writing, I will argue that the array of conflicting voices which constituted the New Journalist approach to truth helps to explain the awkward relationship with science still evident in the present-day mass media.

Before going any further, it is important to mention that although the X-rays are a highly convenient example for this argument, I don't wish to claim any kind of special status for them. The *fin de siècle* was a rich time for physics, and one might as easily examine the discoveries of, say, Marconi, Rutherford, or Einstein for insight into the dissemination of new science throughout the genres of the periodical.[9] X-rays do have some particular attractions as a case study, though, partly because of their prominence in some of the clichés of later SF (X-ray goggles and scores of similarly unlikely twentieth-century creations), but mostly because they are a distinctly *visual* technology with an immediate and obvious impact on print culture's aesthetic. Roland Barthes theorised that affective photographs are those which combine the elements he calls *studium* and *punctum*, respectively the routine affect of human interest and the surprising element 'which rises out of the scene, shoots out of it like an arrow' and invests a picture with its poignancy.[10] One particularly 'good symptom' of this second characteristic is an 'incapacity to name' (p. 51): X-ray photographs, considered in this regard, were striking precisely because of their testimony both to an abject (and previously invisible) reality and because of the *je ne sais quoi* factor caused both by their novelty and by science's inability to fully explain their operation.

From the perspective of this study, X-rays highlight not only the relationships between science and fiction but the relationships between text and image and, ultimately, between the press and the truth. X-rays were decorative and artistic as well as ghoulish and unsettling, but they were at the same time scientific portrayals of a previously inaccessible yet powerfully concrete reality. Taking account of their first appearances in print culture therefore naturally brings a whole range of areas – journalism, literature, print history, images, advertising, science, technology, celebrity, and the supernatural – into contact with each other. The discovery of X-rays 'proves an important moment in literature', says Grove, 'as it blurs the boundaries between ghost fiction, science fiction and scientific reality'.[11] Stephen Kern points out that the X-rays' new perspectives on the human interior formed 'part of a general reappraisal of what is properly inside and what is outside in the body, the mind, physical objects, and nations' which took place in the closing years of the nineteenth century.[12] These amalgamative characteristics, which mirror the amalgamative properties of the general magazine, make X-rays an excellent example of cross-genre conversations in the mass media.

Most of the primary material in this chapter is taken from the two years immediately following the discovery of X-rays, 1896 and 1897, a narrowness of chronological focus which allows me to concentrate on a broader spectrum of genres than I have so far taken account of. Over the next few sections, a number of complimentary and contradictory uses of and attitudes towards a cutting-edge scientific breakthrough will emerge, bolstering the picture I have been painting of *fin-de-siècle* periodicals as dense networks of complex interrelationships which both articulate and subtly alter the literature/science dynamic. But when we examine these various pieces, something else becomes clear: New Journalism sought its truth-authority in a range of places, science being just one of these, and the tensions detectable as a result were thus an intrinsic part, rather than an unfortunate by-product, of the *fin-de-siècle* media. Putting these estranged items back alongside each other, then, reminding ourselves that they originally appeared as bedfellows in the general magazines, does more than simply highlight the complexity of the network of exchanges between various genres: it also sheds light on the conflicts which continue to characterise the relationships between science, fiction, and the media.

Visible invisibility: sales, satire, and spiritualism

My discussion opens with examples of three very different non-fictional treatments of X-rays: their commercial appropriation in an advertising supplement, the humorous use made of them by satirical columnists Barry Pain and W. L. Alden, and the reaction of the occultists, whose interest in X-rays I have already mentioned. The writers of each use X-rays very differently; what they have in common, I suggest, is an interest in focussing on practical or aesthetic ends rather than on technical means. Despite the necessarily scientific nature of their subject matter, they are all discussions in which the science itself is rendered invisible, an implied process rather than an explicitly discussed breakthrough in human understanding.

X-rays reached the advertising section less than six months after the appearance of Röntgen's *Nature* article. A lavish image advertising the oral hygiene product 'Sozodont' appeared in the *Strand* (among other places), depicting a fresh-faced young lady sitting in the consulting chair of a dentist's surgery. Illuminating her is a beam of X-rays, which also lights up the dentist himself, reading some notes on the right hand side of the picture. 'Dr. Van Buskirk applies the Röntgen Rays in his Dental Practice', says the caption, 'and finds that those habitually using SOZODONT have perfect Teeth, hard Gums, and sweet Breath' (Fig. 3.1).[13] The advert suggests several important things about the ways in which X-rays were understood, not just in the inaccuracies of its text (X-rays may be useful for examining teeth, but are far less so for breath) but also in the way the image itself is composed. The equipment behind the woman's chair is the room's only light source, which seems at odds with one of the most well-known facts about the new rays – that they were invisible to human eyes. The intense beam which lights up doctor and patient casts into shadow the rest of the equipment in the room, as well as two iconic pictures which hang on the wall of the surgery: X-rays of a hand and foot respectively.

Images of a hand and a foot seem strange things to display in a dental surgery, but crowing over the advertisement's scientific absurdities is less important here than realising that the rays are being used primarily for their aesthetic. The visible beam is not literally Röntgen's discovery but the figurative light of the truth which that discovery enables the doctor to see: instead of two skeletons, it reveals a sensible medic and a robust, smiling patient, healthy because of her choice of dental products. Kate Flint uses this same advertisement (which she encounters in the *Illustrated London News*) to highlight the extent to which photography 'promised an enhanced role for ocular proof' in late-Victorian Britain.[14] Exploring the limitations of human sight, Flint evokes Walter Benjamin's notion that photography discloses the 'optical unconscious'; '[i]t is indeed a different nature that speaks to the camera from the one which addresses the eye', Benjamin tells us, 'different above all in the sense that instead of a space worked through by a human consciousness there appears one which is affected unconsciously'.[15] The Sozodont advertisement is an illustration rather than a photograph, but the vehicle of its metaphor is the proof-authenticity of photography (in this case, X-ray photography), and via its consciously composed aesthetic focus on end results, it shifts scientific process into implication. Despite apparently being made visible, the X-rays themselves are harder to see here than ever. Though their

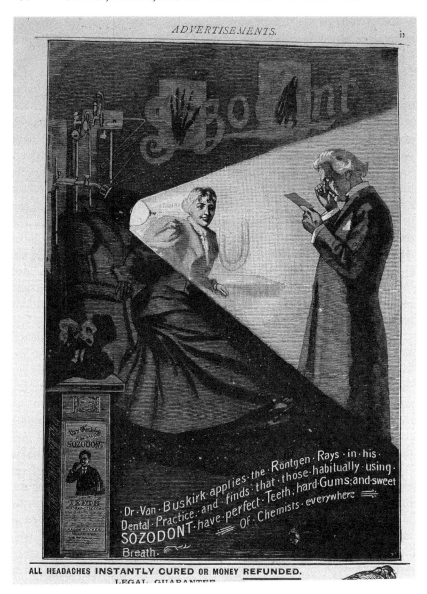

3.1   X-rays used to advertise Sozodont in *The Strand Magazine* (July 1896). Courtesy of the Bodleian Libraries, The University of Oxford.

iconography abounds in this image, they themselves, with their incomprehensible extra-sensory properties, their unnerving display of a patient's living bones, and, of course, their long exposure and development times, are absent. What remains to encourage potential consumers of Sozodont is a distillation of their newness and their effectiveness. Flint summarises the 'optical unconscious' by speaking of photography's ability 'to make us realise what we see without realising that we have seen it': here, we see the reverse of that proposition.[16] An actual photograph may bring truth out of the unconscious, but the concept of photography can still be used to displace it. In this advert, and many others since, we realise what we see without realising *how* we have seen it.

This observation reveals an intriguing parallel between X-rays and the periodical press itself. If the X-rays are at the same time ostentatiously on show in the advert and entirely missing from it, they share this characteristic with advertising *per se*, which accounted for many of the most arresting images printed in the illustrated monthlies, and which, as Warren Chappell and Robert Bringhurst note, 'formed the primary market for new type designs', yet which many readers would presumably have skipped past, confined as they typically were to a long supplement at the beginning of each issue and a shorter section at the back.[17] Many research libraries have removed these sections, and almost no advertisements are scanned when monthlies are digitised, so for the present-day researcher (attempting to get a scan of, say, Fig. 3.1) the advertising sections remain an equally present absence: literally invisibled by our conservation decisions, yet also the main economic driving force behind the developments in print technology without which these publications could not have existed.[18]

These developments themselves constitute a similar kind of present absence. Mass printing had only very recently reached the point where indulgences such as this three-quarter-page image could affordably appear in the pages of general magazines. The technologies needed to produce these publications had been constantly improved throughout the nineteenth century. The *Strand* was printed using a state-of-the-art R. Hoe & Company rotary perfecting press onto super-calendered paper which had been invented specifically to bear the increasingly high-resolution halftone images which were print technology's leading advance of the 1890s. These rapid developments permitted a significant increase in volume as well as quality of illustration, responsible, in David Reed's assessment, for the fact that 'production costs were being decimated'.[19] As Reed points out, advertising revenue was the driving force behind these leaps forward, with publishers capable of standing out

3.2   Advert for Patent Sound Discs, taken from *The Strand Magazine* (July 1896). This ad faces the one reproduced as Fig. 3.1. Courtesy of the Bodleian Libraries, The University of Oxford.

in either quality or quantity of images able to expect higher sales and demand higher advertising rates (pp. 20–23). While X-rays were being discovered in 1895, the processes were being refined which would eventually allow Alfred Harmsworth's *Daily Mirror*, in 1904, to become the first periodical illustrated solely with photographs.[20]

Two layers of image, then, attest to the quality of Sozodont: the X-ray pictures on the dentist's walls (in the picture) and the large, detailed, aesthetically appealing engraving (in the magazine). In both cases, the technology which makes the imaging possible and attractively new is fetishised by the elision of its mechanics of production. With X-rays, it is literally impossible to see the process, which takes place on wavelengths the human eye cannot detect; the process of printing, meanwhile, is geographically removed from the leisured reader, taking place, in the case of the *Strand*, not in the public art gallery of the Newnes offices on Southampton Street, which displayed some of the magazine's most notable illustrations on its walls and offered prints for sale, but in the private, state-of-the-art industrial printing facility elsewhere in the building.[21] Only final products are visible to the reader.

I will return to the relationships between X-rays and printed images in due course. For now, I want to focus on this Latourian idea of the 'black box', the circumscription of a mechanical or digital technology into an integrated device the operations of which need not be seen or comprehended by the end user.[22] Epitomised in today's smartphones (for instance), and surely one of our own most basic technological fantasies, it is clear from this glance at periodical advertising that something like the black box also governed imaginations in the *fin de siècle*. On the page facing the Sozodont advert, a much smaller image advertises the benefits of new patent sound discs for the hard of hearing. These remarkable new devices are, apparently, 'the same to the ears as glasses to the eyes. Invisible' (Fig. 3.2).[23] It is, perhaps, a corollary of Arthur C. Clarke's famous third law of prediction – 'any sufficiently advanced technology is indistinguishable from magic' – that invisibility is a desirable characteristic in any technology which wishes to seem futuristic.[24] This is certainly true of photography which, as Susan Sontag observed, was sold to consumers from the 1880s onwards on the basis that mechanical and technical aptitude were not necessary to take pictures: 'Popular taste expects an easy, an invisible technology'.[25] This bears on radiographs in two ways, since they are both an invisible technology and one which reveals invisible forms inside the body.

The Sozodont advert, in short, is not so much an engagement with recent scientific advances as a fantasy of a near-future when such advances can be taken for granted. It enacts this fantasy by taking advances for granted itself, be they the ability to photograph living bones or the ability to reproduce images on a mass scale with new printing techniques (such advances are also taken for granted elsewhere in the *Strand*, where an X-ray is incidentally used to solve a fictitious crime in an instalment of L. T. Meade and Clifford Halifax's provocatively titled *Adventures of a Man of Science*).[26] In this respect, the advertisers had common ground with some of the satirical columnists writing in the monthly magazines. They, too, were more interested in what the X-rays meant (or should mean) for society than in what they revealed about the universe. An excellent example of this is the sixth in Barry Pain's 'Nature's Next Moves' series in *Pearson's Magazine*. Supposedly assembled from the notes of a scientific free-thinker named Archibald Mosely Damstruther, Pain's jocular pieces offered supposed anticipations of forthcoming changes in the world of science, particularly biology. The running joke was that Nature, rather than human agency, was responsible for new developments. The 'Treble-X Rays', claims Damstruther in this instalment, 'seem to me to be due about now'. They are similar to the X-rays already known, but offer a rather different sort of insight: 'The operator presses the bulb and for the hundredth part of a second the Treble-X Rays pass through the head of the subject, and throw the record of his thoughts on the screen'.[27] Whilst the Röntgen rays are for reading the body, the Treble-X Rays are for reading the mind. And Pain was not alone in satirically raising the prospect of photographing thoughts. W. L. Alden, writing his 'Wisdom Let Loose' column (also in *Pearson's*), worries about the consequences of what he calls 'brain photography':

> Instead of asking Lord Salisbury, in Parliament, what he means to do in regard to Venezuela, Mr. Labouchere will surreptitiously photograph the Premier's brain, and publish a 'processed' copy of the photograph in *Truth*.[28]

Polite society will crumble, jokes Alden, as dishonesty becomes impossible. Pain is sensitive to the same concerns – '[o]ne would never be able, with any feeling of confidence, to sell a horse to one's best friend, or to attend as sole legatee the funeral of a distant and very wealthy relative' – but obligingly makes his equipment too bulky to be used covertly.[29]

In both Alden and Pain's pieces, a concern over the future of privacy in the face of new and increasingly intrusive scientific developments masks a tacit assumption about the objectivity of interior truth which is, at first, easy to miss. At some point roughly halfway through the Pain article, the Treble-X Rays stop being a device for photographing thoughts and, that process "invisibled" like the apparatus itself, start revealing incontestable facts. Their use in court would be revolutionary, says Damstruther, for 'the record would give Mr. Sykes's real thoughts, not the thoughts that he would have liked us to think that he thought' (p. 680). Both Pain and Alden extrapolate X-rays into a science-fictional universal lie detector, able to reveal hidden facts about the mind just as their real-life counterparts revealed hidden facts about the body. The notion is a fascinating one, especially when raised by Pain, who spent the whole of the 'Nature's Next Moves' series revelling in the factual ambiguity surrounding his own authorship. The byline to each instalment reads 'SUGGESTED BY ARCHIBALD MOSELY DAMSTRUTHER AND EDITED BY BARRY PAIN' despite the fact that we as readers know the former to be a fictitious creation of the latter, and Pain is clearly enjoying the obvious inauthenticity of the documents he is supposedly merely editing when he writes (as himself) in his short, italicised introduction to the piece that 'no actual guarantee is given as to the exact amount, if any, of pure science in this article' (p. 677). Likewise, Alden's mention of 'a "processed" copy of the photograph in *Truth*' casts a wry smile at the supposed objectivity of the thought-rays: the inverted commas around 'processed' highlight the fact that all photographs are mitigated by reproductive technology and subject to various kinds of editorial control, whilst the italics on '*Truth*' not only denote a publication but place sarcastic emphasis on the concept of truth within the context of the periodical press. *Truth* would not have been a random choice for Alden: its editor, Henry Labouchere, advocated the introduction of the first-person to journalism in the belief that the press should 'be open and candid in its politics, and that it [should] not hide behind a veneer of independence or omniscience'.[30]

Aware of their satire's dependency on ambiguity, Alden and Pain are both anxious to address the philosophical conundrums arising from the idea of ultimate and detectable interior truth. Alden's paragraph on brain photography comes immediately before a section which I will discuss further in Chapter 4: a call for Antarctic exploration to cease in order that there might be left on Earth one place to which the human imagination can continue to ascribe fantasies. 'Any scientific discoveries that the expedition may make', claims Alden, 'will not be half as interesting as the stories which the romance writers will give us'.[31] In their light-hearted scepticism of science, it is the idea of there *being* a final truth to discover which these two writers find the most alarming. As I hinted at the close of Chapter 2, it is not surprising to find these ideas in some of the more self-conscious writers of the heteroglot periodical press, which thrived on a multiplicity of possible truths, and possible readings of the truth.

Mind-reading was a potential consequence of X-rays which others were taking much more seriously than Pain and Alden. 'There are few persons who have not felt at least a curiosity as to the recent announcement that it was now possible to photograph thought', wrote Stead in his review of occult publications, *Borderland*:

> The presentation of our bones, or the matter of our brain, or the action of the heart, by the 'X' rays would be far transcended in importance, if it were once established that we could procure a permanent record of our passing moods and fancies.[32]

The passage bears distinct resemblance to that in which Pain explains:

> By the X Rays you can detect the bones in the hand or the farthing in the offertory bag. By the Treble-X Rays you will be able to detect the thoughts in the head. Does that not sound useful?[33]

The only real difference between these two passages is tonal, because Pain, unlike Stead, is joking. But *Borderland*, a shilling quarterly aimed at uniting Britain's disparate spiritualists, addressed many of the same concerns and fantasies as the satirists in its purportedly factual coverage of psychic photography. In April 1897, for example, it excerpted a story from *The Light of Truth* (another significantly named publication for my purposes) under the subheading 'Yarns about the X-rays' (a noteworthy title, given the factual ambiguity implied by 'yarns'[34]). The piece relates that J. R. Cocke, blind from birth, was supposedly able to describe the outline of objects held between his brain and a powerful beam of X-rays: 'it seems as if the cortex or outer shell of the brain were rendered fluorescent, like the sensitive plate, and the shadow of these objects was communicated to it and then transmitted to the visual areas at the posterior part'.[35] Here, the brain is part of the photographic equipment rather than simply its object. Technology is therefore invisibled to a whole new degree – it has become integrated with the body, the brain as photographic plate. A technological process is again being elided, this time by being relocated within the mystified human body.

An even more pronounced example, and one with even closer narrative resemblances to Pain's, is to be found in *Borderland*'s reports on the "dorchagraph" experiments of Andrew Glendinning. With the help of a medium, Glendinning purported to be able to conjure photographs without a camera simply by holding on to an undeveloped plate. When developed, the plates showed images (generally profile photographs of people) and, less frequently, text (handwriting) from the mind of one of the subjects. The human brain here becomes the camera itself, and the X-rays are less visible than ever, Stead commenting:

> . . .we have here a discovery which throws that of the X-rays into the shade, for it is much more marvellous to photograph an object that does not exist, save in the thought of an operator, than to photograph a coin that has lodged in a man's throat. . .[36]

This one-upmanship of positivist science – it is 'much more marvellous' here to transcend the drudgery of facts than it is to be medically useful – is aptly expressed using a light/dark metaphor and underlines the fact that both this story and the report from *The Light of Truth* harbour the same distrust of objectivity as Pain and Alden. To Stead, the strongest recommendation of Glendinning's theories is not his evidence but his trustworthiness as an operator ('He is certainly incapable of making any statement that he knows to be false. A more upright man does not live'[37]) whilst Cocke's success as a human photographic plate is due to his exceptional prowess as a perceiver (whether the experiment would work 'in brains less acutely sensitive and magnificently developed is questionable'[38]).

The favouring of witness testimony over verifiable evidence falls in line with *Borderland*'s wider project, outlined in the prospectus Stead published in *Review of Reviews* prior to its launch:

> In *Borderland*, we shall take nothing for granted. Whether on one side or the other, our experience of the immeasurable vastness of the universe, even of material things, and of the constant dogmatism and pharisaic intolerance of men of science when face to face with a new truth, compels us to *refuse to rule out as manifestly incredible even the most incredible statements which are vouched for by trustworthy witnesses.*[39]

The philosophy of this last phrase is the direct opposite of the Royal Society's more famous (and more succinct) 'Nullius in Verba'. Far from not taking anyone's word, Stead proposes to implicitly believe anyone he likes. He opposes this approach to that of 'the men of science', the closed-minded materialists who refuse to entertain the notion that there are more things in heaven and earth. The accusation of hypocrisy implicit in 'pharisaic' is especially interesting given that Stead's declared intention in the previous sentence to 'take nothing for granted' *does* sound similar to the spirit in which the Royal Society was founded, and there are other areas in the same article in which Stead has clearly been deeply influenced by genuinely scientific approaches:

> The wish is so often father to the thought that it is necessary to scrutinise more closely the evidence that seems to tell in favour of a conclusion that we desire than the facts and arguments which point in the opposite direction.[40]

This caution against confirmation bias is a point with which any scientist (of Stead's day or ours) would have no difficulty. As indicated by his use of the phrase 'scientific imagination' in the quotation with which I began this chapter, Stead considered his project to be in many respects an avowedly empirical one. The problem *Borderland* exists to address, he says, is that occult phenomena have not been subjected to 'close systematic and sustained investigation' (p. 675). Far from being straightforwardly antiscientific, Stead explicitly invokes Darwin as a role model; *Borderland*'s function is as an index, and the painstaking nested lists of the different branches of occult investigation in its *Review of Reviews* prospectus are an attempt to bring order to a chaotic and disorganised field of "study" by the imposition of something approaching Linnaean taxonomy. In short, *Borderland* was supposed, by uniting the currently disparate subfields of occultism into common correspondence, to make a science out of the supernatural: to apply 'the methods of research, which have yielded such brilliant results in the material sphere, to the fitful phenomena of the borderland' (p. 675).

The *Review of Reviews* article is perhaps best considered a manifesto for Stead's forthcoming publication, and is significant because it makes clear that *Borderland* was attempting to do with the occult press what *Review of Reviews* was doing with more mainstream publications – provide a continuously updating index from across a spectrum of publications.[41] This taxonomic project conceived journalism *as* science – objectivity came not from adherence to a particular doctrine of empiricism but through a combination and networking of as many pre-existing approaches as possible. As with the satire pieces, this is an attitude which it is not surprising to find coming from the pen of one of the New Journalism's leading lights. The heteroglossia of the general magazine is here shifted to the state of laboratory.

The Sozodont advert, the satirical musings of Alden and Pain, and Stead's coverage of thought photography in *Borderland* are different reactions to the appearance of X-rays, but they have three things in common. The first, as I have argued, is that all share an interest in eliding the scientific side of the discovery, making it "invisible" and focussing on social effects over technological process. The second is that this very characteristic, along with several key details of the way it is expressed (consider again the techno-fetishist aesthetic of the Sozodont advert, the thought-reading machines of Alden and Pain, the brain/technology integration of J. R. Cocke) place them on a similar imaginative plane to SF – as usual, this is not to claim that any of these pieces are "really" SF but, rather, to draw attention to the proximity of different evolving genre strands within individual publications and articles. The third thing which the advertisers, satirists, and spiritualists share, closely related to the first two, is their co-location within the monthly magazines, and specifically their links with the high-tech project of New Journalism. It is this aspect of the periodicals' reception of X-rays that I shall continue to examine in the next section, which addresses itself to that quintessentially New Journalist form, the illustrated interview.

Interviews: fiction stands in for a reluctant subject

H. J. W. Dam's seven-page interview with Wilhelm Röntgen appeared in *Pearson's Magazine* less than three months after the discovery of X-rays had been translated into English. It takes a form which would have been familiar to any *fin-de-siècle* magazine reader: a few pages of introductory biography followed by an editorialised transcription of a laconic chat between interviewer and interviewee. Like most reporters in interviews from this era, Dam writes avowedly in the first person, breaking off occasionally to supply his own interior monologue. The interview takes place in Röntgen's lab: most such chats took place in either the workplace or home of the interviewee, capitalising on the chance to describe their subject's lifestyle as well as their personality.

In one respect, though – illustration – Dam's article is somewhat atypical. Pieces of this kind were typically rife with photographic accompaniments to the reporter's descriptions – pictures of the various rooms of the building, often with the interviewee in situ at a writing desk; pictures showing the exterior, the rest of the interviewee's household;

gator, and not the multiplicity
ion of his tools that breaks new
vast territory
wn. In fact,
s laboratory
three really
ors in one of
scoveries that
eased the
nd the
an—a
il, a
um
nan
for-
un-
had
that
um
lass
nich
een
awn
ains
onth
ere.
e is
the
end,
lec-
e is
ugh
abe,
osi-
ts bands of light varying in
e colour of the glass.

two when the Doctor entered t
hurriedly, something like an an
wind
slen
lim
whos
pear
enth
ener
wea
blue
his l
rose
from
as th
perr
trifie
enth
H
and
spe
and
man
once
track
tery,
dow
rem
an ⟨
patie
are
and
and
cord
He ⟨
fifty years old, but his enthusi
twenty-five. He was born at ⟨

PROFESSOR RÖNTGEN.

VIEW OF PROFESSOR RÖNTGEN'S LABORATORY

The white cross indicates the window of the room in which Professor Röntgen's experiments were conducted.

3.3 Detail of a page from *Pearson's Magazine* showing Wilhelm Röntgen and his laboratory – photographed from outside (April 1896). Courtesy of the Cadbury Research Library, University of Birmingham.

occasionally, photographs from earlier in the interviewee's life, generously provided by themselves – but though Dam's piece is heavily illustrated, only one picture shows Röntgen, and this is obviously a stock photo. Most of the other pictures are X-ray photographs, all of which are from sources other than Röntgen himself: the first two were taken by a Professor Spies, a photograph of whom is also added to bulk up the illustrated content, and the others, commissioned especially for *Pearson's Magazine*, are credited to A. A. C. Swinton, the scientist who wrote the commentary accompanying the translation of Röntgen's original paper in *Nature*. There is one exterior shot of Röntgen's lab, but this is taken from the other side of a rather large fence (Fig. 3.3).

It was not at all unusual for images of an interview subject's scientific work (when the subject was a scientist) to appear in print, but there is something unusual about the lack of personal images to complement them here. Dam is unafraid to draw attention to this, saying, after his offer to buy the table on which the scientist conducted his first X-ray experiments is refused, '[a] photograph of it would have been a consolation, but for several reasons one was not to be had for the present'.[42] After Röntgen demonstrates how, sitting at the table, he first photographed his own hand through it, Dam reports the following exchange:

> 'You ought to have your portrait painted in that attitude,' I suggested.
>
> 'No, that is nonsense,' said he smiling.
>
> 'Or be photographed.' This suggestion was made with a deeply hidden purpose.
>
> The rays from the Röntgen eyes instantly penetrated the deeply hidden purpose. 'Oh, no,' said he, 'I can't let you make pictures of me, I am too busy.' Clearly the Professor was entirely too modest to gratify the wishes of the curious world.[43]

In this room full of imaging technologies – not only the Crookes tubes but the penetrating scientific eyes of Röntgen himself, which here, unlike normal eyes, emit rays as well as receiving them – Dam finds himself unable to get pictures. The professor is scarcely more forthcoming about his personal history. After a three-sentence summary of his subject's career to date, Dam notes:

> These details he gave me under good-natured protest, for he quite failed to understand why his personality should interest the public. He declined to admire himself or his results in any degree, and laughed at the idea of being famous. He is too deeply interested in science to waste any time in thinking about himself.[44]

Röntgen wants to demonstrate the X-rays, and whilst Dam is clearly interested too, he is also invested in shoring up the "great man" narrative and providing the public with insights into the private life of a scientific celebrity. The comparison between the two men and their preferred types of photograph is an apposite one – Röntgen, with his penetrating gaze and X-rays, wants to get at interiors; Dam, with notepad and camera, is interested in surfaces. The last sentence of this second quotation even suggests that Röntgen's love of science and his unwillingness to give out personal images can be equated with each other. Casting himself as an objective observer of the world, he has no interest in being someone else's subject.

Subjectivity, however, was at the heart of the celebrity culture into which Dam was trying to introduce Röntgen. This is vigorously expressed in George Griffith's short story 'A Photograph of the Invisible', the earliest piece of fiction in English I have been able to find which makes use of the discovery of X-rays. It should be regarded as a companion piece to Dam's interview for several reasons: not only does it appear in the same issue of *Pearson's Magazine* (April 1896) but it is actually mentioned by Dam, who devotes a paragraph of his introduction to it:

> Not long ago [Griffith's] story would have been read with utter incredulity, possibly not unmixed with ridicule, but by the time the reader has reached the end of this article he will have learned that the story might, without the alteration of a single detail, be accepted as a narrative of actual fact.[45]

Notwithstanding the argument of this book, which is based on the idea that implied genre conversations were ongoing in these publications, explicit inline linkages like this between two items in the same issue were extremely rare. I suggest in what follows that Griffith's fiction fulfills some of the gaps in the X-ray imagery created by the New Journalism's format, gaps which Röntgen was disinclined to fill himself.

'A Photograph of the Invisible', unlike the Dam interview, revels in the full gothic potential of X-ray images. Griffith's Professor Grantham, 'a chemist and physical investigator by profession, [. . .] a photographer by hobby' comes to the aid of his friend, Denton, who has been wronged in love by an unnamed woman and seeks revenge.[46] Grantham's scheme is scientifically up-to-the-minute. Capitalising upon his reputation as a society photographer, he offers to take a portrait of the lady. Unbeknownst to her, he substitutes X-ray equipment for his regular camera. As anticipated by the two men, the unexpected sight of her living skeleton has a profound effect on the woman, who ends up in a private asylum. There is a lot which could be said about this story, which is racist as well as sexist (the woman's crime is to have married a 'German Jew brute and his millions' instead of Denton), and in which amoral, dispassionate science is the source of narrative justice ('I can give you a revenge that shall be purely scientific. . .', p. 376) but my wider argument here is best served by concentrating on the tale's use of images.

The dénouement comes with the horrifying X-ray photograph arriving at the breakfast table of its unfortunate victim and her now-husband, Mr Goldsberg. 'Neither of them said anything when they first saw what was underneath', Griffith tells us, and indeed, from this moment onwards there is no more dialogue in the story (p. 379). Griffith first describes the Goldsbergs' physical reaction to the image, then he describes the image itself. The two complement each other, for both are presented as 'stills' – the couple's reaction is devoid of sound and movement, described in purely

The blood died out of her face till it was grey and white and ghastly.

3.4   Illustration from George Griffith's 'A Photograph of the Invisible', in the same issue of *Pearson's* as Fig. 3.3 (April 1896). Courtesy of the Cadbury Research Library, University of Birmingham.

visual terms, he becoming 'almost purple', she 'grey and white and ghastly'. The pair are as static as the picture they regard, a picture of the lady whose dress is described in similar terms, 'diaphanous and transparent'. Mrs Goldsberg's X-rayed skull 'seemed to stare at her out of the sockets in which two ghostly eyes appeared to float', and this is a stare which the real Mrs. Goldsberg returns, her face becoming that 'of a corpse, but for the two bright, glaring eyes that stared out of it' (p. 380). Mrs Goldsberg's similarity to her distorted likeness is emphasised by the presentation of her reaction, and that of her husband, as a tableau – a literary device complimented by the story's final illustration, the work of G. G. Manton, which shows the couple freeze-framed, the X-ray turned away from the viewer's perspective (Fig 3.4). They gaze at a particularly overpowering manifestation of Barthes's *punctum,* albeit one intended by the photographer: an image the sight of which causes madness, a moment of 'piercing' which requires a second image to testify to it on the page of the magazine.

Griffith considers the new X-rays by offering a fictitious moment in which a number of crossing gazes are foregrounded. The couple stare at the X-ray; the X-ray stares at the couple; we, the readers, stare at both. In the next paragraph, we learn that the moment is also keenly regarded (within the story's world) by readers of the society journals, and it is through their far more distant eyes that we find out what happens after the intricately described tableau: 'A day or two afterwards Society was startled by an amazing piece of news concerning the golden idols which it had most recently set up...' (p. 380). This is a distance in time as well as in space – in the space of a few lines, readers have gone from being in the narrative presence of events to learning of them after the fact. Another property of the photograph, of course, according to Barthes, is its ability to turn life into history.

This news is not quite the last word of the story. There follows an italicised editorial note:

> *Although this is of course a purely imaginative story, it may be as well to say that such photographs as that of Mrs. Goldsberg have been shown by actual experiment to be possible.*[47]

The insistence on plausibility here is counterpart to the testimonial which Dam gives in the introduction to his piece: despite being fiction, Griffith's story wields the narratives and, more, the iconography of fact. Unlike the material discussed in the previous section, Griffith's is a story in which the processes of early radiography are scrupulously observed and reported, the middle of the story being a meticulous and reasonably accurate description of the methods by which Grantham takes his X-ray pictures. The tacit and overt assertions of realism from both Griffith and Dam draw attention to the fictive feel the X-rays engendered in a world not used to them, but they also serve to legitimise the story as a companion piece to Dam's interview.[48] With its abundance of sensational images, both textual and visual, Griffith's story more than compensates for Röntgen's reticence. Where Röntgen will not give details of his personal life, Griffith's story is almost entirely given over to Grantham's extracurricular pursuits. Where Röntgen wants carefully to detail scientific ideas, Grantham says 'I can see you are impatient, and no doubt naturally. We'll let the explanation go for the present'.[49] Where Röntgen is unwilling to provide his companion with images, Grantham suggests the scheme for the reluctant Denton's photographic revenge himself, and is active in persuading him to go through with it.

Safe in the realm of fiction, a realm designated by, among other things, its style of illustration (typically hand-drawn rather than photographic), Griffith's story nonetheless functions partly as a factually empowered piece of wish fulfilment for the interview in which Röntgen resists Dam's strong desire to sensationalise. The bleed area between the two pieces is considerable; it is certainly not obvious from the titles 'A Wizard of To-Day' and 'A Photograph of the Invisible' that the latter is the one which is fictitious. Although readers would have been unlikely to approach a magazine so large and varied as *Pearson's Magazine* in strict page order, it is also tempting to suppose that Griffith's appearance much closer to the front of the magazine (his is the third item in the issue; Dam's is ninth) belies an editorial preference for narrative over fact. This is supposition, although some weight is given to it by the editorial at the end of the previous number which advertised the two pieces by saying:

> Mr. George Griffith will contribute a very striking story, which he calls 'A Photograph of the Invisible', and which *is emphasized by* an important interview with Dr. Röntgen...[50]

Regardless, however, of how Pearson himself conceived the relationship between the story and the interview, their co-incidence in the same issue of the magazine certainly allowed each to support the wider project of New Journalism, Dam's science authenticating Griffith's fiction, Griffith's fiction sensationalising Dam's science. The implied collaboration also demonstrates the relentless newness of *Pearson's Magazine*: Dam highlights the effect of scientific development on the authority of fiction when he remarks of Griffith's piece that further X-ray developments 'will have removed it from the region of romance to that of the commonplace'.[51] And by drawing attention to the fact that these pieces can be consumed in either order (or not at all) the linkages between them underscore New Journalism's most important subjectivity, that of the reader. The 'chat' takes place not just within Dam's interview but between it and the rest of the magazine, as well as between the entirety of the magazine, the individual who reads it, and the imagined community to which they implicitly belong. It is noteworthy, though, that the supportive role in which science is deployed here is not compatible with an abstract scientific worldview – Röntgen's agenda, in this issue of *Pearson's*, is disadvantaged in a way that Griffith's isn't.

Interviews: breadth of images support an enthusiastic subject

On the seventh of the eighteen pages of Roy Compton's interview with the artist and war illustrator Frederic Villiers in the September 1897 *Idler* – another New Journalist 'chat' – an X-ray photograph sits in the midst of text which makes no reference to it. The radiograph, which is of Villiers's right hand, is taken by the well-known physicist Silvanus P. Thompson – this

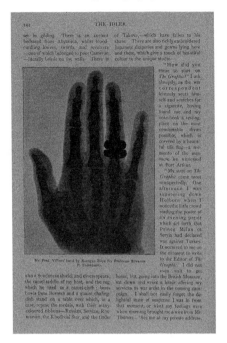

3.5 A page from the *Idler*, showing a radiograph of the hand of the artist Frederic Villiers (September 1897). Courtesy of Cambridge University Library.

much the caption tells us – but it is left to the reader to guess as to why the image might be deemed interesting or relevant (Fig. 3.5). The obvious conclusion is that it is intended to provide insight: this is, after all, an interview piece, its purpose to give the reader depth of vision into the life and work of a celebrity. The never-before-seen rendition of the hand with which Villiers executed his work is implicitly an insight into the skill which made him famous, a penetrative glance at his body supposed to penetrate his craft also.

We, who are more used to X-rays of hands and prepared for the reality that those of skilled artists look similar to those of everyone else, perhaps find the inclusion of this image curious. But there are perspectives from which its appearance makes perfect sense. Villiers is not Röntgen. Indeed, his pliancy in interview makes him appear almost the opposite. For the whole chat, he leads the way with anecdote after anecdote about his long career. Sentences are long and colourful: 'It was in the historic town of Belgrade I first heard the clang of war, the noise of the smith's hammer, the tramp of troops, the clinking of orderlies. . .'.[52] The actual process of painting a picture, the closest thing to an equivalent of the science on which Röntgen wishes to dwell, goes entirely unmentioned. Unlike Röntgen, Villiers recognises that he is being interviewed as a personality, and presents himself as such.

The images on display in the interview form an embarrassment of riches. Of twenty-four pictures in this article, sixteen are examples of Villiers's artwork (sketches and paintings); four are photographs of Villiers himself, his studio, or both; three are photographs taken by Villiers on his travels around the world; and one is the radiograph just mentioned. The images are dispersed fairly evenly throughout the piece. Five of them are whole-page images – more or less normal in an interview with an artist, especially in the post-1895 *Idler*, but still extravagant compared to most other articles. Implicitly, the pictures are all sourced directly from Villiers, or with his permission.

These images do not simply suggest that Villiers was a more willing subject than Röntgen. They also show us that articles like this one drew some of their strength from a collage effect, variety in *types of* image as well as in their images' subjects.[53] The vast majority of the images here are paintings and sketches – after all, they are the basis of Villiers's celebrity – but the variation in tone provided by the others is a key part of what made the New Journalism unique, according to Gerry Beegan:

> This kind of [written] material had been a feature of the working-class press since at least mid-century. [. . .] What was novel in the 1890s was the bringing together of all of these elements for a broad middle-class audience in a lively visual format that incorporated more illustration.[54]

Beegan is talking about more than simply quantity of images here. Arguing against the idea that the advance of printing technology resulted in photography simply replacing older types of illustration, he says:

> . . .overall the photograph was one of a range of different kinds of image used. Line and halftone processes added to the imaging possibilities, making the visual content of periodicals more abundant, complex, and increasingly hybrid.[55]

David Reed has remarked this same tendency in the *Strand*, Newnes's combination of halftones, diagrams, cartoons, and line drawings creating in his estimation a 'more energetic or lively' effect than the stentorian artwork of forebears such as *The English Illustrated Magazine*, an effect 'reinforced by the visual disjunctions'.[56] In the terms of this book, one might say that variety of visual genres was as crucial to the success of Standard Illustrated Popular Magazines as variety of textual genres. The X-ray encountered in the Compton article is therefore part of the *Idler*'s visual hybridity, another way of stressing the newness of New Journalism, print technology's ever-improving ability to deal with different types of image alongside each other. Genres of illustration, of which the X-ray was an example particularly charged with science and technology, were as chaotically mixed in the pages of these magazines as genres of writing.

James Mussell, arguing that the main function of photography in the magazines of the 1890s was to engender a sense of simultaneity, has noted that it was the X-rays' value as curiosities rather than any actual enhancement of perception which made them attractive to editors: 'these images [. . .] presented familiar objects in strange ways'.[57] As well as stressing the unique level of access to the subject which the *Idler* has managed to attain, then, the radiograph in the Villiers interview uses the iconography of science to assert the magazine's location in the present tense – not just a photograph, mass reproduction of which was itself extremely new, but a specific *kind* of photograph which was unheard of less than two years ago.

Mussell stresses that these magazines sought to entertain rather than to inform, and this explains the variety of images and kinds of image on display, not just in the 'Curiosities' section of the *Strand* (the example Mussell uses; a section at the back of each issue which reproduced strange reader-submitted photographs with minimal commentary), but throughout. As a part of this spectrum of images, X-rays were useful because of their scientific currency (in all senses of that word). The crucial point is that their visual appeal and newness were more important to editors than their scientific application. This much is evident from the way the radiograph of Villiers's hand is inserted without comment – it "goes without saying" that such an image is an important way of understanding a celebrity, whilst the visual diversity of the article to anyone flipping through the magazine is very much in the foreground.

It was the iconography of X-rays, then, rather than the X-rays themselves, which often lent interest to articles. This can be seen even in places where X-rays are never used or mentioned by name. A good example is Marcus Tindal's curiosity piece for *Pearson's Magazine*, 'Skeleton Leaves'. Published in the November 1897 issue, this article instructs the reader in the basics of stripping the flesh away from leaves so that only their veins remain. Particularly effective with ferns and ivy, this hobby is reported as being an excellent way of creating objects which appear 'carved in white ivory, so delicate are the veinings'.[58] This is not simply about craft, though, but perception also: 'no human hand was ever skilful enough to imitate the wonders of nature *hidden away beneath* what one is tempted to look upon as merely "ordinary leaves"' (pp. 494–95, my emphases).

If this were all, the visual links to Röntgen's discovery – the glances into nature's interiors attained by human craftsmanship – would be clear enough. But the images which Tindal puts alongside his words make the resonances even stronger. Over its five pages, the article contains twelve photographs of skeleton leaves which have been arranged as decorative borders for pictures of celebrities including Queen Victoria, Gladstone and Pope Leo XIII (Fig. 3.6). 'The accompanying illustrations will prove', Tindal remarks, 'that there are few more effective frames for photographs than a tasteful arrangement of these delicate skeletons' (p. 495). Here, in a display which befittingly embodies the attitude of the press to X-rays outlined earlier, these quasi-scientific bouquets provide ornamentation and interest to snapshots of famous personalities. This fact is enhanced by a diversity of types of image, for as they come to us in the magazine these are photographs *of* photographs (or woodcuts, when the celebrity being displayed predates photography). Images here frame other images.

The chaotic effect of this profusion of layered images has been mediated with consistent editing. All the photographs have been cropped in the same stylised fashion with the top two corners rounded off – their contents are diverse, yet they have been harmonised by the formatting decision. This is very much in line with Stead's ideal of the editorial process, in which the personality of the editor is the reconciling force between the various and superficially conflicted interests of their paper.[59] The treatment of the skeleton leaves in Tindal's piece highlights the fact that photographs in the 1890s press, like everything else, were inevitably subject to editorial control. It is worth remembering that this was partly out of mechanical necessity: the (by our standards) primitive reproduction technology still required physical craftsmanship to create well-balanced images, just as the leaves required careful human intervention to be attractively skeletonised. Due to this material fact, and to the far-from-unrelated journalistic ideals of the day, photography was more often about narrative truth than literal truth, as Beegan points out. Photographs in 1890s magazines, he says:

> ...were created within the existing reporting practices of the illustrated magazine, and, as such, they aimed to produce a meaningful representation of an event rather than 'capture' a fragment of reality.[60]

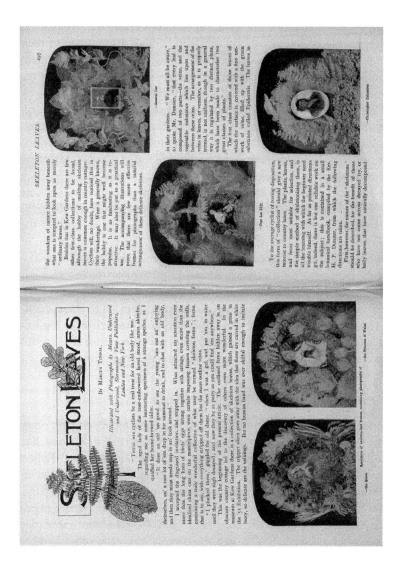

3.6   Double-page spread from Tindal's 'Skeleton Leaves' piece in *Pearson's Magazine* (November 1897).
Courtesy of the Cadbury Research Library, University of Birmingham.

We can also see journalism making a more than usually overt appearance in Compton's interview, for as well as the assertive first person of the interviewer's voice, there is the fact that Villiers, a battlefield illustrator, is himself a kind of journalist – one who specialises in producing a variety of images in order to propagate a specific kind of truth about the frontier for the press. Villiers and his colleagues placed importance on a certain code of authenticity in their reporting, but were nevertheless unlikely to produce (or at least, see printed) images of, say, the British concentration camps in South Africa during the Boer War.[61] Equally, Tindal's piece is empowered to a certain extent by scientific ideas (the camera, the X-ray, natural history, and the related concept of collecting, which has remained closely attached to photography ever since), but not ultimately in thrall to them. Indeed, the images he presents, in which skeletons surround a photograph – the medium of image which, Grove says, 'itself is a type of ghost, a spooky throwback to the past' – against a solid black background cropped into the unmistakable shape of a tombstone, speak more to the gothic imagination than to the scientific.[62] Even before eerie X-rays of living skeletons, gothic and scientific images had already aligned by the invention of photography, itself 'a kind of *Tableau Vivant*, a figuration of the motionless and made-up face beneath which we see the dead'.[63]

Over the last few sections I have been beginning to make the case that it is the insistence on harmonised diversity, both in images and text, which makes scientific interest subordinate to imaginative entertainment in these magazines. I will now carry this notion into a reading of some more overtly science-fictional stories, tracing in their fear of the X-rays not a scepticism of science so much as a scepticism of the totalising world view which accompanies it.

The other invisible man

L. T. Meade's series of detective adventure stories *The Brotherhood of the Seven Kings* was serialised in the *Strand* from January to October 1898. Written, like much of her work, in collaboration with a scientist (in this case Robert Eustace), the stories tell of the adventures of Norman Head, who battles an ancient secret society in an attempt to bring its leader, the cunning Mme. Koluchy, to justice. Despite Eustace's involvement, Meade's engagement with science is often decidedly superficial, and the scientific knowledge employed by Head and Koluchy in their contest with each other is more often elementary physics than anything decidedly new or technologically sophisticated. However, in the June 1898 instalment, 'The Star-Shaped Marks', the X-rays make an appearance. The striking twist is that Meade conceives them not as an imaging technology but as an assassination device.

It is unnecessary to sum up the entire plot of this rather convoluted story. What matters is that during the investigation of a crime, a person whom Mme. Koluchy wants silenced, a Mr Durham, suddenly sickens without any apparent cause. Lady Faulkner, an accomplice of Koluchy's unaware of her murderous plans, is in a position to explain the original crime to the detectives. As she is strong of will, though, nothing can induce her to make a confession until she sees Durham apparently on his death-bed. She tells all to Head and his associates, who then set about finding out why Durham is dying. Head finds the titular star-shaped marks on the sick man's body. They remind him of those he has noticed on photographic plates during X-ray demonstrations. Breaking into the adjacent house, they find 'an enormous focus tube, the platinum electrode turned so as to direct the rays through the wall' into Durham's bedroom. Head explains:

> Constant powerful charges of cathode and X-rays, such as must have been playing upon Durham for days and nights continuously, are now proved to be so injurious to life, that he would in all probability have been dead before the morning.[64]

This discovery is the dramatic climax of the story, and takes place on its final page. Koluchy's baseness is in her subversion of the X-ray technology, which she uses to produce imagery of death on the living body rather than on the photographic plate. But beyond a straightforward scepticism about the possible applications of radiography, it is possible to observe in Meade's ordering of the narrative a similar de-prioritisation of objective truth to that I have already shown taking place in various non-fictional magazine articles.

With the X-ray revelation coming only at the end, the bulk of Meade's story is geared not towards detecting the manner in which Durham is becoming ill (he develops symptoms only two thirds of the way through) but rather towards extracting a confession from Lady Faulkner. Head's method of investigation is, in this respect, curious. Lady Faulkner has no information as to how Durham is being killed – her information only helps Head understand the other, original crime, the crime which the murder of Durham is intended to conceal. When he gets around to it, Head discovers the mode of assassination in a (rare) demonstration of his own scientific abilities, and with no outside help. However, he does not even attempt this until *after* Lady Faulkner has been led into a separate room and told him the entire back-story. This takes nearly three pages to relate, and all the while Durham is dying upstairs.

Why does Head stop to listen to this detailed exposition when he already has everything he apparently needs to save a man from a slow, painful death? This is not the only time in his adventures when he is slow to act, and his lack of speed typically seems to stem from the fact that he needs to be in control of the *narrative* elements of a case before he can solve it, regardless of whether or not all of those elements are clues. In other words, this scientific detective's struggle is for comprehension of a story, not for comprehension of a set of facts around a case. Only with the narrative understanding of the events leading up to the attempt on Durham's life is Head released by generic conventions.

Immediately after the narrative revelation comes the moment of Head's epiphany:

> Once more I bent over Durham, and as I did so the memory of where I had seen similar markings returned to me. I had seen them on photographic plates which had been exposed to the high induction action of a brush discharge of high electro-motive force from the positive terminal of a Plante Rheostatic machine.[65]

The 'once more' at the start of this extract shows how well the narrative revelation has served to refresh Head's memory – only *this* time is the truth printed on Durham's body legible to him (and, consequently, to us). The following burst of jargon about 'high electro-motive force from the positive terminal' (which is incongruous with the rest of the story's tone, and which we may perhaps safely attribute to Eustace) demonstrates that in Meade's universe scientific truths, like the marks of the X-rays, are comprehensible only after narrative truth has been determined. This is equally so when the X-rays are on the side of good rather than evil: in an earlier detective story written by Meade in collaboration with Clifford Halifax (mentioned earlier as the story that occurs in the same issues as the Sozodont and patent sound discs adverts, Figs. 3.1 and 3.2), X-rays are used to confirm an already strong suspicion about the location of a jewel, providing evidence for the authorities in the story but doing nothing to further the narrative (which has already more or less concluded before the X-rays make an appearance). That story celebrates both the newness and the forensic utility of X-rays, but also includes a dangerous character who has stolen some anhydrous hydrocyanic acid – apparently a by-product of X-ray experiments – from the narrator: 'It causes death by inhalation, and the process of making, without certain precautions is fatal'.[66]

Meade's various tales, then, ultimately present a conflicted attitude towards the X-rays: knowledge of them thwarts crime, but can also abet it. A story with less equivocal opinions appeared in *Longman's Magazine* in September 1896. 'Röntgen's Curse', by C. H. T. Crosthwaite, is one of the earliest stories which deals with the idea of 'X-ray vision', but this is no Superman-style fantasy about perfect depth of gaze. The narrator is scientist Herbert Newton: 'I had found at last how to make a liquid which, applied to the eyes, might make them sensitive to the X-rays, and perhaps to other waves of ether yet unknown'.[67] Newton first applies the preparation to the eyes of his faithful dog, and then, failing to be dissuaded by the creature's subsequent insanity and eventual death, to himself. Finding himself in a 'fantastic and ghostly' world in which his wife and children are hideous grinning skeletons, Newton attempts to combat his guttural fear with higher scientific reasoning, but, failing, has a reaction similar to that of the Goldsbergs in George Griffith's 'A Photograph of the Invisible' and is on the verge of complete mental collapse when the effects of the potion unexpectedly wear off. No-one will believe that his tribulations were not the result of a delusion brought on by working too hard, and even Newton himself has doubts: '[i]f it had not been for the fate of my poor dog, who had not shared in his master's scientific labours, I might have persuaded myself that I had been the sport of a diseased imagination' (p. 484).

With its romantic and magical language (from the 'curse' in the title onwards), Crosthwaite's is a tale in which the scientific ideology fares badly. Though Newton's final conclusion is simply that he is himself 'not the stuff of which the pioneers and heroes of science are made' – an inadequate test subject, in other words – Crosthwaite has a deeper distrust, closing the narrative by having Newton send his formula to an elderly German professor judged to be a more dispassionate and capable investigator (p. 484). That professor's death, which is reported in the story's final paragraph, not only shows the depth of Crosthwaite's scepticism (it is not just that Newton is inadequate; not even a seasoned and initially optimistic Professor can handle the horror) but is also finally ambiguous. In a manner akin to the future-prediction texts delighting in ambiguity which were my subject in Chapter 2, Crosthwaite's final sentence revels in its unanswerable question: 'Whether he died from natural causes, or whether he found life under such conditions a burden not to be endured even by a German savant, who can tell?' (p. 484). Even people who are convinced that nothing has actually happened to Newton believe that his scientific investigations are the cause of his breakdown. Both his doctor, to whom he tells the truth, and his wife, from whom he conceals his X-ray vision, are of the opinion that his obsession with his work has made him delusional: 'you are rather run down from too much work and too little air and exercise' (p. 481). When Newton is at his lowest, incapacitated in bed, his wife destroys his laboratory, convinced that scientific endeavour is what is driving her husband to despair.

Like the satires of Pain and Alden, fiction invested in final ambiguities of this kind might be expected to look unfavourably on any ideology of final truth. This distrust of science is more overt in Crosthwaite than in any of the other pieces of writing I have yet discussed, and it is therefore fitting that it appears in *Longman's*, a magazine which, unlike the other monthlies I have been focussing on, remained unillustrated through the 1890s. '*Longman's* always looked old-fashioned and thus never represented what it offered', says Mike Ashley, blaming the editors' resistance to change for the magazine's eventual collapse.[68] The most wholeheartedly conservative piece of writing discussed in this chapter carries no images of any kind.

Also unillustrated, and also sceptical of the psychological effects of experiments with visibility, was H. G. Wells's *The Invisible Man*. This novella was serialised in *Pearson's Weekly*, the precursor and sister-publication of the monthly *Pearson's Magazine*, from June to August 1897. The first instalment, then, appeared a year and a half after Röntgen's X-ray research first appeared in English. Griffin, the invisible man of Wells's title, is himself explicit in denying that his research is related to Röntgen's, but the fact that he even has to make this denial, the appearance of the apparatus he uses, and the unnerving and profoundly visual consequences of his work, to say nothing of the timing of the novella's appearance, make the comparison a straightforward one.[69] It is also a comparison explicitly encouraged by a selection of celebrity vignettes which appeared on the same page as the novella's last instalment, in the 7 August 1897 issue, which includes a paragraph on William Crookes: 'It was he [. . .] who practically paved the way for the discovery of the Röntgen rays, for he came very near discovering them himself'.[70]

Griffin's mania is more disturbing than Newton's: rendered invisible to human eyes by his experiments on himself, he swiftly abandons his attempts to find a scientific "cure" and embarks rather on a campaign of theft, terrorism, and finally murder. But as in the way Crosthwaite concludes his tale, there are moments of ambiguity, including a gap in the story at the point of the supreme crime, details of which are provided only as conjecture after the fact:

> If it is our supposition that the Invisible Man's refuge was the Hintondean thickets, then we must suppose that in the early afternoon he sallied out again, bent upon some project that involved the use of a weapon.[71]

The story is told by a third-person narrator who often seems omniscient, but becomes on the whole less so as the novella continues (in parallel with

Griffin, who becomes on the whole less and less a scientist). 'Our supposition' and 'we must suppose' in this passage attest to this gradual change. In the next sentence, the interposition of an unexpected 'me' makes us really wonder who is telling the story: 'the evidence that he had the iron rod in hand before he met Wicksteed is to me at least overwhelming' (p. 41).

This is one of many points at which the story appears to become a testimonial rather than omniscient fiction, but the narrator never seems to be any of the characters actually named in the novel. Moments where a narrator seems personally manifest are also hard to reconcile with the prosaic language of some of the descriptive passages. This is, after all, a novel which starts with the decidedly omniscient-sounding sentence:

> The stranger came early in February, one wintry day, through a biting wind
> and a driving snow, the last snowfall of the year, over the down, walking, as
> it seemed, from Bramblehurst railway station, and carrying a little black
> portmanteau in his thickly gloved hand.[72]

Passages such as this one seem to come not from a character in the book but from the plane of omniscient objectivity inhabited by the narrators of much fiction. However, by the book's climactic moments ('There was, *I am* afraid, some savage kicking') we realise that this narrator is actually subjective; that there is a second 'invisible man' at the heart of the story, on display at all times, like the X-rays in the Sozodont advert or the editor of the Tindal pictures, taken for granted, absolved from the necessity of actually appearing.[73] There are places where this mysterious voice seems reminiscent of a scientist – meticulously collecting the best data available and only coming to conclusions cautiously, with talk of 'evidence' – but there are more where it resembles that of a journalist. A specific kind of journalist who interviews bystanders, puts the pieces together, and is unafraid to add subjective embellishments (and images) to his relations, often passing them off – almost convincingly – as unbiased. A New Journalist.

Paradoxes

The epilogue of 'The Invisible Man', which appeared only when the novella was published in book form, shows Mr Marvel, Griffin's unwilling assistant, attempting to learn the secret of invisibility. He has carefully concealed the notebooks containing the discovery from the authorities, and every night, in solitude, he examines them. The quest is a hopeless one – not only does Marvel lack the intellectual capacity to break the cipher in which the books were originally written, but some of the pages have themselves become irretrievably invisible, 'washed blank by dirty water'.[74] Science here is untranslatable: ravaged by material conditions, written in code legible only to its author. Unlike the novella's protean storyteller, Griffin is a deliberately recalcitrant narrator, full of secrets from the very beginning until long after his death, the only character whose thoughts are inaccessible to the tale's narrator. Even Griffin's name is not revealed until chapter 17. The drive apparently felt by every other character to find out about him, to render the invisible visible, befits the story's initial appearance in the New Journalist press, as does the shifting status of the narrator, who, despite forays into subjectivity, is still able to close with assured foreknowledge – 'none other will know of them until he [Marvel] dies' – and get away with it (p. 279). These words, with their omniscient access to both the future and to Marvel's private life, are impossible for a character in the world of the book. Wells is having his cake and eating it here, for thanks to the narrator's ambiguous position in the text, Marvel's secret is both assuredly safe forever and immediately and effectively communicated to every reader.

Basic though all this may seem, it underscores some crucial points: New Journalist approaches to fact were evident in fiction as well as news reporting; they were often deeply concerned with visibility; and they were the product of *variety*, both of images and voices.[75] Allen W. Grove's 'Röntgen's Ghosts', of which I have made much use in this chapter, maintains that the periodical press 'portrayed a skeptical, even paranoid public, grasping to understand the implications of the penetrative powers of these new rays', but I have tried to show a more diverse picture, albeit one in which scepticism was a strong theme.[76] Perhaps this diversity (and its sceptical component) is part of the development of Habermas's public sphere, which was notionally in this period moving away from a model of general interest predicated on the shared importance of a 'rational approach to an objective order, that is to say, of truth'.[77] As the New Journalism continued to broaden public discourse beyond its bourgeois roots, the multiplicity of truths to which "general interest" could appeal necessarily widened.

Attitudes towards the X-rays were conflicted within individual publications and often even within individual articles and stories. Many shared Stead's sense of optimism, garnered from the feeling of being on the cutting edge of a tremendous discovery which could be of enormous use in medicine and forensics. When voices were raised in fear, it was not necessarily fear about privacy, death-images, and ghosts; it could be a deeper fear of precision, anxieties over objective truth. These are anxieties which are, Susan Sontag reminds us, inherent in the mixture of discourses embodied by photography:

> ...despite the presumption of veracity that gives all photographs authority, interest, seductiveness, the work that photographers do is no generic exception to the usually shady commerce between art and truth.[78]

X-rays are a kind of photography which make these generic anxieties peculiarly explicit. They unsettled people because they seemed to make truth itself a murkier, more subjective concept – but, as I have been suggesting, this very fact is precisely what made them appealing to the eclectic periodicals of the New Journalism.

If the X-rays illuminated any one concern in the periodical press it was, so to speak, the concern of there being only one concern. The invisible man is abhorrent because he wants to establish a reign of terror: 'He must take some town, like your Burdock, and terrify and dominate it'.[79] The fear is of totalitarianism, of one individual voice becoming dominant, and it is understandable that such an anxiety was articulated in a press which thrived on so many different genres of writing and image. 'Mr. A', the medium with whom Glendinning developed his dorchagraphs, as reported by W. T. Stead, was himself sceptical of Spiritualism: 'I do not believe an objective reality can or has been presented to the plates'.[80] Objective reality is a distasteful idea to a media (or medium) so committed to pushing variety for the sake of entertainment; one which, to maximise profits, needs to appeal to as many different types of reader as possible, and which is working hard to create more.

When it did not speak of 'X-rays' or 'Röntgen rays' (respectively, the name their modest discoverer gave them and the name he would never use), the magazines had another name for this fictive new technology. They called it 'The New Photography'.[81] The term is a fitting one, for it not only shows the emphasis placed by the mass media on novelty but sets the discovery alongside Matthew Arnold's label for the *fin-de-siècle* mass media itself. Like the New Journalism, the New Photography was powered by enormous strides forward in technology; like the New Journalism, it was both explicitly of its time and a site of frenzied cultural activity. It is unsurprising, therefore, that in the writing and images printed by the New Journalism, X-rays were used figuratively to help with what printing was being used to do literally – draw disparate things together. '[O]ne of the most impressive accomplishments of such connective technologies', Aaron

Worth has written, 'may have inhered in their power to bind together what seem to us hopelessly contradictory, even paradoxical ideologies': he was writing of communication technologies such as the telegraph, but X-rays too can be connective when situated in the magazines, bringing into contact the multifarious and paradoxical concerns of the New Journalist press.[82] 'The co-presence of these domains of knowledge', says James Mussell of a dispute in another 1890s periodical, which incorporates astronomy, scripture, geography and philosophy, 'not only denies a single authoritative standpoint, but also ensures that a single author cannot authoritatively pronounce on an issue'.[83]

Of course, Röntgen's discovery was not primarily oriented around this cultural work. It was a genuine scientific breakthrough which widened human understanding of the universe, but to emphasise that would have been to run contrary to Stead's policy of believing anybody he deemed trustworthy. It would have been, against the wishes of W. L. Alden, to explore Antarctica. Science, once confirmed, delegitimises other voices – the voices from the borderland, the voices of fantasy and of the imagination. To do science justice, it is necessary to deny authority to a range of readers and writers on a scale which was at odds with the journalistic and commercial values of variety and entertainment held dear by the magazines. These publications need not be considered antiscientific any more than Stead himself – science, exciting and new, was welcome – but they were reluctant to accord a higher truth-authority to science than to any other kind of discourse.

Though such openness was surely good for business, this was about more than purely the commercial value of mass appeal. Another thing for which the New Journalist publications are known, especially those under the auspices of Stead, is their passionate advocacy for democracy. Stead believed strongly that a free and responsible press should have a core and even a governing role in any democratic society.[84] One of the press's key roles, he suggests in an 1886 essay, should be to use technological mastery of facts to influence government policy for the better:

> Even now, with his imperfect knowledge of facts, the journalist wields enormous influence. What would he be if he had so perfected the mechanism of his craft as to be master of the facts – especially of the dominant fact of all, the state of public opinion?[85]

Stead's insistence on the ideal newspaper's final reliance on absolute access to the truth is significant. More so is the belief he espouses that the greatest of these truths isn't an objective truth at all, but the subjective fact of public opinion. It is worth comparing this quotation to one I have already cited, from Stead's writing on the X-rays a decade later:

> The presentation of our bones, or the matter of our brain, or the action of the heart, by the 'X' rays would be far transcended in importance, if it were once established that we could procure a permanent record of our passing moods and fancies.[86]

The similarity between these two passages – calling respectively for a journalism and a science capable of providing access to current, interior truth – suggests that quantifying 'the public opinion' in the name of a truly representative democracy was the driving aim of all of Stead's various publications. In many of their activities, including, I suggest, their choice of subject matter, a key emphasis was on an equality of voice, an equality of right to newsworthiness: 'No one is too exalted to be interviewed', Stead maintained, 'no one too humble'.[87] Stephen Kern identifies the media as a component of 'a general cultural reorientation in this period that was essentially pluralist and democratic'.[88] My contention is that science's special claims on truth are at the heart of its conflicted relationship with the media, a relationship far too involved to be expressed in terms simply of "pro" or "anti" science. Perhaps, then, it was their vagueness rather than their newness which really made X-rays appealing – the fact that, still so poorly understood by science in those first years, they remained so open to the interpretation of "public opinion".

Throughout this book, I have so far been presenting the polyphony of the *fin-de-siècle* periodical press, as well as its accompanying ambiguities, as roundly beneficial. The elasticity of the boundaries between categories in these magazines provides us with a glimpse of a world before extreme specialisation, when different kinds of knowledge and art were freer to cross-fertilise each other and where, consequentially, far less energy was wasted on fighting. This position, however, has now run into a serious difficulty. How can one declare that a strength of the press was its democratic nebulousness when that nebulousness was inevitably responsible for the press's misrepresentation of science, its demotion of the objective truth which science has at its heart?

This is a crucial question and, in attempting to answer it, it is useful to start by noting – as I did in the introduction – that holding contradictions in suspension is certainly something that New Journalism can teach us more about. Roger Luckhurst points out that it was Stead's enthusiasm for connecting discourses which was behind the breadth of his activities (his wide-ranging enthusiasm, to advance on Chapter 1), and he implicitly invites us to recapture a wider sense of the late-Victorian period by retracing those connections ourselves:

> Stead's apparently diverse interests in mass democracy, spirits and phantasms, an Empire-wide penny post, telepathy, imperial federation, new technology, astral travel, and popular science were the result less of individual foible than of a wider *episteme*, a network of knowledges in which forms of the occult promised to make revelatory connections across the territory of late Victorian modernity, rather than a consolatory exit from it.[89]

These words can serve as a reminder that the diaspora represented by the magazines was to some degree a cohesive one. Indeed, the function of the magazines, some of them wildly different from each other in terms of political stance and editorial philosophy, was arguably to render it so. In this chapter I have mentioned periodicals as diverse as *Nature*, *The Idler*, and *Borderland* – publications with obvious and even fundamental differences – but by pointing out their various engagements with X-rays I hope I have shown that there is something to be said for considering these publications in light of their similarities, too. All jostled for attention in the same commercial environment, faced the same material and financial demands – in short, existed in the same moment. Luckhurst's passage emphasises the value of stressing connections, rather than differences, when attempting to come to terms with that society.

Nevertheless, the realisation that science and fiction could have detrimental as well as supportive effects on one another when closely entangled in print is an important one. It does not reaffirm the conception of a two-culture division, for the simultaneous existence of positive and negative connections is further testimony to the complexity of their relationship, a complexity for which I have been arguing throughout. But apprehending the magazines' shortcomings in conveying *fin-de-siècle* science is important because our present-day mass media is very much their descendant. As the inheritors of Stead, Newnes, Harmsworth, and Pearson, we still have a press that prefers individual anecdotes to statistics; a press which will both favour and provide narrative over facts; a press obsessed with celebrity gossip; a press whose approach to science is generally enthusiastic but seldom rigorous; a press which operates in time cycles with which science is often incompatible; a press which tends to see "truth" as the midpoint of the two most extreme views; a press committed to the freedom of its own multiplicity of voices over and above the accuracy of any individual story. A press which, despite all of this, still manages to idealise objectivity, and convince people that it practices it. In June 2011, the *Independent* columnist Johann Hari was censured by his peers, by the public, and eventually by himself, when it came to light that he had, more than once, replaced the words said to him in interviews with equivalent passages from the interviewees' books. His defence was that by enhancing clarity, he was delivering a more important, less literal truth to his readers: 'I only ever substituted clearer expressions of the same sentiment, so the reader knew what the subject thinks in the most comprehensible possible words'.[90] Replying on his *Telegraph* blog, Brendan O'Neill was unequivocal: 'The notion that one can reach "the truth" by manipulating reality should be anathema to anyone who calls himself a journalist'.[91] By focussing on the complexities of *fin-de-siècle* journalism, this chapter has hopefully shown not only the naivety of both of these viewpoints, but also that, despite O'Neill's professed shock, there is nothing new about the conversation between them.

Susan Sontag points out that one possible use of photography is to 'imply a pseudo-scientific neutrality similar to that claimed by the covertly partisan typological sciences which sprang up in the nineteenth century like phrenology, criminology, psychiatry, and eugenics'.[92] Those typologies, now widely discredited, carried the authority of the scientific voice precisely because of the unequivocal objectivity implied by the images they produced. Sontag moves from this point into a discussion of photography's role in the subjugation of Native Americans – the camera is, for her, a tool of imperial subjugation, empowered as such by the particular claim it makes on and for reality. Having reached the stage where we can acknowledge that there are still moments of profound tension between the formats of the media and of science without returning to the monolithic binary opposition of the two-culture model, it is now time to follow Sontag's lead and focus directly on an arena in which the territorial negotiations between genres become explicitly political. The next and final chapter of this book examines the complex interactions between mass media literature and science specifically in their relation to ideas of empire and conquest.

CHAPTER 4

Further northward
Polar exploration and empire in the fact and fiction of the popular press

Of Nansen and Sherlock Holmes

Fridtjof Nansen left Christiania on 24 June 1893 aboard *Fram*, a custom-built ship constructed to withstand being frozen into the polar ice. Nansen (Fig 4.1) was already famous as the leader of the first expedition to have crossed the interior of Greenland in 1888, but his objective this time was bolder still: to travel into the heart of the Arctic, perhaps becoming the first person to reach the North Pole.

Nansen's voyage and its prospects generated an enormous amount of interest in London, as might be expected of an undertaking with the potential to bring one of the last remaining unexplored places on earth within humanity's grasp. 'In America, the census of 1890 declared that the frontier was closed', notes Stephen Kern, 'and by the end of the century the dominant world powers had finished taking the vast "open" spaces of Africa and Asia'.[1] The Poles, 'the last great frontiers of the world', were therefore major loci of the public imagination in the *fin de siècle* (p. 166). Through both fact and fiction, the periodicals speculated avidly about the potential of Arctic exploration, and Nansen's proposed voyage attracted a great deal of attention – not all of it optimistic. '[U]nless Dr. Nansen wishes to commit suicide, he had better remain at home', said W. T. Stead, summarizing the opinions of several polar explorers in the *Review of Reviews*. Stead described Nansen as 'young [and] comparatively inexperienced' but also said that he was 'very courageous' and praised him for his intention 'to put his theory to the test of experience'.[2]

The theory referred to here was a bold one. Nansen explained it to the British public in a lavishly illustrated article written for the *Strand* magazine when *Fram* was already underway, dispatching the copy to London from the Barents Sea 'just before he and his brave companions

4.1   Fridtjof Nansen. Courtesy of the Prints & Photographs Division, Library of Congress.

disappeared, for years, into the unknown regions of eternal ice'.[3] In the article, he describes the idea underpinning his expedition as follows:

> [T]here must somewhere run currents into the Polar region which carry the floe-ice across the Polar Sea, first northward towards the Pole, and then southward again into the Atlantic Ocean. [...] I shall try to find the place where the heart of this current has its origin, and shall go north there until I am beset in the Polar ice, and then simply let the current have its way, and let it carry us across the unknown region and out into the open sea again on this side of the Pole.[4]

Previous attempts at the Pole had started in the Western hemisphere, making slow progress northwards because of the constant resistance of the southbound Arctic currents. Nansen's idea that these currents originated from the Eastern hemisphere, and could effectively be 'ridden' to the Pole if approached from the right direction, seemed to him a 'very simple conclusion' (p. 614), but not everyone was convinced. Despite its official support of the expedition, many members of London's Royal Geographical Society (RGS) thought the idea of deliberately freezing a ship into an iceberg and allowing it to drift at the mercy of the ocean (Fig 4.2) self-destructive folly. For Nansen, though, it was merely slightly dull: 'If we

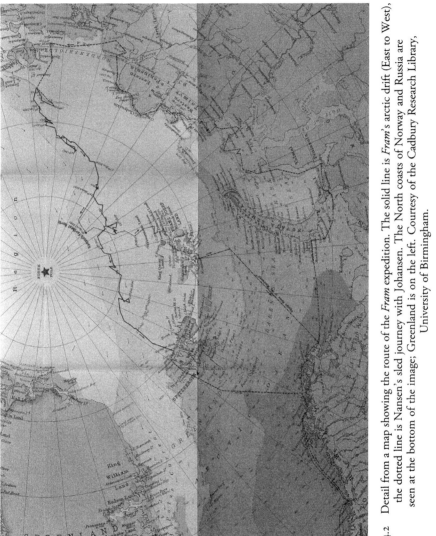

4.2 Detail from a map showing the route of the *Fram* expedition. The solid line is *Fram*'s arctic drift (East to West), the dotted line is Nansen's sled journey with Johansen. The North coasts of Norway and Russia are seen at the bottom of the image; Greenland is on the left. Courtesy of the Cadbury Research Library, University of Birmingham.

drift many years in this way the life may become somewhat monotonous, but we shall have plenty of things to do to pass the time' (p. 620).

In spite of the sceptical voices at the RGS, the British reading public keenly consumed a myriad of articles, interviews, and stories inspired by the Norwegian expedition. Aside from the interest that Arctic exploration generated in and of itself, there were many reasons for Nansen's particular appeal, not least his powerful character, good looks, and the earnestness with which he embodied the ideals of exploration (on the latter, much more later). As significant, perhaps, was the breadth of his expertise. A neurologist and zoologist as well as a regarded sportsman and hunter, he had the intellect to conjure up the voyage as well as the bravado and tenacity to complete it successfully. 'In an age beginning to glimpse the approaching domination of the specialist', remarks his biographer, 'he personified the universal man'.[5] He was also 'a creation of the press' (p. ix), and as I have already suggested in this book, those two characteristics are not necessarily unrelated.

Nansen's farewell to civilisation appeared in the *Strand* in December 1893, in the very same issue in which another hero fêted for his wide-ranging enthusiasm – Sherlock Holmes – vanished into the wilderness for many years. 'The Adventure of the Final Problem' finds Holmes battling the evil Professor Moriarty atop the Riechenbach falls, both plunging to their apparent deaths. The *Strand*'s publication of this story marks the beginning of the period known by Holmes aficionados as "The Great Hiatus", a decade during which Arthur Conan Doyle resisted the enormous public pressure to bring his detective hero back to life, finally capitulating in October 1903 (*The Hound of the Baskervilles*, serialised in the *Strand* in 1901, was set prior to Holmes's death). Read with the benefit of hindsight, Holmes and Nansen are a fantastic match in this issue of the *Strand*. Not only are both characters objects of significant public affection going beyond the circuit of the magazine's readership, but each pens his own farewell with conviction, flair, and grace under pressure. '[M]y career had in any case reached its crisis, and [...] no possible conclusion to it could be more congenial to me than this', writes Holmes to Watson of his imminent fight to the death, while Nansen reacts to the possibility of the destruction of *Fram* by suggesting offhandedly that he and his crew can live quite comfortably on the lifeboats: 'And in case the big boats should also be lost, we can build snow-huts on the ice'.[6] Both farewells are written prior to a daunting physical challenge – years surviving the Arctic, a clifftop *baritsu* struggle with an arch-nemesis – yet both men are also deeply calm, rational, and intellectual. 'There is much scientific work to be done in these unknown regions', says Nansen (p. 620); 'Of late', muses Holmes, summing up his career, 'I have been tempted to look into the problems furnished by Nature rather than those more superficial ones for which our artificial state of society is responsible'.[7]

In the story in which Holmes miraculously returned to life in 1903, he reveals that one of his aliases whilst "dead" was a Norwegian explorer, Sigerson. The reference is glancing, and nothing suggests that Conan Doyle is thinking of Nansen explicitly – "Sigerson" explores Tibet, not the Arctic. However, given their proximity in the periodical press, in which Sigerson also implicitly makes an appearance (Holmes is able to assume that Watson 'may have read' of his adventures), this is at the very least a gratifying coincidence.[8] It may be more than that: Conan Doyle was extremely interested in the Arctic sea, had been there himself aboard a whaler in 1880, and wrote several articles on the subject – including one published in the *Strand* itself in January 1897, shortly after Nansen returned to civilisation and whilst Holmes was still apparently dead, his body tantalisingly absent.

I shall return to this article later on. For the moment, my point is that public interest in feats linking physical derring-do with a cool, scientific intellect were manifest in both factual and fictitious narratives in the periodical press. 'No explorer since Franklin has gained so great a hold upon the imagination of his contemporaries', wrote J. Arthur Bain of Nansen in the *Strand*.[9] The public clamoured for Holmes's return even as they devoured accounts of real-life polar exploration; all appeared, materially entangled, in the pages of the New Journalist monthlies. There was also a sense in which polar writing partook of fictive language. Nansen took large numbers of cameras with him to the Arctic, but remained unable to describe the extraordinary landscapes of the polar seas without recourse to passages like this one:

> To give those who have not seen this world of ice an idea of what it looks like is not easy, as it is so different from anything else. It is a strange thing with this region, that when you are there, you think it sometimes monotonous perhaps ; but when you are away from it, you long to get back again to its white, vast solitude.[10]

Whether expressed in fiction or not, the solitude of the arctic exerted a considerable imaginative pull. SF's most oft-cited nineteenth-century forebears all had investments in the polar regions: Jules Verne's Captain Nemo had placed 'a black flag, carrying a golden *N* quartered on its bunting' on the South Pole in 1868, whilst Edgar Allan Poe's only novel, *Arthur Gordon*

Pym of Nantucket (1838), attains most of its science fiction qualifications in its cryptic closing pages set amidst the Antarctic ice.[11] Most pertinently, Mary Shelley's *Frankenstein* (1818) is told against the backdrop of Robert Walton's (fictitious) voyage to the North Pole, the failure of which provides an apposite keynote against which Victor can relate his story of scientific hubris.

Frankenstein opens with Walton's hope that he may find at the Pole 'a land surpassing in wonders and in beauty every region hitherto discovered on the habitable globe', and it is the possibilities of this new land which 'are sufficient to conquer all fear of danger or death and to induce [him] to commence this laborious voyage'.[12] Here, on the first page of a book about internal truth-discoveries, about the soul of man, a crucial link is formed with exterior voyages of exploration. These voyages and the promise of "strange new worlds" at the end of them have become routine fascinations of SF. Before the map of Earth was filled in, those new worlds could be islands across the ocean (as in Thomas More's *Utopia* and its descendants); as real exploration made such finds decreasingly plausible, they were pushed up to the poles, and eventually displaced from the surface of the planet entirely, finding their home among the stars (a transition sketched in a little more detail later). SF has repeatedly dealt in the metaphorical underpinnings of the voyage of discovery, and at the *fin de siècle* it engaged busily with numerous theories of what might be at the Poles and how they might best be reached.

The quest for discovery is generally seen as one of the nobler goals of both SF and its protagonists. But just as the supposedly curiosity-driven researches of Victor Frankenstein have a considerable dark side, it is difficult to consider either real-life voyages of exploration or their fictional counterparts entirely altruistic, even and perhaps especially when they seem motivated solely by the spirit of scientific discovery. Nansen tells his readers at one point '[I]t is to explore that we go out', but elsewhere he closes a paragraph about electric power with the suggestive phrase '[i]n this way man must conquer Nature'.[13] His non-fictional description of the Arctic sits comfortably within a proud tradition of imaginative treatments which used polar climes, Jen Hill has argued, as 'a blank page on which to draft different national and imperial narratives that either embraced or critiqued Britain's increased investments in imperial or colonial projects'.[14] In these narratives, exploration and conquest are never too far removed from each other. The purpose of this chapter is to situate this specifically imperialist construct within the network of periodical discourses articulated in the rest of this book.

In what follows, I examine a range of periodical pieces of both SF and non-fiction which engaged with polar exploration during the time Nansen was away (1893–96) and in the years following his return. As usual, I will present a network of genre interchange that complicates the proposition that science and fiction function as opposites in the pages of the *fin-de-siècle* press. This time, though, I will also focus on the political idea of *territory* which underlies both Western imperial expansion and the metaphorical basis of genre discourses. There is the literal territory of the Arctic – blank, unmapped, and increasingly the subject of Imperial attention – and the figurative territory of colluding and competing genres. Both were enacted in the general magazines, and by treating them as analogous my intention is to highlight the colonial attitudes inherent in traditional ways of cat-egorising writing. Though I therefore seem more interested in what Bernard Porter identifies (and condemns) as the 'sentiment' rather than the '*reality*' of imperialism, my focus on the cultural side of the question is a function of my desire to observe the resonances between a tangible empire and abstract systems of organisation such as genres, disciplines, and, indeed, magazines.[15] These abstract systems have bases in material reality, and my contention in this chapter is that imperialism is one such.

For this reason, I draw in particular on material from strongly pro-imperial publications such as the *Strand* and *Pearson's Magazine* in this chapter. I want to show that locutions of both fact and fiction can be made equally complicit in the imperial project (that their use together, rather than as opposites, remains politically subjective); I want to argue that an obfuscatory approach to the location of final truth is a characteristic means by which this linkage is affected; and I want to demonstrate that the emergent genre of SF was so thoroughly caught up in imperialism that it is no wonder its inheritors remain so today. The polar regions turn out to be an excellent place to observe these things in action, since they were provably real places which remained – just – outside the grasp of the European empires in this period. They had not yet had flags raised on them, but by the 1890s it was clearly only a matter of time: in the end, the North Pole was probably reached Peary in 1909 (this is disputed) and the South by Amundsen in 1911.

For the most part, I focus in what follows on the imperial aspects of fictitious treatments of polar exploration, returning frequently to maga-zine coverage of Nansen's real-life expedition for comparison. I begin by tracing the close relationship between SF and non-fiction written about the Pole, drawing attention to the tangle of fact and fiction which almost inevitably surrounds tales of exploration. I demonstrate that these stories retain a colonial interest in race; argue that the Pole also represents a potent *symbolic* target for imperial expansion; then focus on the more prosaic aspects of empire in the form of trade and commodity culture. The chapter goes on to unite the arguments of these three sections with the Arctic's factual ambiguity, concluding a running argument that science, fiction, imperialism, and polar exploration are all materially entangled by the magazine's guiding commitment to the heteroglot ambiguity described at the end of Chapter 3. Two further sections advance my conclusions on this subject: firstly, I track SF's departure from the planet, arguing that tales of space exploration take imperial baggage with them from their terrestrial analogues which cannot be lightly ignored; secondly, I contemplate the extent to which periodicals were complicit in the imperial project, and argue for a nuanced view which takes account of a simultaneous resistance to it.

In general, I focus on source material discussing the Arctic, although the Antarctic occasionally drifts into the conversation as well. Sarah Moss argues in *Scott's Last Biscuit* that of the two 'Antarctica can be less problematically assimilated into a quest narrative because no-one has ever lived there', but this chapter contends that even with no real people, the assimilation, both real and imagined, of a space like the polar regions is still far from straightforward.[16] It was, after all, for the purposes of non-existent natives that W. L. Alden jokingly proposed in 1896 that Antarctic exploration be stopped:

> ...there is still room in the vast and unknown Antarctic continent for all sorts of cities and men. The people who understand the art of flying; who use gold for the most common domestic purposes; who have domesticated most of the animals that are extinct in the other parts of the globe; who receive all strangers [...] as messengers direct from the gods; are still dwelling and thriving close to the South Pole.
>
> Of course, they will not be seen by any members of the Antarctic expedition, and after the expedition has made its report they will vanish for ever, just as the wonderful white Africans have vanished. Cannot science keep its hands from this one comparatively small part of the globe, and leave it to the romancer[?][17]

Alden's sentiments in this passage sound all the keynotes of this chapter: the relationships between fantasy and reality, the connections both have with the British imperial project as expressed in the periodicals, and the underlying resistance to final, definite answers of the sort that imperial exploration supposedly demands. By examining the ways in which the unexplored areas of the planet were used as imaginative spaces, I show how a periodical network of science and fiction shored up the empire, presenting empirical discovery and imperial conquest as inseparable and arguing throughout that few explorers have set out to new lands without explicitly or implicitly saying, as the defiant Nemo does, 'I hereby claim this entire part of the globe'.[18]

Balloons to the Arctic

'The North Pole', says a character in George Griffith's short story 'From Pole to Pole', 'although still undiscovered, is getting a little bit hackneyed'.[19] The voyages of Nansen and other explorers had, by the time this tale was published in *Windsor Magazine* in October 1904, given rise to an enormous crop of stories which dealt with the possibilities offered by the Earth's remotest places. In part, this profusion was the result of the fact that explorers themselves had become increasingly publicity-conscious: 'In the very polar-bear's hug of circumstance they remember their cameras', Richard Le Gallienne had commented in 1897.[20] Another possible cause was the fact that expeditions were by necessity out of communication with the world of print culture for several years (Nansen was away for just over three). As the expeditions attempted to fill in the maps of the polar regions, speculative fiction filled in the temporal gaps in the publication cycle during which new information about real-life Arctic adventures was unavailable.

In consequence, these works of fiction can be used to illustrate the press's dependence on a chain of connections to reality. Through his concept of 'circulating reference', Bruno Latour argues that ordering the wilderness is possible for science only when it preserves a reversible series of links between published findings and the objects of study in their chaotic, outdoor environment. 'A text truly speaks of the world', he suggests, only because of the network of transformations, '[r]eduction, compression, marking, continuity, reversibility, standardisation, compatibility with text and numbers', which connect it to its referent.[21] Latour's example is a part of the Amazon jungle reduced to a diagram (but by the same gesture amplified into knowledge) by soil scientists. I want to suggest that his model can in some respects work for fiction as well; that the strongest fiction is not that which is most dissociated from its opposite, fact, but that which is able to establish a retraceable chain of reference to it, whatever the length of that chain.

One story which demonstrates the possibilities of this kind of understanding is John Munro's 'How I Discovered the North Pole', published in

Cassell's Magazine in June 1894, a little under a year after Nansen's departure. This tale's close relationship with real-life polar exploration, a relationship strengthened by its appearance in a periodical, is paradigmatic of the links between fact and fantasy which exist in an enormous amount of exploration literature.

The unnamed narrator of 'How I Discovered the North Pole' has his own audacious scheme for reaching the latitudes upon which Nansen had set his sights. Circumventing the hardships of travelling personally to the highest latitudes, he releases a series of hot-air balloons, each equipped with automatic cameras, in the hopes that they will drift over the Pole and return with photographs of it. John Munro's reputation as an author was founded on a number of popular non-fictional works about electricity, but he also wrote several tales which may safely be described as SF, and would soon publish the novel *A Trip To Venus* (1897). The byline of his story in *Cassell's* is suggestive, for in addition to containing a dedication to Jules Verne it also bills Munro as 'AUTHOR OF "THE ROMANCE OF ELECTRICITY"'.[22] The title of Munro's previous work, as well as the decision to use it as advertising here (stressing his non-fictional credentials alongside his admiration for Verne), is indicative of the equal weighting accorded to fact and fantasy throughout the piece.

Munro is plainly writing in an attempt to be absolutely convincing, so much so that a present-day reader is compelled to check quite carefully that the events he describes did not actually take place. Some of them, in fact, did – the story opens with a discussion of the last British attempt at the North Pole, commanded by George Nares in 1875–76, and the next page and a half of the tale is a synopsis of some real real-life, contemporary proposals, including a fairly lengthy summary of Nansen's plans. The narrator is in the audience at the Norwegian's presentation to the RGS, and, inspired by the talk, he sits down at home to think the matter over 'with one of Nansen's maps' (p. 484). There follows some speculation about the possibility of running electric cables out behind sledges to provide expeditions with 'heat, light and even motive power' before Munro goes further, saying:

> A submarine vessel *à la* Jules Verne might, indeed, be constructed, and supposing the surface at the Pole to be frozen hard, it might be possible to blast the ice with dynamite, and allow the vessel to emerge from the water.
>
> Again, a steering balloon with a closed and heated car, or a flying machine, were possible means of journeying through the air.[23]

Even without the Verne reference (the second in the piece) the techno-fetishist overtones of this final sentence are obvious. In Munro's opening, the transitions between the historical account of British polar exploration, the survey of Nansen's plan and the futurist science-fictional speculations are seamless, and the whole process takes less than two pages. Munro then rejects the Verne-like methods of transport, saying that '[s]uch conveyances [. . .] belonged to the future' and arrives at the conclusion that 'an automatic explorer in the shape of a balloon' can adequately investigate the Pole for us in the meantime (p. 484). We do not need to actually go to the Pole, Munro suggests, if we attach some cameras with a clockwork timers to balloons and release them in the Arctic sea when the wind is blowing in the right direction. Although it might be said to prefigure the idea of the space probe, and despite the reliance on clockwork automation which has become a part of this period's retrospective aesthetic, this seems a fairly modest novum for a work of SF – but perhaps that modesty is the point. By explicitly keeping its distance from the more outrageous technological fantasies in this fashion, Munro's story maintains plausibility throughout its extensive descriptions of the way in which the balloon is put together. In places, the only real clue that the whole narrative is speculative is in the fact that the accompanying illustrations are drawings rather than photographs (without commenting on the illustrations directly, the piece promises that photographs will eventually follow in a forthcoming book).[24] The narrator's lack of name also adds plausibility, since it makes it easier for the reader to assume that Munro is writing as himself, a man known (and introduced in the byline) as a practitioner and communicator of real science.

Munro's relentless desire to furnish us with a believable narrative is evident in the precision with which he describes the route of his voyage to the Arctic seas, the vividness with which he relates apparently trivial details of the journey, and his provision of coordinates for the release of each balloon. A typical sentence from the middle of the tale:

> There was drift-ice between us and the Seven Islands, but not enough to prevent us forcing a passage to the north end of Parry's Island, where we anchored in lat. 80° 40' N., long. 21° E.[25]

The most diverting appearance of "real detail" in the story, though, comes on the last page, when one of the narrator's explorer-balloons is finally retrieved and its cargo of precious negatives developed:

> In the middle of the white waste of ice it showed a dark blotch, not unlike a ship, with black spots here and there, which I took to be men. On enlarging it, judge of my astonishment to find that it was indeed a vessel caught in the pack, and that in one of the dim figures on deck I fancied I could trace the features of Dr. Nansen, watching the balloon with a telescope to his eye![26]

This is, in a sense, the denouement of the story, since the photos of the Pole itself are 'somewhat blurred and out of focus', and the narrator refuses to describe them (p. 489). To do so, of course, would have been for Munro to stray uncomfortably close to outright speculation. Nansen's cameo is, internally, proof of the success of the balloon scheme; externally, it speaks of the need to fill the gap in the magazine press left by his disappearance into the ice. When the original audience of this tale read about the photograph of Nansen trapped in the ice, that is where he actually was at that moment. 'Especially when over-wintering, explorers of the frozen regions essentially lost touch with the rhythm of daily Victorian life', write Deirdre C. and David H. Stam: Munro's story constructs a way for Nansen to continue to be part of the circuit of periodicals, just as the production of a small magazine aboard *Fram* during her long voyage (*Framjee*) fantasised a similar connection from Nansen's side.[27] Had the climax of Munro's tale been a picture of the Pole itself, it would perhaps have been less satisfying because more clearly fictitious.

In Munro's willingness to abstract the scientific discovery of the North Pole from himself to an automated machine, we have a hint of circulating reference at work. On both internal and external textual levels, the pictures brought back from those fictitious balloons derive their authority from retraceable connections to reality, both through the truth-authority of photography (see Chapter 3 earlier), and through the way they apprehend, depend upon, and reinforce Nansen's voyage, both as scientific endeavour and current event. Without the lengthy chains of infrastructure and scientific theory which connect the Arctic wilderness with Munro's sitting room, his proposition is useless both as science and as fiction. But circulating reference is detectable here in more than simply the descriptions of a scientific scheme: it can also be used to understand the ways in which the story itself is connected to reality. Circulating reference, Latour says, grants science its power accurately to describe the world through a 'movement – indirect, crosswise, and crablike – through successive layers of transformations'.[28] Any datum in a (reliable) scientific paper can be traced back to its source; the "reality" which is supposed under the Cartesian model to be solidly divorced from human perspicacity turns out to be linked to it by a retraceable chain of carefully managed interpretative processes. Using Latour's model here, all I am really suggesting is an analogous link with any story that seeks to relate to the world. Fact and fiction are no more opposites than, for Latour, a published survey of soil conditions and the jungle to which it refers. Munro's story is anchored to contemporary events by its periodical situation, by the authorities to which it appeals, by the language it uses – it is certainly fiction, even (marginally) SF, but it is very far from any notional disconnection from reality which is sometimes evoked when describing imaginative writing. In fact, the links to "our world" are as meticulous as any in realist fiction: the story here is a way of exploring (and conveying) ideas about reality, not a way of escaping from it.

In one sense, this is a simple way of making a point which should be obvious: fiction which has no relationship at all with reality, which was literally its opposite, would be useless except as an intellectual exercise. But Latour's chain does not only problematise the idea of a fact and fiction completely disassociated from each other, nor does it only nuance our appreciation of the complex mechanics through which they might interact. It also hints at the reason that these networks of connections are so important to writers circulating in the periodical press: by using Nansen instead of the Pole, Munro provides a fantasy for the age of the telegraph – instant news from the wilderness – as well as the more straightforward fantasy of Arctic exploration. His story is dependent for its effect on association with an immediate historical context, but also serves that context by buoying up public interest in Nansen at a moment when he is traumatically separated from the periodical circuit, unable to speak for himself. As Nansen's biographer, Roland Huntford, comments, in the era before radio 'isolation descended once the shore had disappeared astern. Conversely, when voyagers vanished out of sight, they were swallowed by oblivion'.[29] Munro uses fiction to bridge this gap in the chain which connects Nansen to the circuit of the periodical press. Uninterested, like the material I dealt with in Chapter 2, in the Verne-esque inventions of the future, Munro provides us instead with a vision of an ultimate, simultaneous present.

Two years after the publication of 'How I Discovered the North Pole' in *Cassell's*, the *Strand* published a piece which further complicates Munro's relationship with reality when the two are read together. This was 'Mr. Andrée's Balloon Voyage to the North Pole', a non-fiction article by Alfred T. Story. S. A. Andrée was a Swedish aeronaut and scientist who became convinced that he and his two companions (including Nils Strindberg, brother of August) could reach the Pole in a balloon. The three made meticulous preparations and departed after giving an in-depth interview to Story. At fifteen pages, lavishly illustrated with photographs, drawings, maps and diagrams, the piece is unusually long for the *Strand*, and it was also the only article advertised on the front cover of that month's issue. Nansen had now been absent for exactly three years, and the public was so far entirely ignorant as to whether he was dead or alive, successful or a failure. Other expeditions were beginning to capture the limelight.

In fact, Nansen would return to civilisation the next month, with all hands alive and well. It was Andrée's voyage which was doomed to end tragically, with the death of all three adventurers.[30] Perhaps the idea of attempting to balloon to the Pole seems more foolhardy to us than Nansen's plan to sit comfortably in his boat, but Story's piece resounds with the same optimism which Nansen had himself deployed when announcing his own undertaking:

> Every attempt to do something that has not been done before looks foolhardy to most people, until the reasons upon which the adventurer acts are justified by results.[31]

Again there is the sense of a theory being put to the test; again the sense of detailed plans being comprehensively worked out; of physical endurance and scientific method united to do the unthinkable, over the objections of conservative commentators. Story's relation of Andrée's voyage shares all of these qualities with Nansen's earlier piece, but also with Munro's fictitious exposition. There are other similarities with Munro: not only do both schemes revolve around balloons, and not only do both dwell at length on nuances of construction and design rather than being urged forwards by narrative, but the schemes themselves have details in common. Most striking is that both rely on the possibility of local help for their success, and both propose to use print to help them access it. Munro explains:

> In order to trace and recover the balloon, I appended an automatic distributor of cards or circulars, bearing instructions in different languages [. . .]. Ejected at regular intervals from the receptacle, these notices fluttered down to the earth, and the finder, reading the inscription, was asked to state in the blank space provided when and where he had picked it up [. . .]. If he had found the balloon itself, he was requested to give particulars of the fact, and to preserve it carefully. . .[32]

Story's piece ends with a description of a similar scheme which Andrée actually put into place (Fig. 4.3):

> Tens of thousands of a circular, of which we give a photographic reproduction, have been distributed broadcast throughout Siberia, instructing all and sundry what to do should the balloon descend in their midst. Similar circulars have been distributed also in Alaska and British North America.[33]

As usual, I am not suggesting that there was a direct correspondence between Andrée and Munro – that the former read the latter, or that the

4.3   Circular distributed in advance of the Andrée polar expedition, reproduced in *The Strand Magazine* (July 1896). Courtesy of the Cadbury Research Library, University of Birmingham.

latter was in any sense "prophetic" of the former. The common traits of these two pieces, as reported by the magazines, say much more useful things about the press itself than they say about their authors. Story comes not only after Munro but after numerous other nineteenth-century tales in which balloon travel was the best method of reaching fantastic lands. The hero of Edgar Allan Poe's 'The Unparalleled Adventure of One Hans Pfaall' (*Southern Literary Messenger*, June 1835) gets all the way to the moon in one. There are also resonances in the other direction, into twentieth-century space travel – three men in a capsule, flying on instruments through the unknown towards a seemingly impossible goal. Andrée's balloon was the *Ornen*, in English the *Eagle*, the same name as Apollo 11's lunar module. Exploration has its own generic traits, which resonate both in fact and fiction.

The Apollo programme, Andrée's doomed voyage, *Hans Pfaall*, and J. Munro may seem a disparate lot at first, but one thing uniting them is the fact that they all considerably engaged the media culture of their time.

Poe's tale was written for a Virginia monthly; the *Strand* and *Cassell's* were amongst the bestselling London magazines of their day; and the worldwide media sensation which surrounded the moon landings requires no expansion here. The four share another trait, though: a complex relationship with fact. *Hans Pfaall* was written as a hoax, fiction couched as fact. Munro's tale does not set out to deceive, acknowledging up-front its indebtedness to Jules Verne, but is still, as demonstrated earlier, keen to stress the absolute plausibility of his scheme by anchoring it in real, current details. Andrée's real-life voyage, meticulously planned by scientists, has numerous precedents in the balloon-voyage narratives of science fiction. And today, paradoxers convinced that the Apollo landings are works of carefully constructed fiction continue to thrive.[34] Both *Hans Pfaall* and Apollo 11 reflect, or cause to be reflected, an underlying consumer interest in exploration which stretches far beyond the confines of material discoveries and will happily improvise when none are available. This interest often shows itself through presences and absences in periodical culture: Munro's tale, Story's article, and even Andrée's expedition are in the magazines of 1894 and 1896 at least partly because Nansen cannot be. References to reality circulate throughout every genre of the periodical press. It is time, now, to consider why the publics consuming this smorgasbord of fact and fiction were so invested in the discovery of new places.

Races to the Pole

The first words of 'How I Discovered the North Pole', taken from the title of a picture which inspires the narrator to set about inventing his balloons, are 'It can be done, and England ought to do it!'[35] The phrase recurs at intervals throughout the story, appearing on the lips of the narrator when he sits in his study drawing up his plans, and again when he is on the verge of releasing the first balloon from the deck of his ship. Its recurrence is suggestive of Munro's real motivations in writing the story, which are patriotic rather than scientific: 'Why should there not be a generous rivalry amongst nations, as amongst individuals, making them compete for renown?', asks the narrator (p. 489). His main concern on the story's first page was that the latitude record set by Albert Hastings Markham, a British Lieutenant on the Nares expedition, had finally been broken after standing for twenty years. Britain no longer lead the world in polar exploration: 'Of several attempts to reach the Pole by all three avenues into the Arctic Basin, that of Lieutenant Greeley, by way of

Smith's Sound, has planted the Stars and Stripes in a higher latitude than "Markham's Farthest'" (p. 489).

Munro's story is captivating not just because it represents a technologically empowered new offensive on Arctic exploration but because it constitutes a distinctly British one at a time when no real British missions were in the offing. 'Britain has been content [. . .] to look on while other nations tried their hands', rues the narrator at the outset (p. 483). By the end of the tale, the prospect of his 'forthcoming book' promises not only data about the North Pole but a reaffirmation of British design, ingenuity, and pluck. Knowing that even if the government did decide to bankroll another expedition, it could never catch up with Nansen – already absent a year – Munro creates a narrative in which Nansen not only features but is also, in a sense, surpassed. Mute in the story, trapped in the ice, the Norwegian explorer can only watch, 'telescope to his eye', as Munro's balloon overtakes him (p. 489). The photo which the balloon brings back therefore represents not just the story's engagement with a contemporary phenomenon; it is also the *coup de grace* in a fantasy of superseding it.

The polar regions were repeatedly an arena for the staging of rivalries between Western nations, and would become so with renewed vividness during the attempts on the South Pole by Roald Amundsen and Robert Falcon Scott in 1911. The imperialist attitudes which underpin this gentlemanly rivalry implicitly emerge in one of Munro's most poignant expressions of his simultaneity with Nansen:

> . . .assuredly there are many who will often picture to themselves that lonely vessel [*Fram*] and its weird electric star of civilisation shining on the frozen roof of the world during the long Arctic night.[36]

This sentence casts the Arctic as a wilderness into which Nansen brings civilisation in the form of, among other things, *Fram*'s electrical generator. As Earth's 'frozen roof', the Pole is the ultimate climbable summit. Nansen's mission becomes an ascent as well as a voyage, with the obvious metaphorical implications of supremacy for the person (and nation) "on top" (earlier, Munro calls for the British flag to be planted 'on the very crown of the planet', p. 483). *Fram*'s 'electric star' in this passage suggests a similarly decorative act – the Earth as Christmas tree. But is also more obviously a light in a dark place, with overtones of moral authority and enlightenment. 'Civilisation', here meaning Western civilisation, acquires in this passage the beneficial metaphors of both height and brightness, underwritten with the scientifically charged novelty of electricity. *Fram*'s electricity, here, is our first sign in this chapter of science being evoked in the service of the imperial discourse.

Unlike many of the territories into which the enlightened explorers and missionaries of Europe carried metaphors like these, the Arctic is at least, for the most part, genuinely a wilderness, with fewer natives to exploit. But this just increased its potential as a venue for the *fiction* by which empire could be constructed: Jen Hill posits that 'the Arctic was a landscape on which assertions and critiques of nation and empire could unroll at a literal "safe distance"', its perceived 'blankness' a slate onto which imperial ideals could be drawn.[37] Julie F. Codell, meanwhile, highlights the particular role of periodicals in this process, saying that their readers 'derived their sense of their own and others' places and spaces from the press, which offered a major site for the production and re-production of national identities'.[38]

As Europe's latest ambassador to the polar regions, Nansen was routinely described by the magazines in highly racialised terms:

> One feels insensibly that he is of the type of men fitted for Herculean tasks, and his physical form in no degree contradicts the record that he can bear fatigue and exposure, and is one of the most accomplished skilobers in Norway.[39]

In an earlier piece, the same author had brought in Eva Nansen, Fridtjof's wife, in order to make a similar point:

> Nansen is more than six feet high. Fru Nansen, on the contrary, is *petite* and dark, and, withal, of as adventurous a spirit as her husband. Indeed, in this respect both are worthy descendants of a noble race.[40]

A few pages before that, the author describes Nansen's earlier triumph – the first crossing of Greenland from East to West – and a rare mention of the Arctic's indigenous population is made:

> At considerable inconvenience and self-sacrifice and shock to his sensibilities – for the stench which arises from the filthy surroundings of the Eskimo is, to a refined European, appalling – Nansen lived their life in his endeavour to obtain an accurate knowledge of their habits.[41]

At this point on his journey, Nansen had crossed Greenland on foot, East coast to West, and was taking refuge in an Eskimo habitation at Godthaab. After his trek, it is hard to imagine him being picky about who offered respite to his party. Nonetheless, Bain makes it sound here as if putting up with the natives is almost as noble an achievement as the crossing itself, an heroic piece of self-sacrifice committed in the name of scientific data-gathering.

Anxieties over European racial supremacy are repeatedly articulated in accounts of polar exploration, despite the comparative lack of native populations. They are highly visible, for instance, in accounts of Nansen's return to civilisation in 1896. The dramatic climax of his *Fram* voyage was his decision to leave the ship, accompanied by only one other member of the party, Hjalmar Johansen, and make a dash for the Pole on dog sleds. It was on this journey, while *Fram* drifted south with the remaining crew, that Nansen attained his highest latitude of 86°13.6′N – but the conditions, damage to the kayaks, and a lack of supplies on the return journey almost had disastrous consequences and the two were forced to winter in Franz Joseph Land. At the end of this gruelling experience, they encountered the Jackson-Harmsworth surveying expedition, financed by the newspaper and periodical magnate Alfred Harmsworth, which was charting the northern reaches of the archipelago. For the members of the expedition, Nansen's appearance was a complete surprise. One of them described him thus:

> He was absolutely black from head to foot. His light hair and moustache were jet black, and there was not a speck of white about his face or hands. He looked for all the world like a nigger, and the brightness of his eyes was accentuated by the grime of his face which had been blackened by the blubber-smoke. His clothes were stiff with blood and oil, with which his face and hands were also covered.[42]

This description from Harry Fisher, Jackson's botanist, quoted in an account of Nansen's voyage published in *The Leisure Hour* in November 1896, is the negative image of the 'tall, handsome specimen of a Scandinavian' described by Bain.[43] Living in the wilderness forced Nansen to adopt many of the survival habits he learned in Godthaab, turning him savage in the eyes of Fisher. Jackson's own description of the moment evokes the more famous meeting between Stanley and Livingstone in central Africa in November 1891, and can easily be read as an attempt to extend the mantle of civilisation into the wilderness of Franz Joseph Land:

> ...I exclaimed, 'Aren't you Nansen?' 'Yes,' he replied, 'I am Nansen.' 'By Jove,' I responded, 'I really am awfully glad to see you!' Then we shook hands again still more heartily. 'Thank you very much,' said Nansen, 'very kind of you.'[44]

This absurd exchange, which is difficult to picture amidst the Arctic desolation without a smile, carries with it some genre markers of what was by the 1890s a legendary moment in the Anglo-Saxon domination of Africa, not only in the language but in the fact that, like Stanley's, Jackson's voyage was financed by the periodical press.[45] The trope had already cropped up in the Arctic in descriptions of the encounter which marked the discovery of the North-West Passage: Jen Hill relates the similar story of an encounter between the crew of the *Investigator* and a Lieutenant from the *Resolute*, initially mistaken for an Inuit, commenting that the incident 'echoes the instability of the landscape [. . .] and under-mines the stability and legibility of national identity Arctic narratives so forcefully sought to assert'.[46]

Once Nansen and Johansen were returned to its emissaries, though, "civilisation" could be asserted extremely quickly. Having proved their credentials with their language, the two were whisked onto Jackson's boat, the *Windward*. They washed off the discolouring grime and sailed back to society, reaching home in record speed to find *Fram* already waiting for them in harbour.[47] Even in an environment where there are no savages (especially not black ones), the potential of the civilised explorer lapsing into becoming one and the need for a ritual reversing that "wilding" seems ever-present.

But it is another kind of "savage", a First Nations Canadian, who plays a role in Munro's fantasy of defeating Nansen with automated balloons. The narrator's first balloon, with its valuable photographic cargo, is recovered when a Dog Rib Indian shoots it down over the Northwest Territories: 'Not knowing what to make of it, and thinking it might be some "strange medicine" of the white man, he and his family had taken it to Fort Enterprise. . .'.[48] The aboriginal presence in Munro's story lasts less than a paragraph, but is underlined by being the subject of the final illustration in the story (one of only six pictures in total). The image (Fig. 4.4) shows a highly stereotyped figure, complete with headdress and long, flowing robes, looking towards the incongruous shape of the balloon floating in the distance. Even the narrator is surprised by the Indian's presence: 'I must confess I had not expected any of the balloons to turn up in that quarter' (p. 489). Why this sudden native appearance in Munro's fantastical story of automated polar exploration by balloon? The superficial answer to this question – amusement and variety for the readership – points towards a deeper explanation: that no tale of derring-do in the wilderness is quite complete without an uneducated native mistaking post-Enlightenment science for magic, the butt of a joke he could never get, whose humour turns on the implied superiority

"A DOG RIB INDIAN BROUGHT IT DOWN WITH A SHOT FROM HIS GUN" (*p.* 489).

4.4   A Dog Rib Indian fails to comprehend J. Munro's automated Arctic probes. Illustration from 'How I Discovered the North Pole', found in *Cassell's Magazine* (June 1894). Courtesy of the Cadbury Research Library, University of Birmingham.

of the white races.[49] My point in this book, of course, is that the superficial and deeper explanations offered here are far from unrelated to each other.

'Imperial discourse', Patrick Bratlinger has written, 'is inseparable from racism'.[50] The racism discussed in this section is in turn inseparable from the ways in which the genres and characters in these periodicals are codified. Their cumulative effect parallels one observed by Jen Hill of wider cultural responses to the polar regions:

> Arctic space was revealed – perhaps as unexpectedly for contemporary Britons as it is to us – to be central to the ways Britons imagined, justified, and even critiqued their nation and empire.[51]

Commentary on exploration, in this analysis, can never be value-free. Even the more innocent fantasies which appeared in the periodicals could not escape the discourses which were irresistibly thrown up by the blank space on the map.

Sir Robert Ball, W. L. Alden, and a system of concentric circles

The quest for the North Pole, then, was addressed both in racialised terms and in terms of a race between European powers. The Pole was an attractive target not only because of the challenge but also because of the metaphorical implications of being the power "on top" of the world. Discourses of superiority, of whatever genre, are at the heart of Arctic exploration. But there was another still more esoteric quality which the Pole offered to provide those who reached it: coherence.

'The North Pole is that hitherto unattainable point on our globe', wrote Sir Robert Ball in the *Fortnightly Review* in 1893, 'on which, if an observer could take his station, he would find that the phenomena of the rising and the setting of stars, so familiar elsewhere, was non-existent'.[52] To Ball's hypothetical astronomer on the Pole it would appear as if the heavens rotated around him; as if he was at the very centre of things. This sensation was the subject of a story by the humourist W. L. Alden, published in the *Idler* in March 1897, which proposes that the illusion of being in the middle of the universe could drive somebody mad with power (an idea which recalls a more famous work from this period, one which treats of the idea of coherence in the wilderness in its very name[53]).

Alden's piece can be read as a pastiche of Munro's style of polar tale, and like Munro's it is written with a certain emphasis on plausibility: ridiculous in its details, it is nonetheless entitled 'Very Cold Truth'. Like *The Time Machine*, discussed in Chapter 2, it is a club story, told to its narrator by a mariner (called Martin) who claims to be the sole survivor of an expedition which discovered the North Pole long before Nansen set off. '[T]wenty-nine years ago come next July' it was, says the Mariner. In the next paragraph: 'Twenty, let me see, I think I said twenty-eight years ago'.[54] Martin's story is as follows: he was on the crew of a whaler commanded by Captain Bill Shattuck, a man who in Martin's retelling, unbeknownst to the crew, has gone mad. Shattuck's delirium causes him to separate his ship from the whaling fleet and seek out the highest latitudes. The route proves dangerous, but Martin, Shattuck and a few survivors of the original crew finally find land. Danish-speaking natives, ignorant of the world beyond their own shores, direct them to 'some sort of stone chair that had been scooped out of the rock' which seems to have been there since before the natives arrived (p. 254). Sitting on the chair, which is, of course, situated directly on the North Pole, Shattuck becomes the observer imagined in Ball's popular science piece. His immediate reaction is that of a coloniser:

> 'All right!' says the old man. 'Thish-yer chair is the genuine North Pole, and
> I take possession of it in the name of the United States of America in
> general, and William G. Shattuck in particular.'[55]

The speech echoes Nemo's claim upon the South Pole, and seems straightforwardly imperial in nature, especially because it is made in the presence
of the natives who have lived on the island for centuries. But the colonising
tone becomes even more explicit with what happens next:

> You see, being as we were at the Pole, the sun and all the stars revolved
> around us, same as a street does when you've had a drop too much. [...]
> Now, Captain Shattuck, being stark mad, considered that when he sat on
> the North Pole we, as well as the sun and the stars, ought to revolve round
> him.[56]

The captain assigns his surviving crew orbits around him, dictates times
that they are to wax, wane, and eclipse each other, and sits at the centre as
they do so. As he has the expedition's only pistols, the crew are compelled
to do as he says. In spite of not speaking English or understanding the
danger the guns represent, the natives also obey the captain's wishes, 'as
meek as a crew of niggers' (p. 256): once again, a glancing dismissal of
"lesser" races seems unavoidable when treating of this subject. When
petitioned to leave, the captain reacts angrily: 'I'm the centre of the solar
system, and I'm not going to throw up a berth like that just in order to
sneak back to New Bedford and to ask somebody to give me a ship!'
(p. 256). Delirious beyond any reason, Shattuck eventually has to be killed
before Martin can escape the island.

Shattuck's obsession with his own centrality, the result of the same
mania which caused him to seek the Pole in the first place, was also
evidently of persistent interest to Alden himself, who was, in writing this
story, re-hashing an idea he had expressed in non-fiction the previous year.
In his 'Wisdom Let Loose' column in the very first issue of *Pearson's
Magazine*, he speculates on the possibility of a British expedition to the
South Pole, adding:

> The moment the captain places himself at the pole, his personal axis will
> coincide with the axis of the earth, and he will immediately begin to
> revolve. His attendants will circle around him like so many satellites,
> and will have their days and nights, their phases, and other astronomical
> characteristics.[57]

In the column, natural forces cause the men to start revolving. In the
story, written later and at greater length, the agency lies solely with the
armed madman. Apart from this change, Alden migrates the concept from

speculation ("will") to fiction ("did") remarkably intact. The satirical nature of both pieces notwithstanding, this is an idea which obviously resonated with Alden, one which interested him enough that he kept it around and developed it.

A possible reason for both this resonance and the change from natural to human agency can be found in the fact that both pieces are fundamentally about structures of command. 'Very Cold Truth', is about Shattuck's abuse of power, returning repeatedly to the reasons for Martin's quiescence ('I didn't say anything, because I had shipped to obey orders, and not to talk').[58] The *Pearson's Magazine* column, despite being far shorter, is equally engaged with the hierarchical dispositions of the revolving sailors:

> The commander will be liable at almost any moment to be eclipsed by an ordinary seaman, or to be forced into occultation with a midshipman.
>
> Whether this sort of thing will please a captain who is a strict disciplinarian may be doubted.[59]

Shattuck's claim that he is the 'centre of the solar system' when he sits on the North Pole seems strange to anyone familiar with the Copernican model, but unlike the naturally occurring arrangement in 'Wisdom Let Loose', his is a man-made system: the sun and stars appear distant servants of Shattuck's gravitational pull, and the nearer revolutions of the island's natives and his crew (organised hierarchically, with Martin, as mate, closest) symbolise the captain's power by the orbits themselves as well as their submission to his humiliating whims. Shattuck becomes the platonic imperial overlord, using both deadly force and a naturalising symbolism to maintain control over his subjects. Without any apparent prompting, the islanders take Shattuck for 'one of their leading gods' – the perfect imperial power structure seems innate to those caught within it, but is artificial to the point of hilarity from an outside perspective such as the reader's.[60] As I argued in the introduction, classification systems of disciplines or genres are at their most intransigent when it is forgotten that they are artificial. This eagerness to *essentialise*, therefore, constitutes an insight into the correlation between taxonomies of knowledge and the language of imperialism.

The Pole is an enticing symbolic target for an empire because the view from it, as Ball notes, grants the illusion of order. The heavens seem less chaotic.

> Each star viewed from the coign of vantage offered by the North Pole would move round and round in a horizontal circle; and the system of concentric circles would be directly overhead.[61]

Alden's tale foregrounds the powerful metaphorical implications of appearing to be in the centre of this natural system. To the language of "height" and "light" used to discuss polar exploration in John Munro's story, we can now add "centrality". The three are a powerful combination in a press based in London, the centre of the British Empire, and once again it is appropriate that the periodical is the medium here. Stam and Stam point out that periodicals produced by crews on polar voyages:

> ...served at least one of the functions of their Victorian counterparts at home, that is, to unify their readers through the presentation of the familiar and comforting assumptions of the Victorian world view.[62]

Just as home-made periodicals on ships provided the artificial voice of the metropole to the explorers, so their commercial counterparts at the imperial centre narrativised into coherence the efforts of polar expeditions. They were not simply discovering knowledge, they were ordering it, and that act of ordering routinely carried with it the language and ideas of colonial dominance. All of this throws into perspective an incidental comment J. Arthur Bain made about Nansen in the *Idler* in 1896: 'confusion is altogether unknown where he is'.[63]

Empire is the fantasy of being in the middle of a series of concentric circles. One of the reasons that the loss of the Franklin expedition had so traumatised Britain in the 1840s and 50s was surely that it showed a wild, incoherent Arctic, one which was in reality very far from the pure white space which Jen Hill argues the Victorians saw it as symbolically. This Arctic was a narrative-free void in which two entire boats full of men could simply disappear. Finding the North Pole was an opportunity to restore that coherence, for those at home as well as for the explorers themselves. It was a target of exploration not only because it represented one of the few remaining unknown places on the Earth, but also because, despite the fact that it had never 'been approached by man within 400 miles', so much *was* already known about it. Through astronomy, it spoke to the empire's fantasy of coherence.[64]

This coherence, though, is ultimately the product of human narrative. As Sarah Moss reminds us, 'there is no final point on the earth's surface at which it can be said that one is at the North Pole'.[65] There are multiple poles, and they move as the earth does; the idea of one, significant geographical North Pole is necessary only for the concept of latitude, for the cartographic processes which made sea navigation reliable, and hence, empire possible. Those navigation systems were equally dependent on astronomy, reliably arranged around the observatory at Greenwich and its meridian. The meridian and the pole are both fabrications: neither inheres in nature, both are in a sense invented. But like the genre discourses which made up the periodicals, which are also anything but essential, they remain powerfully real – real enough, in this case, to enable the charting of the oceans and the subjugation of a territory on which the sun never set. In this regard, we might here remind ourselves of the arguments about Bruno Latour's notions of composition that I made in my introduction, earlier. The Royal Observatory manifests the inseparability of astronomy, sea voyaging and empire, and all of these required a conceptual ordering of space in order to work effectively. They also, of course, needed a conceptual ordering of time: since 1884, Greenwich had been the epicentre of the international collaboration which created world time, an organising principle with an influence even more pervasive than the British Empire. It was also (Stephen Kern has noted) a development essential to modern conflicts such as the First World War.[66]

The ordering of space and time into patterns, rhythms, and concentric circles was a characteristic of empire which it is no surprise to find reflections of in the history of SF. But the conception of a Latour-like chain of circulating reference demands that we pay attention not only to very abstract, enabling concepts such as these, but the more material concerns which link them to create reality. As we start to think about whether the role of science, which was indispensable to the ordering projects I have just described, really was a strictly amoral one (as is usually claimed), it is time to focus on a less esoteric way in which the Pole provoked imperial associations.

George Griffith and tangible commodities

A rather different approach to the Arctic is evident in *Pearson's Magazine*'s publication of George Griffith's 'A Corner in Lightning' (March 1898). So far, this chapter has – perhaps forgivably, in a book focussed on literature – focussed on the ways in which the quest for the North Pole was *metaphorically* resonant with the Imperial project. Griffith's story, though, with its unusually up-front approach, allows us to turn our attention to a more literal way in which the Arctic was attractive: its potential as a source of material wealth. Commerce was, of course, a driving force of the British Empire, and by focussing on the entrepreneurial potential of the Pole through his SF lens, Griffith opens both empire and science to some difficult questions. There is particular relevance in this approach for a present-day reader, since commercial interests continue to have the largest stake in twenty-first century debates over the exploitation of Arctic resources.

'A Corner in Lightning' follows the endeavours of Calvert, a wealthy young man with 'a chilly glitter in the eyes' who, in collaboration with his friend, Professor Kenyon, has developed a scheme to harness the Earth's electrical energy.[67] This involves building a power plant on the Magnetic North Pole which will store up the Earth's electricity, rendering all other generators on the planet useless and thus giving Calvert a complete monopoly over the commodity. His imperialist motivations remain unabashed and straightforward: 'Just fancy what a glorious thing it will be to play Jove to the nations of the earth, and dole out lightning to them at so much a flash' (p. 267). Calvert ignores a warning from his friend the professor, who tells him:

> ...you propose to interfere very seriously with the distribution of one of the subtlest and least-known forces of Nature, and [...] the consequences of such an interference might be most disastrous, not only for those engaged in the work, but even the whole hemisphere, and possibly the whole planet.[68]

The entrepreneur persists regardless, and though the planet does survive it is devastated by storms and plagues, and the story ends with the destruction of Calvert's Arctic plant and the death of his infant daughter: a classic arc of hubris-nemesis, we might think, for the mad scientist.

Crucially, however, Calvert is *not* a mad scientist. Neither is he an explorer. The opposite of Nansen, he is solely a financier, an ideas man hiring scientific expertise from Kenyon and from Orloff Markovitch, the scheme's real scientific mastermind (who dies dramatically at the end but is otherwise absent from the entire narrative). Calvert also outsources his exploring and engineering to others who perform their roles namelessly in the tale's background. Unusually for an Arctic exploration story, the scene of action never leaves London, the imperial centre, in spite of the occasional departure of the main characters to both the Magnetic Pole (exploration) and the south of France (refuge). We hear of the Arctic only via the reports sent back by telegraph. When the electrical chaos unleashed by Calvert's dabbling shuts the telegraph down, we experience the suspense from the home side: what is currently happening with our overseas interests? This kind of suspense is perhaps less common in adventure fiction, but would have been *de rigueur* to the reading public who had, for example, waited three years for word of Nansen.

The most direct instance of imperial language emerges in the story's first scene, an after-dinner chat between Calvert and his wife. Mrs Calvert, like the professor, is opposed to her husband's reckless undertaking, and tries to dissuade him from it. Her first argument is a commercial one: 'surely you, one of the richest men in London, are rich enough to do without it'. She then changes tack, offering a moral objection: 'I'm sure it's wrong, too. What should we think if somebody managed to bottle up the atmosphere and made us pay for every breath we drew?' (p. 264). Only then does she turn to the risk argument which the professor will later recapitulate, albeit in terms of personal risk to her husband rather than risk to the safety of the planet. Calvert, though, sees only financial risk, and is happy to take it: 'I think that quite good enough to gamble on', he later says (p. 266). His immediate answers to his wife are not answers at all. Fobbing off most of her objections on the grounds that 'it isn't fair' that she make them whilst looking at him (women are pretty; it would be unchivalrous of him to actually address the issues she raises), he concludes:

> ...it would be quite impossible to run any business and make money out of it on the lines of the Sermon on the Mount. But, come, here's a convenient digression for both of us. That's the professor, I expect.[69]

The digression is certainly convenient for one of them. Contrary to what Calvert tells the professor when he comes in, the bell does not interrupt an ethical discussion because the two are not having one. With a little casual sexism, Calvert sidesteps the fact that the only objections he is prepared to consider are those couched in terms of a cost-benefit analysis. Calvert is described later as being '...thoroughly fascinated by the grandeur and magnitude, to say nothing of the dazzling financial aspects of the scheme': it is in this combination of grandstanding and profiteering that his ideology can be most obviously seen at work (p. 266–67).

By highlighting the commercial side of imperialism, which sees exploration as an opportunity to exploit overseas interests for capital rather than anything else, this story illuminates the difficult side of the relationship between imperialism and science. When Professor Kenyon first presents himself, he makes it clear that he agrees with Calvert's wife about the moral advisability of the scheme but, after prompting from Calvert, he goes on to promise that his advice about the scientific details will be dispassionate: 'The ethics of the matter are no business of mine, nor have I anything to do with its commercial bearings' (p. 265). Kenyon has been retained to offer an objective, technical opinion. Though he has a moral position, he refuses to let it intrude into (or sever) his professional relationship with Calvert's scheme, and he goes on to provide technical advice without which it could never be put into practice. Since at least the establishment of the Royal Society in 1660, one of the ideals of science had been a healthy separation from the rest of the world. Discussions were to be only on the subject of knowledge:

> 'Their first purpose,' said Thomas Sprat, writing his 'history' of the Society when it was barely fledged, 'was no more, than onely the satisfaction of breathing a freer air, and of conversing in quiet one with another, without being ingag'd in the passions, and madness of that dismal Age'. The rules were clear: nothing about God; nothing about politics; nothing about 'News (other than what concern'd our business of Philosophy)'.[70]

Kenyon operates within this tradition, but it is a position he finds impossible to sustain. As the chaos indirectly caused by his actions goes on, he enters Calvert's sitting room once again with a rather different message:

> I wish to goodness that I had had nothing to do with the infernal business, for infernal it really is. Who are you that you should usurp one of the functions of the Almighty, for it is nothing less than that?[71]

The shift from characterising electricity as one of the 'forces of Nature' to 'one of the functions of the Almighty' alone is suggestive of the change wrought on the professor by his role in the catastrophe. The dispassionate stance he worked so carefully to maintain is precisely what Calvert opportunistically seized upon for financial gain. Latour reminds us that 'the ideal of the transportation of information without discussion or deformation [...] is *not* a description of what scientists do'.[72] Mary Midgley, meanwhile, reminds us that 'the vision of an omnicompetent science – a freestanding, autonomous skill with a monopoly of rationality that does all our thinking for us – is not workable'.[73]

Even if the Polar Storage Company had not failed spectacularly, Kenyon would still have been complicit in holding the Northern Hemisphere to ransom for the purposes of absurd and shameless profiteering. With the peripeteia of Calvert (and that of Kenyon), Griffith critiques both commerce and science for their idealisation of amorality. As well as the nightmare of the (already in 1898 almost unimaginable) world without electricity, Griffith appears to be offering the readers of *Pearson's* the idea that science and business can never be entirely value-free.

Roger Luckhurst and Josephine McDonagh have pointed out that the colonial encounter 'as a structure of dominance and control [...] leant a framework to all kinds of scientific endeavour'.[74] The most common example of this in periodical depictions of polar exploration was the bald heroism with which these scientific endeavours were usually credited. Of Nansen, for example, J. Arthur Bain writes:

> The key of his life can be found in the answer he once made to a hostile critic – an answer that deserves to ring through the ages to comfort the doubters and faint-hearted: 'Man wants to know; when man no longer wants to know, he will no longer be man.'[75]

This sentiment is generally seen as a noble one. The explorer-scientist is, at face-value, a literal embodiment of science's metaphorical struggle in the laboratory: to push back the frontiers of the unknown. But a glance at the voyage of Nansen, in which he shot an enormous amount of wildlife, slept in a bear-skin sleeping-bag, and returned rendered almost unrecognisable by his fight for sheer survival shows how problematic that analogy can be. The tension is discernible in Tony Harrison's recent characterisation of Nansen as a 'modern scientific Viking'.[76] In order to conduct polar science, Nansen needs to be anything but a dispassionate observer. He is a rugged survivor, a polymath who 'contributed articles to both scientific and sporting journals'.[77] The wilderness is not a laboratory. Nansen could not conduct controls or carry out blind sampling: science in the Arctic is red in tooth and claw.

None of this is to argue that Nansen's voyage was not a genuinely scientific one, rather the contrary. Latour repeatedly stresses that 'the more connected a science is to the rest of the collective, the better it is'.[78] Arguing that science conceived as a mere observer is useless, he says:

> Yes, we live in a hybrid world made up at once of gods, people, stars, electrons, nuclear plants, and markets, and it is our duty to turn it into either an 'unruly shambles' or an 'ordered whole'. . .[79]

Once we dispense with Descartes, however,

> [t]he search for absolute certainty becomes less urgent, and thus there is no great difficulty in reconnecting with the relativism, the relations, the relativity on which the sciences have always thrived.[80]

Both Mary Midgley and Latour argue that it need not be to science's detriment to be connected to the rest of the collective. I have already noted the breadth of Nansen's talents, the combination of different aptitudes which helped him to make his mission a success. Bain's articles repeatedly emphasise this characteristic:

> Dr. Nansen is an exceptionally accomplished linguist, speaking several languages fluently. He is also an artist and photographer of no mean order, so much so that at one time it was proposed that he should devote his life to Art.[81]

The same diversity which made Nansen's voyage a scientific success is what made him an attractive figure to the periodicals, with their commercial interest in a wide market. Bain drew attention to the fact that Eva Nansen shares her husband's breadth of expertise: a mezzo-soprano, part of Grieg's musical circle, but also 'one of the most athletic women of the North', a champion skilober.[82] Everything appealing about the explorer, both on his travels and at home, stems from his wide-ranging enthusiasm, the integrity of his different connections to the collective. This can be seen as the basis at once of both his scientific authority and his popular appeal, and it attractively offers a reason that his disconnection from the periodicals in 1893-6 was so keenly felt.

Griffith suggests that science should not ignore its connections to the rest of the world; Latour suggests it cannot. If this is the case, it becomes reasonable to ask why the noble image of objective empiricism is so often thrust upon it. This is too big a question to dwell on here, but it is certainly the case that disconnecting empiricism from the world amply serves the purposes of imperial propagandising. Latour regards the whole conversation as a top-down effort to silence the voice of the mob, a 'dramatic double bind' which has been going on since at least Plato, passed on to us through a modernist settlement at odds with reality.[83] However convincing one finds this view, both imperialism and empiricism are certainly, from their own perspectives, naturalising attempts to order a wilderness.

Although Nansen was not British, the status he and his undertakings attained in the British magazines can certainly be read as indicative of their vested interest in defending the ideals of imperialism *per se*. The 'man wants to know' justification, which seems noble enough at first glance, is charged with the Enlightenment ideology which empowered the most devastating phase of European colonialism as well as all the breakthroughs in scientific research and thinking which we continue to profit from today. When science wasn't an active participant in the imperial project, its ideal of passivity made it easy enough to co-opt, just as Calvert co-opts Kenyon's expertise in Griffith's story. The two are harder to separate than we might like, so much so that we still think of exploration as an intrinsically noble activity: Bain's prediction that Nansen's attitude would 'ring through the ages' has so far been borne out.[84] Hence, for instance, *Star Trek*'s noble (and usually uninterrogated) quest 'to explore strange new worlds' – whatever the consequences for us or them. Hence, also, popular physicist Brian Cox, responding to a question ahead of the National Theatre's 2011 production of *Frankenstein*: 'For me science is literally exploration, in the sense of getting on a boat'.[85] The job of the scientist is to stand on the border between the known and the unknown, taking small steps (as Nansen did literally, pushing away at the highest-attained latitude; as Cox does metaphorically at CERN, for example). After mentioning the role played by amoral science in the Manhattan Project, however, Cox finished his answer by saying: 'What the moral responsibility of the explorer is... is an extremely complex question'. It may be decidedly lowbrow and over a century out of date, but Griffith's story highlights anxieties in the ethics of science which remain extremely pressing, and which are unlikely to diminish as the new frontiers of laboratory exploration (for example, stem cell research) continue to throw new hopes and fears open to both science and popular culture.

Questions of commerce and power continue to resonate in the modern Arctic, which is now supposed to contain 'upwards of 90 billion barrels of oil and 1.7 trillion cubic feet of natural gas reserves', the favourite commodities of the twenty-first century West. Zachary Nathan Schulman has estimated the value of these resources at $7,225 billion.[86] As the ice retreats around the Pole due to global warming and this potential wealth becomes increasingly accessible, the Arctic countries (Norway, Denmark, and the USA, but especially Russia and Canada) are vying for control over them. Matters came to a head in 2007, when a Russian expedition used a submarine to plant a flag on the sea bed at the North Pole, a move, Schulman notes, 'reminiscent of the grand geopolitics of the late 19th and early 20th centuries' (p. 6). Canadian Prime Minister Stephen Harper responded by announcing the construction of two new military bases in Resolute Bay and Nanisivik, saying 'Today's announcements tell the world that Canada has real, growing, long-term presence in the Arctic'.[87] Technology and global warming may have changed much about the geopolitics of the Arctic Circle, but the straightforwardness of the language in this dispute is still quite remarkable. Sarah Moss sums up our thirst for Arctic resources:

> We burn oil in order to travel further and faster than we could do without it, so that more people can see and know more about more of the world, and the result is that there is less of the world to see and know.[88]

'Science is literally exploration, in the sense of getting on a boat': it is worth bearing in mind what those who got on boats to go exploring actually did, and what they still do.

Ghosts, matter, truth

Griffith's story is helpful because of the self-consciousness with which it approaches the questions of science, commerce and empire, but uncovering those questions in places where they emerge rather in spite of themselves is also valuable. The relationship between Calvert and Kenyon can be read allegorically as that between empire and knowledge, and in less direct ways this conversation can be found playing out in numerous other pieces of writing on polar exploration in the periodical press. One such is Hamilton Drummond's 'A Secret of the South Pole' (*Windsor*, April 1902). I want to use this story as a way into relating the arguments of the preceding three sections of this chapter to those of its second – to argue that there is a distinctly imperial dimension to the close relationship between fact and fiction in these periodical, polar writings.

Drummond's story can be summarised as follows: like Alden's 'Very Cold Truth', it takes the form of a tale told to the narrator by an ancient mariner, in this case a man called Cap'n Towson. Towson, a far less reflective storyteller than Griffith, is asked by the narrator about an 'irregular, flattish fragment' of an unusual substance – not quite metal or glass – found amongst his memorabilia.[89] He replies by telling the story of how, cast away with two others, he came across a hulk adrift in the middle of the Pacific. Apparently several hundred years old yet still mysteriously afloat, the hulk makes the sailors uneasy, but they board it in any case as it represents a better chance of survival than their dinghy. It turns out to have been preserved by Antarctic ice, but it has also been filled with "solid air", an invisible substance in which the unfortunate seaman who descends into the hold "drowns".

Drummond's story fits well into the structural template of a "ghost ship" narrative. The fundamentals broadly mirror an episode in Poe's *Arthur Gordon Pym*, and the tale includes descriptive passages resonant with the tropes of supernatural horror. These include the moment when Towson describes removing a tarpaulin from the roof of the hulk, saying:

> I give you my word it was like strippin' the dead, an' even now there are times when I lie awake o' nights that I can hear the soft rastle o' the rip o' the stuff; an' when I hear it, the skin of my back creeps an' I go cold down the spine.[90]

Shane McCorristine has shown that narratives of polar exploration often have recourse to 'the language of the supernatural and the ghostly', arguing that the Arctic has always had a spectral appeal to both explorers and their readers.[91] Sure enough, when one of Towson's companions, Brady, is in the grip of the solid air, '['t]was all one as if he'd seen a ghost'.[92] Yet despite capitalising on the supernatural template, this is not a ghost story: the hulk is not haunted by spirits, but rather by '[s]ome kind of a gas, maybe, or fluid that turned to gas' (p. 619). Science stands in for the supernatural here: however absurd the idea of 'solid air' seems, its presence nonetheless reflects an attempt from Drummond to articulate a material basis for his apparently supernatural adventure. By some definitions, this aligns 'A Secret of the South Pole' more closely with SF than with the ghost tale.

At the same time, the scary thing about the ship is not her spectral, departed crew but her threatening new cargo from an unknown place. Like 'A Corner in Lightning', and despite its title, Drummond's tale never actually visits the polar regions, discussing the South Pole only in terms of its "export". The Pole is present only in the 'solid air', a cargo which has no apparent commercial value and which kills those who would try to exploit it. This commodity anxiety opens the tale to being read in terms of trade and empire. 'It's a noble calling is the sea, and I reckon England sucks her Empire out o' the salt water', reflects Towson on his career choices, but there is little nobility in his actions in the tale and his refusal to reveal why he and his two fellows were cast away in the first place suggests that his character was far from above reproach (p. 614). The narrator speculates that Towson probably never earned the title "captain": even a mariner with his dubious credentials, however, can recognise the intrinsic links between seafaring and colonisation.

'A Secret of the South Pole' is driven by the inscrutability of the new substances which it describes: the solid air and the container which originally held it, part of which is the fragment which prompted the narrator's initial question to Towson. But as well as being an imperial anxiety, this is also a scientific concern, in that new discoveries always carry the risk of unhorsing pre-existing systems of understanding by their failure to fit into them. Hence Towson's penultimate sentence: '...we don't know everything our side the world, for all our cocksure ways' (p. 620). This line too could be from a ghost story, but here the suggestion is not of a transcendental "spirit realm" (or something like it) which can *never* be understood, but of an actual, physical type of understanding which the British Empire (for all its cocksure ways) currently lacks. Towson announces to the narrator that he intends to leave the baffling relic of his adventure to the British Museum on his death: 'I s'pose they'll pound it to bits to see what it's made of. Even then they won't be any the wiser...' (p. 614). This is an unsettling prospect because the investigative tools of high empire (appropriately embodied by the British Museum) have been broken: Enlightenment atomism threatens to prove useless in the investigation of a piece of physical matter. The anxiety this generates implicitly binds science and empire together.

Regarding Drummond's story as being fundamentally about tangible matter rather than intangible horror (reading it, we might say, as SF rather than as a ghost story) throws new light on the amount of time his narrator spends – nearly the whole of the first page, the story being only nine pages long – discussing the plausibility of the tale and the reliability of Towson as a source of information. For once again, we are dealing here with a club story. 'As to his experience, I have only himself as witness', says the narrator, after stressing that he is himself a landsman and not qualified to judge the man's seafaring claims (p. 612). These doubts are presented long before any hint of what the story is actually going to be about, and they strike a key-note of dubiousness which is quite perplexing – after all, we, as readers, know that the story is not true, don't we? The dubiousness is compounded when the narrator adds that he believes Towson in spite of his doubts, saying:

> Those of my friends to whom I have retold his tales have not scrupled to call him liar, and certainly his stories were at times largely capable of disbelief. But for my part I always found it hard to doubt him ; he was so circumstantial, so fluent, so calmly level, so credulous of himself. There was no assertiveness, no subtle doubt lurking in an appeal for belief, but just a quiet assurance that disarmed incredulity. Your habitual liar has a way of calling the gods to witness that is in itself suspicious. With Towson there was none of that. The thing was so because it was so. It was as if Galileo said the sun moved because it moved, and not all the Pope Urbans in the world could make it a lie.[93]

Here, as in all fiction, the surety of truth lies in the conviction of the performance rather than at large in the world. The innocent-looking 'as if' in the final sentence completely reverses science in its Baconian sense: Towson speaking is the equivalent of Galileo observing. This is the piece's stronger, subtler claim to the mantle of SF, within which science is always subject, to some extent, to narrative diktat.

Griffith's 'Corner in Lightning' story cautions us about the involvement of amoral science in the machinations of imperial commerce. But my reading of Arctic stories from the periodical press reminds us that fiction was itself equally amoral and subject to complicity in the project of imperialism. By confusing or reinterpreting truth, fiction can explicitly and implicitly further the goals of the imperial project, weaving out of complexity the apparently basic order which was a vital component of empire's vision of itself. These tales were particularly well-positioned for two other reasons: they were published in general magazines, in the same pages as non-fictional material and with almost no distinction from it, and they were science-fictional insofar as they adopted a narrative architecture where fact appears to supersede narrative, but is in fact always junior to it. If SF carried this imperial baggage to the pole, it was certainly prepared to carry it beyond as its ambitions, ahead of those of real-world scientists, widened to include exploring the stars. At last, it is time to focus on this transition.

Stepping-stone to the stars

Reading through the monthlies of the 1890s and 1900s, one is immediately struck by the abundance of tales of the sea. Given the nautical adventure's resonances with the culture of any empire, especially Britain's, this is perhaps to be expected, although the quantity is still a little humbling. It is dramatically easier to find a nautical adventure than it is to find a story with science-fictional elements, although, of course, many SF stories *are* nautical adventures, and nautical adventure in its various forms can also potentially incorporate historical fiction, romances, ghost stories, detective fiction, and many other kinds of tale. Interest in maritime subjects is no less apparent in the non-fiction published by these magazines: for example, the very next item after 'A Secret of the South Pole' in *Windsor Magazine* is a documentary of a "cable hospital" consisting of a lavishly illustrated series of interviews with the crew of a ship which maintains and repairs transatlantic telegraph cables. Towards the end of this article, one crewmember reflects on the fact that the ice often renders work on the cable impossible for lengthy periods of time, during which the crew is idle. He says:

> Here is a photograph taken off Nova Scotia, which depicts our happy little band engaged in a mild picnic on the ice. Cables and cable-repairing are at this period of enforced inactivity as remote from us as the North Pole![94]

This chapter's central argument about exploration, colonialism, and science fiction could have been made by recourse to almost any of the vast archive of maritime articles – fictitious and otherwise – offered to us by the periodical press. But the idea of the Pole's "remoteness", even to someone who has been much closer to it than the majority of his readers, is just one of the characteristics which gave it a particular place in the public imagination. Thus, McCorristine:

> Of much concern to first-time explorers were the haunting epistemological uncertainties that the polar experience inculcated: with mirages, optical illusions, and sensory nightmares an almost daily occurrence, commanders were keen to stress the new aesthetic realities in the Arctic theatre, realities which seemed destined to scupper the coping mechanisms learnt back in England.[95]

The Pole is not only a blank space on the map, to be explored and conquered by Europeans, but also an imaginative space in which science appears to be confounded. Its spectrality, the way in which those who attempt to reach it encounter the uncanny folded alongside the scientifically explicable, the real alongside the fantastical (McCorristine calls this "the Arctic sublime") make it an ideal staging-post for nautical fiction's departure from the planet. The transition from the North Pole to a distinctly new world seems entirely natural.

For an example of nautical writing inching its way towards the condition of SF, it is worth returning to the author this chapter opened with, Arthur Conan Doyle. The creator of Sherlock Holmes was an ardent imperialist who, as mentioned earlier, wrote several articles on the subject of his own Arctic voyage on a whaler in 1880. It is possible to discern in these articles several telling suggestions of the links between real Arctic and fictional space exploration. The first clue is in the title of one of the articles, 'The Glamour of the Arctic' (*The Idler*, July 1892). The glamour here is not just the excitement of brave adventurers on ships, or the nostalgia of a worthy trade which was by now on its last legs (although, for an imperial reading, it is also both of those things). It is also the glamour of the landscape itself, which Conan Doyle describes as a 'region of romance'.[96] The ethereality implied by 'romance' here goes nicely with McCorristine's 'Arctic sublime', as does the word 'glamour' itself, whose original Scots meaning of 'magic, enchantment, spell', was still current in the 1890s.[97] 'It is a region of purity', Conan Doyle says:

> ...of white ice and of blue water, with no human dwelling within a thousand miles to sully the freshness of the breeze which blows across the icefields.[98]

He spends some time discussing the mystery of the open polar seas and the possibility of reaching the Pole, relying frequently on the testimony of whaling captains, and admitting that allowances must be made 'for expansive talk over a pipe and a glass' – the same ambiguity extant in the fiction of Drummond and Alden. Not only is there the same vagueness seen in the fictional pieces, but Conan Doyle ends with discussion of the 'medical and curative side' of the Arctic climate:

> Davos Platz has shown what cold can do in consumption, but in the life-giving air of the Arctic Circle no noxious germ can live. The only illness of any consequence which ever attacks a whaler is an explosive bullet.[99]

With this kind of restorative magic in the air (and the adventure implied by 'explosive bullet'), the Arctic seems a perfect venue for fantastical adventure. It is surely not impossible, in these circumstances, that a lost European civilisation flourishes on the other side of a barrier of polar ice:

> Have they preserved some singular civilisation of their own, and are they still singing and drinking and fighting [. . .] or have they been destroyed by the hated Skraelings, or have they, as is more likely, amalgamated with them, and produced a race of tow-headed, large-limbed Esquimaux? We must wait until some Nansen turns his steps in that direction before we can tell.[100]

The 'they' in this quotation are lost Danes from centuries ago, and Conan Doyle wasn't the only one to hypothesise about their continued existence – the fact that Alden's natives in 'Very Cold Truth' are Danish speakers suggests that he too is thinking of them. Many others have been interested in this posited ideal Scandinavian culture, isolated from decadent society behind a wall of cleansing ice. Yet Conan Doyle's treatment of it here is especially interesting since, we need to remind ourselves, this is purportedly a non-fictional piece about the whaling industry. Yet it also lapses into a distinctly science-fictional speculation about the future when Conan Doyle mentions an unfortunate seafarer who became tangled in a chain and dragged into the ocean by a whale's carcass:

> Some æons hence those two skeletons, the one hanging by the foot from the other, may grace the museum of a subtropical Greenland, or astonish the students of the Spitzbergen Institute of Anatomy.[101]

It's only with a handful of words in this one sentence, but Conan Doyle here implies a much wider consideration of the future than the inevitable demise of whaling. Here we have, potentially, continental drift, global warming, and the rise of a new cultural superpower. As always, my objective in making these points is not to argue that 'The Glamour of the Arctic' is SF in any straightforward sense, but rather to argue that the way in which the Arctic landscape was portrayed, its eerie unquantifiability, lent itself to writing in a way that blended exploration, technology, the future, and other races – all big themes of genre SF.

Conan Doyle's Arctic is made even more surreal by the imposition of human commodity culture on it. In a later article on the same subject, written for the *Strand*, he describes the 'murderous harvest' of sealing:

> It is brutal work, though not more brutal than that which goes on to supply every dinner-table in the country. And yet those glaring crimson pools upon the dazzling white of the ice-fields, under the peaceful silence of a blue Arctic sky, did seem a horrible intrusion.[102]

The focus on the "supply and demand" justification, as well as its effect on the landscape, brings us to what is arguably the most interesting link between these whaling articles and SF: the whales themselves. The creatures Conan Doyle's expedition hunted (specifically, the Greenland right whale, now known as the Bowhead whale) are far more tangible both as entities and objectives than a lost race of Danes, yet they are still tantalisingly difficult to track down and catch:

> That the whale entirely understands the mechanism of its own capture is beyond dispute. To swim backwards and forwards beneath a floe in the hope of cutting the rope against the sharp edge of the ice is a common device of the creature after being struck.[103]

After lingering for a while on the capacities of the whale's 'highly intelligent brain', Conan Doyle continues that should the reader manage to find one, 'he has a taste of sport which it would be ill to match [. . .] To play a salmon is a royal game, but when your fish weighs more than a suburban villa, and is worth a clear two thousand pounds [. . .] it dwarfs all other experiences'.[104] The mention of the commodity value of whales here (Conan Doyle notes in the *Strand* piece that they are worth so much money because their numbers are decreasing so sharply[105]), as well as the straightforward superiority work done by scale, speak strongly to the imperial hunter's instinct – glory, profit, and sport. But it's the frequency with which Conan Doyle returns to the whale's intelligence which is really significant, for it goes beyond merely stressing their worthiness as quarry. After describing, rather vividly, the process of actually killing one, Conan Doyle offers this unexpected reflection:

> Yet amid all the excitement – and no one who has not held an oar in such a scene can tell how exciting it is – one's sympathies lie with the poor hunted creature. The whale has a small eye, little larger than that of a bullock, but I cannot easily forget the mute expostulation which I read in one, as it dimmed over in death within hand's touch of me. What could it guess, poor creature, of laws of supply and demand[. . .]?[106]

Conan Doyle is here face to face (or, rather, eye to eye) with a genuinely alien consciousness, one with strong resemblances to various imagined aliens in later works of science fiction.[107] There may be few human natives in the Greenland seas (other than the speculative ones), but there are certainly natives, perhaps the more empathetic for their entirely unfathomable yet readily apparent intelligence. The empire hunts them anyway. Today, the Bowhead whale remains on the IUCN red list.

Conan Doyle wrote to impress. The glamour of the Arctic is something he evokes by stressing how different the Greenland seas are from the world inhabited by the London-based readers of the periodical press. He describes unfamiliar landscapes where 'night is but an expression', magical, curative air, and giant, intelligent natives who can live up to a century – surely the stuff of fantasy.[108] But he is also keen throughout to emphasise the material chain which connects this fantasy to the reader's reality, the 'long line of seamen, dockers, tanners, curers, triers, chandlers, leather merchants, and oil sellers' who take the whales to the centres of commerce.[109] By this keenness, if by nothing else, Conan Doyle's fantasy world becomes, in certain respects, a science fictional one. His writings show that the division between fantastical adventures in strange lands and the hard daily life of an imperial citizen of the metropole is far from an absolute one. The chain which links them is long, but it is real and can be followed.

With such a chain, we can also link the Pole explicitly to the idea of space travel. I have already mentioned in my discussion of W. L. Alden's 'Very Cold Truth' the perceived link between the Poles and Newtonian cosmology, as elaborated upon by Sir Robert Ball. I have also mentioned the Royal Observatory, described by one magazine piece as 'so intimately associated with our maritime affairs, that it may be said to have contributed, in a very large degree, towards our naval supremacy'.[110] The empire literally brought the heavens into the service of colonialism, co-opted them and the mechanisms by which they were understood for the purposes of navigation, map-making, and the definition and division of territory. The stars are 'put in their harness and made to help our ships', and as with Conan Doyle and the whaling industry, as with so many of the other non-fictional pieces I have focussed on in this book, there is a detectable emphasis on the connection of this process with everyday life. Through an economic chain of circulating reference, the abstract is translated into the tangible:

> ...the most abstruse of the sciences [astronomy] is made of such practical effect, that, working hand in hand with commerce, it has conduced to the cheapening of figs and to the putting of tea on the poor man's breakfast table.[111]

Historically, the objective, empirical, scientific attempt to understand the movements of the heavens led to the understanding of longitude, the development of precision timekeeping, and the cartographic techniques without which the British Empire would have been an impossible project.

It is no coincidence that today, the National Maritime Museum and the Greenwich Observatory are one institution, two buildings on the same site. Given the romanticised connection between seafaring and the heavens epitomised in John Masefield's 1902 poem 'Sea-Fever' ('all I ask is a tall ship and a star to sail her by'[112]), and given the imperial press and society in which this connection was popularly articulated, it is unsurprising the SF took the imaginative leap necessary to travel to the stars as well as by them. As the location in the northern hemisphere around which the heavens appeared to cohere (Polaris, the North Star, the one fixed point in the night sky), the Pole was a natural channel through which this leap would take place.

Summing up Nansen's endeavour, Roland Huntford writes: 'After the scramble for Africa, the polar regions were the last great blanks upon the map. They saw the last act of terrestrial discovery before the leap into space'.[113] The Arctic, I want to suggest, is a stepping-stone to the stars, a place where spectrality and science, known and unknown, intersect with exploration and colonialism in a way which empowers a genre to leave the planet. We can see this happen in front of our eyes in H. G. Wells's *The First Men in the Moon*, which first appeared in serial form in the *Strand* magazine in 1900–1. The novel describes the lunar voyage of Mr Cavor, the scientist, and Mr Bedford, the entrepreneur (and narrator), in an anti-gravity sphere of Cavor's devising. The pair's trip to the moon is undertaken by Cavor in the spirit of scientific curiosity, but is all about profit as far as Bedford is concerned. When Bedford first hears about Cavor's invention:

> An extraordinary possibility came rushing into my mind. Suddenly I saw as in a vision the whole solar system threaded with Cavorite liners and spheres *de luxe*. 'Rights of pre-emption,' came floating into my head – planetary rights of pre-emption. I recalled the old Spanish monopoly in American gold. It wasn't as though it was just this planet or that – it was all of them. [. . .]
>
> 'I'm beginning to take it in,' I said; 'I'm beginning to take it in.' The transition from doubt to enthusiasm seemed to take scarcely any time at all. 'But this is tremendous!' I cried. 'This is Imperial! I haven't been dreaming this sort of thing.'[114]

Bedford views the enterprise as a form of prospecting, a way of unlocking the untold mineral wealth of other worlds. Cavor, a few lines earlier, has characterised the proposed voyage thus: 'After all, to go into space is not so much worse, if at all, than a Polar expedition. Men go on Polar expeditions' (p. 698). The comparison is tantalising in a novel at least as thoughtful about empire as Griffith is in 'A Corner in Lightning'. When Bedford, who is bankrupt, joins forces with Cavor, it is an attempt on his part to do as Calvert did to Kenyon; to capitalise on the fact that Cavor's quest for knowledge has given him tunnel-vision, that Cavor is only capable of displaying interest in distinctly scientific subjects. 'It isn't one man in a million has that twist', Bedford will later tell him, in frustration. 'Most men want- well, various things, but very few want knowledge for its own sake'.[115]

Having escaped from the clutches of the moon-dwellers, the Selenites, whom Cavor has stayed behind to try and understand (his straightforward curiosity will end up costing him his life), Bedford sits on the moon and contemplates exploration in a passage which explicitly underlines Wells's main interests in the novel, and which is worth quoting at length:

> What is this spirit in man that urges him for ever to depart from happiness and security, to toil, to place himself in danger, to risk even a reasonable certainty of death? [. . .] Sitting there in the midst of that useless moon gold, amidst the things of another world, I took count of all my life. Assuming I was to die a castaway upon the moon, I failed altogether to see what purpose I had served. I got no light on that point, but at any rate it was clearer to me than it had ever been in my life before that I was not serving my own purpose, that all my life I had in truth never served the purposes of my private life.[116]

In the book version Bedford continues: 'Whose purposes, what purposes, was I serving?'.[117] Bedford's interrogations – of Cavor and of his own motivations – cast Nansen's heroic proclamation, 'Man wants to know; when man no longer wants to know, he will no longer be man' in a more sinister light. If Bedford has co-opted science's disinterestedness, this passage suggests, then his own material interestedness is also serving another, less overt, ideological purpose.

There are numerous other moments in *The First Men in the Moon* which speculate on the practices of exploration and empire-building,[118] and to detail all of them would distract from the main argument I want to make here, which is that the moon in Wells's understanding is not just another world, visited imperially, but also refers to the Arctic as part of the trajectory by which its colonial protagonists leave Earth. Aaron Worth reads in Wells's moon echoes of British southern Africa, and whilst these comparisons are arresting, I believe that equally powerful associations with the North Pole can be made, associations which only add weight to Worth's general argument about the vivid links between imperialism and technology in Wells's writing.[119] Cavor's comment at the outset is not the only time that we are invited to consider the voyage in the Cavorite sphere as a form of polar exploration. 'Think yourself a sort of ultra-Arctic voyager exploring the desolate places of space', he says later, when the sphere is descending towards the moon.[120] It eventually lands, at dawn, in a vast Arctic snowscape (Fig. 4.5):

> As we saw it first it was the wildest and most desolate of scenes. [...] a disordered escarpment of drab and greyish rock, lined here and there with banks and crevices of snow.[121]

This 'snow' is actually 'mounds and masses of frozen air' (p. 33), which is evaporated by the rising sun shortly after the sphere lands to create an atmosphere: 'the Arctic appearance had gone altogether' (p. 35). A short

32   *THE STRAND MAGAZINE.*

" WE WERE LYING IN THE DARKNESS OF THE SHADOW OF THE WALL OF THE GREAT CRATER."

4.5   A lunar dawn in H. G. Wells's *First Men in the Moon*, as it appeared in *The Strand Magazine* (January 1901). Shades of the polar regions here? Courtesy of the Cadbury Research Library, University of Birmingham.

while later, plants begin to grow before the eyes of the adventurers. Their life cycle, it appears, is to remain dormant through the lunar night, but with the coming of the sun and atmosphere there springs up a forest at remarkable speed:

> Imagine it! Imagine that dawn! The resurrection of the frozen air, the stirring and quickening of the soil, and then this silent uprising of vegetation, this unearthly ascent of fleshiness and spikes. Conceive it all lit by a blaze that would make the intensest sunlight of earth seem watery and weak. And still around this stirring jungle, wherever there was shadow, lingered banks of bluish snow.[122]

The Arctic is still recalled by details like the intensity of the sunlight, and the lingering snow serves as a reminder of the speed with which the desolate polar landscape has been transformed into a rich, fantasy world. That this transformation takes place before the eyes of the two adventurers draws attention to the fact that Wells does not just take them to the moon by putting them in a spacecraft, but also brings the moon to them by transforming one of the last wildernesses on earth into his alien world. The contact zone between the moon – fantasy – and Mr Bedford's sitting room – reality – is the ethereal wasteland of the Arctic. The Arctic here is a gateway, passed through to get to the real discoveries.

Jam tomorrow

So far, I have contended that much of what the Victorian reading public found fascinating about polar exploration can be traced back to the imperial project tacitly supported by the majority of the press. From the increasingly nightmarish prospect of being disconnected from modern communication networks – fiction rising up to fill the gap left by the simultaneous absence of Arctic voyagers – to the racial, metaphorical and commodity obsessions of both the fiction and non-fiction which concerned itself with exploration, the Arctic regions were a flashpoint for all manner of imperial concerns, both practical and ideological. I have tried to show these concerns at work in the complex, overlapping spheres of factual and fictional discourse which constituted the spawning ground of SF as a commercial genre. Latour's model of circulating reference suggests a mechanism for connecting abstract concerns of genre territory to tangible concerns of physical territory, laid out both on sea charts and the pages of the magazines. The place of science itself in this elaborate network is a complicated one, but it is very far from an objective bystander, some form of it often actively involved in the service of pro-imperial rhetoric.

Whether deliberately, as in stories like Griffith's 'A Corner in Lightning', or less so, as in Drummond's 'A Secret of the South Pole', *fin-de-siècle* SF frequently dealt with themes of exploration, capital (both cultural and material), technology, aspiration, and privilege. Particularly when it did so in the spectral space of the Arctic, and in the material space of the periodical press, the connection to empire was unavoidable. I have also argued that it was at least partly via the space of the polar wastelands, with all of these concerns very much in play, that imaginative literature was able to leave the surface of the planet and explore the stars. It would be ridiculous to suppose for a moment, given the weight and number of connections outlined earlier, that it left its attachment to empire behind when it did so – even the cursory reading of Wells undertaken earlier shows a relentless engagement with questions of colonialism, exploration and conquest, questions from which, as John Rieder has so comprehensively documented, SF has remained far from distant.[123] The genre's continuing postcolonial associations are attested to by the recent publication – from the magazine *The Future Fire* – of an anthology described in its introduction as a collection of 'speculative fiction in which the viewpoint is that of the colonised, not the invader. We want to see stories that remind us that neither readers nor writers are a homogeneous club of white, male, Christian, hetero, cis, monoglot anglophone, able-bodied Westerners'.[124] Here, once again, the periodical format holds a contradiction in suspension by simultaneously insisting on diversity and enabling the emergence of a highly specific individual voice, in this instance the sub-genre of postcolonial SF.

Periodicals, as I have now been arguing for some time, play an important formal role in the emergence of new genres, providing a hybrid environment and, through specialist publication, a means of segregating a new discourse from it. It is reductive to think of them simply as transmitters of content – they are active in shaping the fluctuating internal boundaries of public discourse, and there are tangible connections between the metaphorical territories of genre and the real communities of readers formed and re-formed by this evolving process. The British Empire was at least partly a creation of the periodical press, in that the pro-imperial magazines fabricated an essentialised norm which worked to rhythmically reassure its readers of its continued existence. 'The serial format', writes David Reed, 'returning every week or month, reassures its audience [...] that there is a base of reliability and predictability that can be touched in a dangerous and unstable world'.[125] The reassuring rhythm of seriality is something I already pointed out in my discussion of *The Time Machine* in

Chapter 2. In the light of these Arctic readings, though, such reassurances take on darker associations: it is not merely constancy of which the magazines reassure us, but also "civilised" constancy. Periodicity offers a regulated alternative not only to the blank, timeless future of *The Time Machine*, but also to the "savagery" of contemporary societies against which the empire was set up as a bureaucratic, civilising, regulated alternative. Magazines were a part of this large project. Recognising this, we can see the links between the esoteric territories of genre and the real life territories at stake in the Arctic and elsewhere.

Magazines 'offer a cynosure, a parenthesis in which to shelter, a home from home' (p. 10) – they not only play a role in shaping the literal and figurative territories into which we divide the world, but they are also a territory themselves. Reed, through Leon Festinger's theory of cognitive dissonance, identifies in periodical specialisation a symptom of 'the extensively documented human need to avoid contradiction, with either the self or others' (pp. 10–11). We return to the organised territory of the magazine not primarily for information or entertainment but for comfort, to reaffirm our own senses of self and society. Readers of general magazines were routinely valorised in a certain worldview – that of their particular imagined community, per Benedict Anderson – which legitimated the colonial goings-on in distant parts of the world. Yet this is not to claim that the periodical is inherently the tool of empire any more than science is. I have already discussed the fact that, unlike Reed's magazine reader, a general magazine is remarkable in its insistence on a diversity of content, in its ability to hold contradictions in suspension. Reed's point is that most readers habitually blind themselves to this: 'we filter out that which does not suit us and retain that which does' (p. 10).

That argument is attested to by the work I have had to do in this study to make visible the magazine's (and the human being's) exceptionally self-evident capacity for tolerating, and indeed insisting on, a certain plurality of contradictory locutions. One of the biggest contradictions of the general magazine is that it can maintain this very characteristic even whilst aiding the imperial processes of segregating both the world and our knowledge of it into isolated territories. But if the periodical does this work, then it can also help us to retrace it, and understanding the real, historical involvement of magazines in the formation of territory is an important first step in this process. A second step, I suggest in this final section, might be to pay attention to ways in which the periodical resists the project of authoritarian completeness on which empire is embarked even as it assists it.

Nansen never reached the North Pole. Perhaps that's just as well: it is unmarked in a featureless ocean. We, of course, have the privilege of living in an age where this is evident. But whilst we are clearly the better for knowing, a remarkable passage in Richard Le Gallienne's review of Nansen's book may justly give us pause:

> "To travel hopefully is better than to arrive." When the North Pole is at length actually reached, these words of Robert Louis Stevenson will be found written upon it, or "writ in water" on that mathematical point of polar sea where it is conjectured the north end of the earth's axis may well come out: "To travel hopefully is better than to arrive." Arctic explorers, of all people, should remember that – let them just think for a moment how dull their lives will be when their great aim is at last accomplished. And if they don't mind, a day will come when there'll be no North Pole to find.[126]

Fear of an anticlimax also lay beneath the Reverend Andrew A. W. Drew's prediction when discussing Nansen's voyage in the *English Illustrated Magazine* just after the explorer set off:

> ...the stout little *Fram* may come through in the summer of 1894, and he [Nansen] may tell us that he steamed up to N. latitude 90° and found there absolutely nothing to mark the fact that he alone of living men had reached the North Terrestrial Pole.[127]

The passage reads curiously after five pages advocating heroism and derring-do amongst the ice, but Drew is far from alone here. His sentiment recalls W. L. Alden's demand, quoted at the start of this chapter, that the Antarctic be left for the romancers, assailable by a variety of imaginations, none of them as binding as ordinary scientific fact.

Patrick Bratlinger has written influentially of the way in which nineteenth-century imperial discourses were caught up in the 'vanishing of frontiers, the industrialisation of travel and warfare, the diminishing chances for heroism. . .'.[128] Empire needs those frontiers to justify its expansion, and therefore cannot be satiated by final discoveries. This may go some way towards explaining the retreating goalposts of exploration across the twentieth century. In 1911, humanity reached the South Pole (Amundsen used *Fram* for his trip to Antarctica), and found it a desert. The Apollo programme took us (or rather, took twelve white, male pilots and geologists) to the moon, which was also something of an anti-climax. The reaction? 'As I stand out here in the wonders of the unknown at Hadley', said Dave Scott, commander of Apollo 15, 'I sort of realize there's a fundamental truth to our nature. Man *must* explore'.[129] Spoken in July 1971, this echo of Nansen's 'Man wants to know' proclamation shows a certain persistence of rhetoric, but of course it is the reference to 'fundamental truth', ever exploration's stalwart companion, which is really interesting.

Mars is next, already being explored with probes – the spiritual descendants, perhaps, of the balloons which Munro proposed to send to the Arctic with their cargo of automated cameras. One of them, *Opportunity*, stopped off to explore the Fram Crater, named after Nansen's ship, in April 2004. 'Fram' is Norwegian for 'Forward'. A manned mission to Mars is repeatedly mooted in our contemporary mass media – SF has rehearsed it many times – and whilst the scientific value of such an undertaking is undeniable, it will be through the vexed rhetoric of exploration that we take off for wherever is next after that (there's the possibility of life under the ice of Europa, Jupiter's sixth moon. . .). The push/stretch trajectory of human exploration, and the fictions which have inspired it, suggest an observation from Barbara Fuchs's *Mimesis and Empire*:

> Viewed through the lens of chivalric romance, the conquistadors' advances in America seem the by-product of frustrated desires. Spanish expansion consists of a series of incidental conquests in a romance mode: the explorers set off for El Dorado and instead find Bolivia; they conquer Florida while seeking the Fountain of Youth. The perverse refusal of the landscape to furnish the exact object of desire does not stop the expansion, but instead propels it forward.[130]

Fuchs is writing about seventeenth-century Spanish romances, not nineteenth-century British SF, but the parallel is exact. SF in the periodical press helped to set up the cycle of 'frustrated desires' which empowered the ideology of the British Empire at its zenith, pushing explorers ever further northward towards the fathomless, receding objective of the Pole. As Paul Fayter puts it: 'Science fiction not only reflected contemporary trends, but in suggesting new scientific and technical possibilities and applications, it helped create the expectation of change'.[131] 'Expectation' is the key word in this sentence; 'jam tomorrow', to borrow an idea from Lewis Carroll. You can promise all you want for the future as long as you then keep it in the future – and the future, as I argued in Chapter 2, is something which SF and the periodicals always push away, even as they engage with it.

But if this pushing away of definite answers helps actuate the imperial impulse for continuing outwards expansion, it simultaneously constitutes an opportunity for second thought. The periodical, as I discussed in Chapter 3, distrusts unitary, definite answers. And the "definiteness" of empire was often questioned by the very publications which helped shape it. One example of this is to be found in Jerome K. Jerome's *Letters to Clorinda*. Published serially in *The Idler* when Jerome was still editor, each letter is an eclectic mix of Jerome's thoughts that month; a series of ruminations, often connected only extremely loosely, characterised by their quick wit and the occasional moment of profundity. In the April 1896 issue, from which this example is taken, Nansen had been unheard of for almost three years. Jerome begins the piece light-heartedly, wryly discussing the New Woman and bicycles, and slowly his discussion moves round to the idea, one he sees as backed by science, that human progress is a cumulative process building to a glorious, undefined future. 'Through sorrow and through struggle', he writes, 'by the sweat of brain and brow, he will lift himself towards the angels. He will come into his kingdom'.[132] This is the philosophical (and evolutionary) equivalent of the pattern of cumulative exploration which I have outlined, but Jerome is not slow to question it:

> But why the building? Why the passing of the countless ages? [. . .] Why the Pict and Hun that I may be here? Why me, that a child of my own, to whom I shall seem a savage, may come after me? Why, if the universe be ordered by a Creator, to whom all things are possible, the protoplasmic cell? Why not the man that is to be? Shall all the generations be so much human waste that he may live? Am I but the soil preparing for him?
>
> Or if our future is in other spheres, then why the need of this world?[133]

Here, in the *Idler*, a less establishment-driven periodical than the others examined in this chapter, the "jam tomorrow" approach of the political orthodoxy is really on trial. Jerome's answer to his own question is a curious one – maybe it is not for us to understand, he says: 'May be, we are as school children asking, "Of what use are these lessons?" [. . .] So perhaps when we are a little more grown up, we too may begin to understand the reason for our tasks' (p. 474). Immediately after this optimism, though, he turns abruptly to nostalgia:

> I shall be half sorry if it prove true that Nansen has discovered the North Pole. The world grows so small, and with its shrinkage life grows small, also, to us. Think what existence must have meant to the lad of two thousand years ago who dared and dreamed. All things were possible to him.[134]

Jerome concludes his letter, offhandedly, with the line 'Wells is pushing rapidly to the front. In some of his shorter stories he is as good as Kipling at his best' (p. 475). This is a joke about the evolutionary ideas which Jerome has just been playing with, but there's also the hint in it that approval of empire (Kipling) is beginning to be overtaken by a voice which sought to subject its ethos to scrutiny (Wells).

'May Nansen live to make more such expeditions', wrote Le Gallienne, after the explorer completed his adventure, 'but, for his own sake, may he never reach the pole'.[135] If this speaks to the imperial need never to meet its own mythic goals (*Fram*; forwards), it also speaks to the periodical's formal resistance to the notion of being defined by one, overriding coherence – whether of truth or of empire. In the very act of giving it a voice, the periodical also cautions us to be sceptical of that very human impulse to continually organise things into estranged, warring, mutually exclusive territories. This is a way in which the *fin-de-siècle* periodical speaks to its twenty-first century readers as well as to its contemporaries. It reminds us, among other things, to think carefully about the voice which tells us, always and forever, that the *next* hurdle is the big one, that the *next* peak, island, or planet is the final goal. Jam tomorrow. It's possible to know everything. All it will take is one more little step, further northwards.

Conclusion: bad science and the study of English

Throughout this book, I have been arguing that the hybrid textual space provided by Standard Illustrated Popular Magazines has an important place in the history of both science fiction and the "two culture" divide. In the last two chapters, though, I have also suggested that although diverse in the spread of genres represented, these publications were far from *limitlessly* inclusive. They gave only seriously stymied expression to women, offered no voice at all to ethnic minorities, were pitched firmly and finally at middle class readers, and edited almost exclusively by white, male imperialists; they echoed entirely the 'segregated cultural space' which Richard Ohmann identifies in American magazines of the same period.[1] For all the commitment to democracy which made them such an awkward site for science, they were nevertheless thoroughly enmeshed in the overriding discourses of empire.

Habermas found things to admire in the eighteenth-century public sphere even whilst condemning its elitism, and I hope it is no huge surprise to find elitism on display in these magazines too: this is an historically specific discussion, and the New Journalism was primarily a commercial enterprise producing reading for metropolitan consumers at the zenith of the British Empire. Precisely these commercial concerns, though, combined with the wide-ranging enthusiasms of the implied readers, necessarily led to a print environment that was simultaneously conservative and experimental, homogeneous and heterogeneous, homophonic and polyphonic, chaotic and clear. They reified a colonial ideal which they also sometimes undermined, and they thrived commercially whilst laying the conceptual groundwork for their own obsolescence.

This is all testimony to a claim I have been repeating from the start: magazines have a formal advantage in their ability to hold contradictions in suspension. The magazine is conflicted – never more so than when active in the service of both heteroglossia and empire – but able to function despite that conflict and perhaps even because of it. It's a claim that, after book-length scrutiny, I am inclined to try making from a slightly different angle: the fact that the magazines worked, that they cohere in spite the variety of material entangled within them, suggests that there is mileage in not taking very seriously binary pairs like those mentioned in the previous paragraph. The magazines' suspended contradictions might conceivably say less about their power to resist binaries than it does about the fact that, intrinsically to the human condition, these binaries do not exist at all. We have built them round ourselves, enrolled them, assumed they were real, and acted accordingly. Both as an analogy and as an historical process, magazines allow us to see that fact.

We think in binaries for good reason and with productive results, and the division of knowledge into a series of either/or propositions, as I said at the start, has on the whole been beneficial. But it shows how far down this road we have come that the 1882 speech which declares that '[a]*ll* knowledge is, as I said just now, interesting' is currently seen as the opening salvo in the debate which would forever sunder literary and scientific thought.[2] Matthew Arnold, the author of those words, is now supposed (following enrolment) to have been prefiguring the fundamental opposition which C. P. Snow would cast into infamy in 1959: his speech was part of a spat with T. H. Huxley, and spats are easy to think about and to remember. Read in full, though, Arnold actually sounds more like George Levine, whom I quoted on this subject in Chapter 1 (p. 61, earlier), especially at the moment when he holds that no person is as simple as an oppositional hierarchy of knowledges presupposes:

> [E]very one knows how we seek naturally to combine the pieces of our knowledge together, to bring them under general rules, to relate them to principles; and how unsatisfactory and tiresome it would be to go on for ever learning lists of exceptions, or accumulating items of fact which must stand isolated.[3]

The general magazine imperfectly reflects the complexity of our inner voices, its commercial impetus for mass appeal producing an object which can address many sides of an individual as well as many individuals in a society. Yet for all its insistence on this array of difference – different subject matter, different ontologies, and different genres – the periodical still reaches us as a coherent single entity, rendered commensurate by the eliding circumstances of editing, materiality, and politics of which it is a product. The periodical, then, shares with binary opposition (and human individuals) the quality of appearing (and therefore being) coherent on a macro level but fostering enormous inner complexity once examined up close. Perhaps this is what bestows upon it that powerful contradiction-suspending ability.

My notion has been that we may ask the periodical to hold one more contradiction in suspension: that we may ask it to teach us about the historical processes of division and subdivision – the imperial processes of enrolment, categorisation, and exploration which it both documented and materially contributed to – *and* to provide us with a model by which these processes may be exposed and resisted. The construction of opposites is an invitation to conflict: the magazine, meanwhile, offers a formal opportunity for peace whilst at the same time preserving difference. Its commercial insistence on variety is translatable into a theoretical framework which revels in, rather than deplores, the diffuseness of human thought and experience. I said early in this book that I am arguing for complexity: for nuance over generalisation and for inconsistency over the fantasy of coherence. We all need generalised categories in order to advance and order our thinking in this world – there is already too much for any one of us to know – but remaining aware of the histories and mechanics of those categories, or at least of the fact that they *have* histories and mechanics, can prevent us from using them imperially, from shutting down conversation. In this aspect, studying the periodical can augment a role which Patrick Parrinder has long claimed for the study of SF more widely: 'SF may provoke reflection', he suggests, 'on the social and historical contingencies which have led to an arts/science split where rationally none need exist'.[4]

Addressing that 'split' specifically, it may at first seem as if my focus on contradiction is symptomatic of a typical literary-critical failure to understand science properly. In science, there is surely no room for productive vagaries like those I have suggested: certain questions about the universe have unambiguously right and wrong answers. To assume this, however, is to confuse the process of science with the verifiable body of knowledge which it generates. In fact, that body of knowledge is augmented rather than restricted by a culture in which all pronouncements are open to contradiction:

> . . .real science is all about critically appraising the evidence for somebody else's position. That's what happens in academic journals. That's what happens at academic conferences. The Q&A session after a postdoc presents data is often a blood bath. And nobody minds that. We actively welcome it.[5]

GP and author Ben Goldacre here highlights a foundational aspect of the scientific process. Scientific truth is, Latour would say, 'composed' out of the prevailing discourses in a storm of discussion and exchange, not out of blank, incontestable facts nakedly arising in a sterile laboratory. As I argued in Chapter 2, it is this characteristic which makes the journal the format of scientific progress, which is best thought of as an ongoing construction rather than a list of definite answers. When I began this study, I was not expecting to find an abiding interest in the location of truth so routinely at the centre of any periodical encounter between science and fiction, but each of my four themes eventually led me back there. Magazines provided a staging ground for debates around truth by materially entangling the voices in a conversation which would set the precedent for twentieth-century publishing on both sides of the "two cultures". Themselves partial in this conversation, magazines established an imperial tone for the genre exchanges between facts, fictions, and knowledges whilst at the same time furnishing us with formal and historical tools with which to resist it.

A straightforward binary is always hiding something, as Goldacre, whose catchphrase in *Bad Science* is 'I think you'll find it's a bit more complicated than that', is keenly aware.[6] Goldacre's understanding of this complexity is evident in the fact that, despite his declared scepticism of the humanities, he acts in his book as an adroit cultural critic, seeking social as well as empirical solutions to a problem – the media's mishandling of science – which is ultimately as much about the activity of science in culture as it is about scientific practices. Throughout the book, Goldacre problematises media reporting of supposed new miracle treatments by drawing attention to the complex social dimension of disease. This underlies his explanation of the placebo effect, in which social expectations effect measurable medical outcomes (pp. 81–82), and it is also in focus when he turns to the political dimension of pseudoscience, pointing out that bogus research is often conducted or publicised in order to reinforce dominant ideologies, especially those of class (pp. 132–33). He is strongest on the cultural roots of bad science, though, in an early passage which links detox regimes to religious cleansing rituals, worth quoting at length:

> The presentation of these purification diets and rituals has always been a product of their time and place, and now that science is our dominant explanatory framework for the natural and moral world, for right or wrong, it's natural that we should bolt a bastardised pseudoscientific justification onto our redemption. Like so much of the nonsense in bad science, "detox" pseudoscience isn't something done *to* us, by venal and exploitative outsiders: it is a cultural product, a recurring theme, and we do it to ourselves.[7]

The problem to which Goldacre addresses himself has an enormous cultural dimension. That scholarship in the humanities can contribute to understanding it – its precedents, mechanics, and solutions – has been an implicit argument of this book, and I have been trying to show in my examination of the media portrayal of science at the *fin de siècle* what such a study might look like.

For all his personal disavowal of the practices of the humanities, Goldacre actually makes a sustained and persuasive argument for critical reading – of the press as well as of scientific papers.[8] *Bad Science* has at its centre the message that science in the media needs to be approached anything other than passively, that the general readers to whom today's press addresses itself lack the skills and/or motivation rigorously to follow up on specious claims, investigate the studies quoted in the news, or interrogate the politics which may underlie a specific reporter's choice to emphasise or deemphasise certain kinds of story. Repeatedly, Goldacre stresses that niche expertise is not necessary to perform this kind of basic reading. At the same time, media figures such as Patrick Holford and Gillian McKeith, whom he identifies as charlatans, are significant not so much because of the damage they can do to impressionable individuals as because they represent 'a menace to the public understanding of science'.[9] It is at this point, perhaps, with the cultural valency of disease, the media's implication in the spread of scientific misinformation, and the value of acute reading all prominently on the table, that the study of English Literature is positioned to be of significant use.

Matthew Arnold was keen to point out that the study of *belles lettres* was not necessarily limited to canonical works: 'Literature is a large word; it may mean everything written with letters or printed in a book. Euclid's *Elements* and Newton's *Principia* are thus literature'.[10] Despite the cultural turn, this epiphany has yet to fully emerge into public perceptions of English Studies, and even undergraduate curricula remain largely – although very far from wholly – populated with those literary works which were self-consciously written as such. Rightly so: the many merits of studying capital-L literature are not at issue here. But a sense that the skills honed in such study are applicable also to the myriad texts encountered outside university is something comparatively few literature students seem to take away with them, even though universities proudly vaunt the capacity for critical thought as one of the principle benefits of humanistic study.

When I bring this up with my own students, as I frequently do when we discuss Victorian literature and science, their reaction is often discomfort.

At least where I teach, English undergraduates are instinctively historicists: they want to learn about Literature and about past societies, and science occurs to them most frequently as yet another context through which to illuminate the great works. It is not routinely their desire to reverse the proposition, treating "great works" as a lens through which present-day public disputes might be rigorously analysed. Yet the literary critic's eye is as usefully turned towards this morning's internet adverts as it is to the yellowing pages of a Hugo or a Dickens, and the processes which make the two activities seem so different are, as I have been suggesting, themselves historical, themselves the product of work which is open to interrogation. My undergraduates report that their historical and literary proclivities – the ways in which they conceive their work and its purpose – create frequent moments of social tension with their scientist peers despite shared flats, shared social groups, shared romances. English students don't work hard or produce anything valuable, we all know that; equally common knowledge is the dogmatism, or insularity, or damaging narrow-ness of focus of the scientist. Conceive of the bizarreness of this situation: that a group of people with so much in common should so seldom be able to see it.

Seeing it, and thinking about it head-on, should be something that English Studies is good at. It should produce graduates who can think clearly and critically about the way knowledge is constructed around us, who can and do read acutely those constructions wherever they may emerge, and who do not allow their preconceptions to get the better of them whatever their eventual walk of life.

With his emphasis on the damage caused by ignorance and unwillingness to learn, and his keenness for the introduction of evidence-based medicine into schools and museums, Goldacre is fundamentally interested in *education*; it is too often forgotten that educational policy (rather than abstract disciplinary demarcation) was the subject of the original two cultures debates between Arnold and Huxley, Snow and Leavis. It is also a favourite subject of Stefan Collini who, in a recent book about the purpose of universities, writes that '[t]he mind is engaged much more fully by trying to understand something that initially resists our categories than by encoun-tering a further instance of what is already familiar'.[11] Collini's book is also a reminder that the battles between disciplines are about economics as much as territory: the increasingly corporate nature of British universities casts them as rivals rather than allies to each other, pits departments and individual scholars against each other in competition for funding, and measures the worth of research in terms of its measurable economic and cultural "impact".[12] All of this is a profound distraction from the wide-ranging enthusiasm underlying the claim that 'all knowledge is, as I said just now, interesting'.

When scrutinised, general magazines of the *fin de siècle* evince a similar weakness before the authoritarian (fiscal) power discourses of a totalising ideology. But such scrutiny also gives the lie to the notion adopted for intellectual and bureaucratic convenience that human modes of pursuing knowledge are necessarily and fundamentally divergent. As Ludmilla Jordanova has written:

> We know all too well that we are the inheritors of long, weighty traditions that separate out types of knowledge, institutions and practices, making it necessary for us to join, by scholarly means, what was put asunder by historical processes.[13]

Jordanova stresses that this is not an easy enterprise. I suggest that the classroom is where it could most profitably be conducted. Goldacre – correctly, in my view – places much of the blame for the media's poor understanding of science on the shoulders of the humanities graduates who run journalism, people who leave university having never been asked to question the assumptions of the two culture divide, having never been invited to find science interesting, having been implicitly instructed (often since primary school) that no aptitude can encompass the mutually exclusive fields of art and science.[14] Specific ignorance of scientific facts is less damaging here than a general failure to apprehend the ways in which science goes about making its claims. Despite its track record in perpetuating this state of affairs, English Studies is nevertheless ideally positioned to improve it, to produce graduates capable of critically reading science and fiction as they appear in culture, materially entangled in the media. Without claiming expertise in scientific subjects – without thinking imperially – we can show connections, reveal historical associations, shed light on ideological commonalities. A first step in doing so is to avoid the language of conflict, to caution against the easy opposition of categories of knowledge.

One way of resisting the marketisation of the academy is to continue to think outside the boxes in which its institutional architecture places us. By the same token, the path to be beaten in improving relations between disciplines and the universities' standing with the general public is to educate our students – on both "sides" – about the deficiencies of dyadic division, and about the complex nature of the general interest afforded by the study of people and things.

Notes

Introduction

1 Ashley, *The Age of the Storytellers*, 197.

2 Stableford, Clute, and Nicholls, 'Definitions of SF'.

3 My use of 'material entanglements', here and throughout this book, was developed in ignorance of N. Katherine Hayles's 2011 article of that name. Hayles does not develop the term, which occurs only in her title, except by implication: it concerns the relationship between materiality and the database in a 2007 slipstream novel by Steven Hall. A different focus from mine here, but not a contradictory one – indeed, I believe that the two of us are grasping at some of the same issues, and so elected to leave my phraseology unchanged. C.f. Hayles, 'Material Entanglements'.

4 Collini, 'Introduction', lx–lxi. Emphasis original. **Unless otherwise stated, all italicised words within quotations in this book are original.**

5 Latour, *Pandora's Hope*, 17. For an account of the 'science wars', see for e.g. Sokal, *Beyond the Hoax*, 115–17.

6 Grove, 'Universities "worse than Bankers"'.

7 Habermas, *The Structural Transformation of the Public Sphere*, 50.

8 Goldacre, *Bad Science*, 224–25. For more on this work, please refer to the conclusion of the present volume.

9 Ohmann, *Selling Culture*, 13.

10 1891 was the year that the *Strand's* appearance changed magazine publishing; it was changed again by the appearance of the first pulps (*The Grand Magazine* and *The Novel Magazine*) in 1905. These incidents set my notional start and end dates, but I have no wish to isolate the period they demarcate and have not been puritanical in sticking to them.

11 See Ashley, *The Age of the Storytellers*, 3.

12 Ashley's *The Age of the Storytellers* has full entries on all of these magazines. In general, I refer to explicit publication details only when they are directly relevant to my arguments.

13 Reed, *The Popular Magazine in Britain and the United States*, 98.

14 Ashley, *The Age of the Storytellers*, 197.

15 Good circulation data for Britain in this period are hard to come by, and 300,000 is a conservative figure. See Reed, *The Popular Magazine in Britain and the United States*, 96.
16 Arnold, 'Up to Easter', 347.
17 See Mussell, 'New Journalism', 443.
18 Reed, *The Popular Magazine in Britain and the United States*, 17.
19 For the variegated appeal of New Journalism, see Wiener, 'How New Was the New Journalism?', 55–56. On general interest and wide-ranging enthusiasm as a scholarly paradigm, see pp. 53–61 of this work.
20 Turner, 'Toward a Cultural Critique of Victorian Periodicals', 112.
21 Holquist, 'Introduction', xxi.
22 'The prehistory of the novelistic word is not to be contained within the narrow perimeters of a history confined to mere literary styles'. Bakhtin, 'From the Prehistory of Novelistic Discourse', 83.
23 Liddle, *The Dynamics of Genre*, 153.
24 Frow, *Genre*, 48.
25 Anderson, *Imagined Communities*, 35.
26 Reed, *The Popular Magazine in Britain and the United States*, 16.
27 For yet another defence of noting shared interests over proof of direct influence, see Kern, *The Culture of Time and Space*, 8.
28 Parrinder, *Science Fiction: Its Criticism and Teaching*, 136–37.
29 Gernsback, 'A New Sort of Magazine', 3.
30 Parrinder, *Science Fiction: Its Criticism and Teaching*, 2.
31 'How good this magazine will be in the future is up to you. [...] We will welcome constructive criticism - for only in this way will we know how to satisfy you'. Gernsback, 'A New Sort of Magazine', 3.
32 Ashley, *The Time Machines*, 4.
33 Moskowitz, *Science Fiction by Gaslight*, 11.
34 Bould and Vint, *The Routledge Concise History of Science Fiction*, 2.
35 See Latour, *The Pasteurization of France*.
36 Bould and Vint, 'Learning from the Little Engines That Couldn't'.
37 Bould and Vint, *The Routledge Concise History of Science Fiction*, 6–16.
38 On Gernsback's loss of control over SF, see Ashley, 'Science Fiction Magazines: The Crucibles of Change', 63–64. There are critics who would doubtless say that I have given Gernsback far too much individual credit in my account – see, for instance, Westfahl and Mullen, 'An Exchange: Hugo Gernsback and His Impact on Modern Science Fiction'.
39 'Unfortunately today the very existence of the SF magazine is largely unknown to the vast science fiction market'. Ashley, 'Science Fiction Magazines: The Crucibles of Change', 60.
40 Brake, *Subjugated Knowledges*, xi.
41 This process is further abetted by research libraries, many of which remove paratexts such as contents pages and advertising supplements. It is also unusual for those digitising periodicals to spend time scanning things deemed 'ephemeral'. See 101 of the present volume for more discussion of this.

42 Bowker and Star, *Sorting Things Out*, 9. John Rieder precedes me in applying Bowker and Star's understanding of categories to SF – see Rieder, 'On Defining SF, or Not', 203.
43 Beer, *Darwin's Plots*, 2.
44 At time of writing. For an up-to-date figure, see www.sf-encyclopedia.com/ entry/statistics.
45 Latour, *Pandora's Hope*, 1–3.
46 Anderson, *Imagined Communities*, 6.
47 See Stableford, Clute, and Nicholls, 'Definitions of SF'.
48 Kincaid, 'On the Origins of Genre', 409–10.
49 Aldiss, *Billion Year Spree*, 8.
50 Frow, *Genre*, 2.
51 Baldick, *The Oxford Dictionary of Literary Terms*, 140.
52 Rieder, 'On Defining SF, or Not', 199.
53 Frow, *Genre*, 2.
54 Miller, 'Genre as Social Action', 159.
55 Bakhtin, 'Epic and Novel', 33.
56 Miller, 'Genre as Social Action', 153.
57 Frow, *Genre*, 140.
58 '[T]he relationships here [are] no longer [. . .] those of extension, from exemplary individual to species, from species to genre or genus or from the genre of genre to genre in general; rather, as we shall see, these relationships are a whole order apart'. Derrida, 'The Law of Genre', 58–59.
59 White, 'The Four White Days'; White, 'The Four Days' Night'; White, 'The Dust of Death'; White, 'A Bubble Burst'; White, 'The Invisible Force'; White, 'The River of Death'.
60 'The knowledge a century hence that London derived its water supply from an open river into which many towns conveyed its sewage will be recorded with pitiful amazement'. White, 'The River of Death', 619.
61 Fleming, 'The Problem of Inebrity'; MacCracken, 'An Antiphony in Orange and Red'; Stead, 'Government by Journalism'.
62 It is on this point – the social insight available through a genre reading of demotic rather than capital-L literary fiction in periodicals – that my argument most closely resembles that of Richard Ohmann, whose study of American magazines in the same period has different priorities but nevertheless reads very well (I hope) alongside the present volume. For a view on the role of periodicals in the USA's *fin de siècle*, in particular as they reflected embedded ideologies of class, I therefore commend to the reader Ohmann's *Selling Culture*. On the specific issue of literary value, see p. 337 in particular.
63 Luckhurst, *Science Fiction*, 16.
64 For a recent book-length summary of activity in this field, see Willis, *Literature and Science*.
65 The American Society for Literature, Science, and the Arts (SLSA) was founded in 1985 (as the Society for Literature and Science). The British Society of Literature and Science (BSLS) followed in 2005. The BSLS is closely

associated with the *Journal of Literature and Science* (published electronically from the University of Westminster), the SLSA with *Configurations* (Johns Hopkins University Press). The inauguration of the BSLS and the differences between it and the SLSA are discussed in Dawson, 'Literature and Science under the Microscope'.

66 Whitworth, 'Roundtable: Versions of History, Versions of Chronology', 72.
67 Sleigh, *Literature and Science*, x–xi.
68 Westfahl and Slusser, *Science Fiction and the Two Cultures*.
69 Cantor et al., *Science in the Nineteenth-Century Periodical*; Mussell, *Science, Time and Space in the Late Nineteenth-Century Periodical Press*.
70 See, for instance, Fyfe and Lightman, *Science in the Marketplace*.
71 Sell, *Sell's Dictionary* (1891), 12; Sell, *Sell's Dictionary* (1907), 8.
72 'Rather than the principal means through which readers accessed representations of the world and so made sense of their place within it, these print genres become reduced to series of individual articles, standing alone against an undifferentiated cultural background'. Mussell, *The Nineteenth-Century Press in the Digital Age*, 31.
73 '...not all or even most instances of text in a genre need to be read closely because most uses of a genre – especially journalistic ones – only reproduce ready-made meanings already contained in the genre itself'. Liddle, *The Dynamics of Genre*, 154.
74 Kern, *The Culture of Time and Space*, 4.
75 Bakhtin, 'Epic and Novel', 33.
76 Smith, *The Journalism of H. G. Wells*.
77 McLean, *The Early Fiction of H. G. Wells*, 1.
78 On the interdependence of nineteenth-century markets of books and serials, see Brake, *Print in Transition*.

Chapter 1

1 Addison, 'Is Mars Inhabited?', 442.
2 For a detailed account of Galton's life, see Galton, *Memories of My Life*; Pearson, *The Life, Letters and Labours of Francis Galton*.
3 Galton, 'Sun Signals to Mars', 7.
4 Ibid.
5 Galton, 'Intelligible Signals', 657.
6 Galton, 'Draft Letter to the "Spectator"'.
7 Galton, 'Intelligible Signals', 657.
8 Ibid.
9 Ibid., 660.
10 Ibid., 663.
11 See Turner, *Trollope and the Magazines*, 121.
12 Saintsbury, *A History of Nineteenth Century Literature (1780–1895)*, 382.
13 *Fortnightly Review* 1, no. 1 (May 15, 1865): inside cover.
14 Galton, 'Intelligible Signals', 658.

15 See Rubery, *The Novelty of Newspapers*, 23–45.

16 Galton, 'Intelligible Signals', 659.

17 Rubery, *The Novelty of Newspapers*, 14.

18 On the 'novum', see Suvin, *Metamorphoses of Science Fiction*.

19 Poe, 'The Murders in the Rue Morgue', 99.

20 Rubery, *The Novelty of Newspapers*, 12.

21 Wells, 'Popularising Science', 301.

22 Galton, 'Intelligible Signals', 661.

23 Ibid., 658.

24 Galton, 'Signals', 16; 17.

25 Galton, 'Intelligible Signals', 659.

26 Ibid., 662–63.

27 Arnold, 'Up to Easter', 348.

28 Wiener, 'Papers for the Millions', xii.

29 Beer, *Darwin's Plots*, xxv.

30 Courtney to Galton, 2 October 1896.

31 I have not seen Galton's reply, but Courtney's response to it was to write again, saying: 'By all means let your article stand as it is at present. Mine was only a suggestion for you to consider'. Courtney to Galton, 12 October 1896.

32 Fayter, 'Strange New Worlds of Space and Time', 257.

33 Galton, 'Signals', 18–19.

34 See, for example, Bleiler, *Science-Fiction, the Early Years*, 796–97.

35 Wells, 'Human Evolution, An Artificial Process', 592.

36 Wells, 'Popularising Science', 300.

37 Wells, 'Human Evolution, An Artificial Process', 595.

38 Wells, 'Popularising Science', 300.

39 Ibid., 301.

40 Wells, 'Human Evolution, An Artificial Process', 594.

41 Wells, 'Stories of the Stone Age: Ugh-Lomi and Uya'; Wells, 'Stories of the Stone Age: Ugh-Lomi and the Cave Bear'; Wells, 'Stories of the Stone Age: The First Horseman'; Wells, 'Stories of the Stone Age: The Reign of Uya the Lion'; Wells, 'Stories of the Stone Age: The Fight in the Lion's Thicket'.

42 Suvin, *Metamorphoses of Science Fiction*, 7–8.

43 Wells, 'Stories of the Stone Age: Ugh-Lomi and Uya', 418.

44 Wells, 'The War of the Worlds', April 1897, 364.

45 Galton's article is mentioned in *The First Men in the Moon*, whose heroes attempt a similar means of algebraic communication with the Selenites. This is yet another example of Galton's non-fiction resonating with popular culture – and of Wells using current scientific thinking as a basis for his fiction. The most fascinating thing about this reference, though, is that Wells treats the piece as non-fiction, describing it as a 'paper', with no hint given of its fantastical or narrative components. Wells, 'The First Men in the Moon', March 1901, 281; McLean, *The Early Fiction of H. G. Wells*, 132–33.

46 Worth, 'Imperial Transmissions: H. G. Wells, 1897–1901', 72; Wells, 'The War of the Worlds', April 1897, 370.

47 Wells, 'The War of the Worlds', May 1897, 488.

48 Worth, 'Imperial Transmissions: H. G. Wells, 1897–1901', 70–71.

49 Broks, *Media Science before the Great War*, 30.

50 Ibid., 131.

51 Lightman, 'The Voices of Nature', 189.

52 Crossley, *Imagining Mars*, chapter 7.

53 [Stead], 'News from Mars', 406.

54 'Probably most persons will agree in regarding these communications as a confirmation of Tennyson's judgment' – this judgement apparently being (Stead quotes Tennyson's son) 'that the spectroscope was destined to make much greater revelations even than it had already made'. Ibid.

55 Ibid.

56 Ibid., 408.

57 Habermas, *The Structural Transformation of the Public Sphere*, 50.

58 Galton, 'Signals', 23; Galton, 'Intelligible Signals', 658.

59 Crossley, *Imagining Mars*, 89.

60 Galton, 'The Just-Perceptible Difference', 8.

61 Broks, *Media Science before the Great War*, 101.

62 Menke, *Telegraphic Realism*, 6.

63 Fyfe, 'Signalling through Space', 114.

64 Henniker Heaton, 'Postal and Telegraphic Progress under Queen Victoria', 845.

65 Stead, 'My System', 296.

66 'Let us bear two facts in mind, the one is that a very large quantity of telegraphic information is daily published in the papers, anticipating the post by many days or weeks. The other is that pictorial illustrations of current events of a rude kind, but acceptable to the reader, appear from time to time in the daily papers. We may be sure that the quantity of telegraphic intelligence will steadily improve and be more resorted to'. Galton, 'The Just-Perceptible Difference', 7.

67 All of this, of course, bears intriguingly on the subject of empire. See Worth, 'Imperial Transmissions: H. G. Wells, 1897–1901', 78. See also Chapter 4 of the present volume.

68 Galton, 'Intelligible Signals', 664.

69 Galton, 'Signals', 24.

70 Galton, 'The Just-Perceptible Difference', 4.

71 'Carl Sagan'.

72 Ruston, 'Introduction', 6.

73 Holmes, *The Age of Wonder*, xvi.

74 Schmidt, 'Pearson's Magazine', 311.

75 For more on Cecil Arthur Pearson and the founding of his magazines, see Dark, *The Life of Sir Arthur Pearson*.

76 Galton, 'Intelligible Signals', 658.

77 *Fortnightly Review* 1, no. 1 (15 May 1865): inside cover.

78 Turner, *Trollope and the Magazines*, 106.

79 Rubery, *The Novelty of Newspapers*, 12.

80 Broks, *Media Science before the Great War*, 131.
81 Mussell, *The Nineteenth-Century Press in the Digital Age*, 18.
82 Liddle, *The Dynamics of Genre*, 5.
83 Levine, 'Looking for the Real', 15.
84 Calhoun, 'Introduction: Habermas and the Public Sphere', 25.
85 Levine, 'Introduction', 2.
86 Galton, 'Intelligible Signals', 664.

Chapter 2

1 Moskowitz, *Science Fiction by Gaslight*, 12.
2 Beaumont, *Utopia Ltd.*, 194.
3 '...the differences between the style of dress and furniture of the two epochs are not more marked than I have known fashion to make in the time of one generation'. Bellamy, *Looking Backward*, 45.
4 Wells, 'Anticipations', 747.
5 Brake, *Print in Transition*, 16.
6 Ashley, *The Age of the Storytellers*, 3.
7 'We treat the title of a periodical or newspaper as if it names a single, coherent work and treat individual issues as if they manifest this corporate identity. However, as the definition of the work depends on the material artefacts that document it, the identity of the work changes with the publication of every issue'. Mussell, *The Nineteenth-Century Press in the Digital Age*, 10.
8 Turner, 'Periodical Time in the Nineteenth Century', 192.
9 Turner, 'Time, Periodicals, and Literary Studies', 311.
10 Sawyer, 'Tales of Futures Passed', 117.
11 Kipling, 'With the Night Mail', December 1905, 52.
12 Ibid.
13 Ibid., 66. My emphases.
14 See Sawyer, 'Tales of Futures Passed', 121.
15 Sawyer glosses the superficial differences between the three texts. He has taken the volume edition as his preferred text, and therefore (writing in 2005) makes something of the millennial associations. I have favoured the *Windsor* version – the first appearance of the story before a London audience. However, as Sawyer also notes, there seem to be no substantive discrepancies between the actual texts of the different versions. Ibid., 272 (note 14).
16 Kipling, 'With the Night Mail', December 1905, 52.
17 The American version of the story is Kipling, 'With the Night Mail', November 1905.
18 Kipling, *With the Night Mail*, 1909.
19 For example, in Kipling, *Actions and Reactions*.
20 On this and what follows, see Sawyer, 'Tales of Futures Passed', 119–20.
21 Robinson, 'Chronicles in Cartoon', 35.
22 Ibid., 51.

23 Bull, 'An Artist in Bermuda', 80.

24 Kipling, 'With the Night Mail', December 1905, 54.

25 Bull, 'An Artist in Bermuda', 80.

26 A first-hand account of Kipling's early career can be found in Kipling, *Something of Myself*, 36–57.

27 On infodump, see Clute, Wessells, and Langford, 'Infodump'.

28 Sawyer, 'Tales of Futures Passed', 118.

29 For instance, Luckhurst, *Science Fiction*, 45; Bleiler, *Science-Fiction, the Early Years*, 408.

30 Bell, 'A Journey Through Space', 111.

31 Kipling, 'With the Night Mail', December 1905, 57.

32 Periodicals, George Levine reminds us, are 'more important than books to practicing scientists'. Levine, 'Why Science Isn't Literature', 180.

33 Cox and Forshaw, *Why Does E=mc²?*, xv–xvi. My emphases.

34 Levine, 'Defining Knowledge', 15. For more on how the present tense unites science and fiction, see Beer, *Darwin's Plots*, 43.

35 Bell, 'A Journey Through Space', 115.

36 Kipling, 'With the Night Mail', December 1905, 64.

37 [Ward], 'London in 1930: A Forecast', 573.

38 Ibid., 574.

39 Ibid., 572.

40 Sawyer, 'Tales of Futures Passed', 125.

41 Nicholls and Langford, 'Prediction'.

42 [Ward], 'London in 1930: A Forecast', 575.

43 Arkas, 'A Twentieth Century Dinner', 362.

44 Burgin, 'The Horseless Future', 581.

45 Oswald, 'Cities of the Future', 424.

46 Ibid., 421.

47 Medawar, 'An Essay on Scians', 4.

48 The first weather map appeared in the *Times* on April 1, 1875. It was prepared, incidentally, by Francis Galton, whose wide-ranging enthusiasm is the subject of Chapter 1.

49 Oswald, 'Cities of the Future', 424.

50 Ibid., 422.

51 Ibid., 423–24.

52 Nicholls and Langford, 'Time Machine'.

53 Wells, 'The Time Machine', January 1895, 98.

54 Legg, 'New Review'.

55 Wells, 'The Time Machine', January 1895, 98.

56 The January 1895 *New Review* can be read online by those with access to ProQuest's *British Periodicals Collection 2*, although at the time of writing Wells's contributions have been redacted for copyright reasons. http://search .proquest.com/docview/6948417.

57 Some characters are also changed: Filby is no longer described as a poet, and the Rector has been replaced with a 'Very Young Man'. There is also the addition of a 'Provincial Mayor'. Wells, *The Time Machine*, 2005, 1–7.

58 Wells, 'The Time Machine', January 1895, 100.
59 Turner, 'Time, Periodicals, and Literary Studies', 311.
60 Wells, 'The Time Machine', January 1895, 100.
61 Zangwill, 'Without Prejudice', 153.
62 Wells, 'The Time Machine', April 1895, 456.
63 Wells, 'The Time Machine', May 1895, 579.
64 Ibid., 584.
65 Printing fourteen of Wells's articles in 1893 alone. See Smith, *The Journalism of H. G. Wells*, 76–77.
66 Wells, 'The Time Machine', May 1895, 586–87.
67 Mussell, *Science, Time and Space in the Late Nineteenth-Century Periodical Press*, 95.
68 My point about the contemporary audience's lack of plot foreknowledge is complicated in this specific instance by the prior publication of *The Chronic Argonauts* (also in a periodical, *The Science Schools Journal*, April–June 1888), in which Wells rehearsed many of the ideas which would eventually make their way into *The Time Machine*. This earlier work, however, was never concluded – a danger of the modern serial format's qualities of suspense with which present-day television viewers will also be familiar.
69 Levine, *The Serious Pleasures of Suspense*, 3.
70 See Dawson, 'Literary Megatheriums and Loose Baggy Monsters'.
71 Levine, *The Serious Pleasures of Suspense*, 47.
72 Suvin, *Metamorphoses of Science Fiction*, 7–8.
73 Wells, 'The Time Machine', January 1895, 102.
74 Levine, *The Serious Pleasures of Suspense*, 9.
75 Wells, 'The Time Machine', May 1895, 584.
76 Wells, 'The Time Machine', January 1895, 109.
77 Clute, 'Club Story'.
78 Bakhtin, 'Epic and Novel', 15.
79 Ibid., 30.
80 Bakhtin, 'Forms of Time and of the Chronotope in the Novel', 84.
81 See also Brake and Codell, 'Encountering the Press'.
82 Bakhtin, 'Epic and Novel', 27.
83 Ibid., 23.
84 Mussell, *The Nineteenth-Century Press in the Digital Age*, 31.
85 Wells, 'Anticipations', 747.
86 [Ward], 'London in 1930: A Forecast', 574.
87 Moskowitz, *Science Fiction by Gaslight*, 13.
88 For one account of the history of Steampunk, including (chapter 2) its relationship with Verne and Wells, see VanderMeer and Chambers, *The Steampunk Bible*. For a sense of Steampunk's aesthetic impact beyond literature, see Dr. Grymm, *1000 Steampunk Creations*.
89 Sawyer, 'Tales of Futures Passed', 125.
90 Latour, *Pandora's Hope*, 172.
91 Sawyer, 'Tales of Futures Passed', 127.
92 Kern, *The Culture of Time and Space*, 29.

Chapter 3

1 [Stead], 'Throughth', 426.
2 For a summary of Stead on the occult both in the *Review* and elsewhere, see Luckhurst, 'W. T. Stead's Occult Economies', 127.
3 [Stead], 'Throughth', 427.
4 Porter, 'The New Photography', 116.
5 Dam, 'A Wizard of To-Day', 419.
6 Röntgen, 'On a New Kind of Rays', 276.
7 Grove, 'Röntgen's Ghosts', 142.
8 Luckhurst, 'W. T. Stead's Occult Economies', 125.
9 For a discussion of Einstein in popular fiction, for example, and one which also discusses the 'fourth dimension', see Price, 'On the Back of the Light Waves: Novel Possibilities in the "Fourth Dimension"'.
10 Barthes, *Camera Lucida*, 26.
11 Grove, 'Röntgen's Ghosts', 142.
12 Kern, *The Culture of Time and Space*, 7.
13 'Sozodont Advertisement', ix.
14 Flint, *The Victorians and the Visual Imagination*, 30.
15 Benjamin, 'A Short History of Photography', 7.
16 Flint, *The Victorians and the Visual Imagination*, 30.
17 Chappell and Bringhurst, *A Short History of the Printed Word*, 195.
18 On the value of ephemera, particularly in 'strip[ping] away the aura of neutral disinterestedness from what is now defined as the high culture of its day', see Brake, *Print in Transition,* xiii.
19 Reed, *The Popular Magazine in Britain and the United States,* 42. See pp. 28–45 of this work for an in-depth discussion of this subject.
20 For more on the changes in commercial printing during this period, see Twyman, *Printing 1770–1970,* 95–97; 104.
21 Beare, *Index to the Strand Magazine, 1891-1950,* xiv.
22 Latour, *Pandora's Hope,* 304.
23 'The New Patent Sound Discs Advertisement'.
24 Clarke, *Profiles of the Future: An Inquiry into the Limits of the Possible,* 36.
25 Sontag, *On Photography,* 14.
26 Meade and Halifax, 'The Snake's Eye'.
27 Damstruther and Pain, 'The Treble-X Rays', 678.
28 Alden, 'Wisdom Let Loose', May 1896, 524.
29 Damstruther and Pain, 'The Treble-X Rays', 679.
30 Weber, 'Henry Labouchere, "Truth" and the New Journalism of Late Victorian Britain', 40.
31 Alden, 'Wisdom Let Loose', May 1896, 526.
32 Stead, 'Psychic Photography', 317.
33 Damstruther and Pain, 'The Treble-X Rays', 678.
34 '. . .a (long) story or tale: sometimes implying one of a marvellous or incredible kind; also, a mere tale'. *Oxford English Dictionary Online,* s.v. 'yarn', accessed 28 April 2015. www.oed.com/view/Entry/231240.

35 Stead, 'Miscellaneous', 200–1.
36 Stead, 'Psychic Pictures without the Camera', 27.
37 Stead, 'Psychic Photography', 312.
38 Stead, 'Miscellaneous', 200.
39 [Stead], '"Borderland"', 677. My emphases.
40 Ibid., 678.
41 Another early appearance of the idea which became *Borderland*: 'A periodical which surveyed the whole obscure field with the calm and impartial eye of the scientific enquirer, which investigated all phenomena without prejudice or superstition, might considerably enlarge the sphere of human knowledge, and reduce to something like scientific certainty many crude ideas on things now supposed to be almost unknowable'. Stead, 'Preface', 6.
42 Dam, 'A Wizard of To-Day', 418.
43 Ibid.
44 Ibid., 415–16.
45 Ibid., 414.
46 Griffith, 'A Photograph of the Invisible', 378.
47 Ibid., 380.
48 'When it is first advanced, [scientific] theory is at its most fictive'. Beer, *Darwin's Plots,* 1.
49 Griffith, 'A Photograph of the Invisible', 377.
50 Pearson, 'The Editorial Mind', 352A. My emphases.
51 Dam, 'A Wizard of To-Day', 414.
52 Compton, 'Mr. Frederic Villiers', 246.
53 On the mixture of images in American periodicals during this period, and their uses of photography, see Ohmann, *Selling Culture,* 234–36.
54 Beegan, *The Mass Image,* 5.
55 Ibid., 8.
56 Reed, *The Popular Magazine in Britain and the United States,* 96.
57 Mussell, 'Science and the Timeliness of Reproduced Photographs in the Late Nineteenth-Century Periodical Press', 214.
58 Tindal, 'Skeleton Leaves', 494.
59 Stead, 'The Future of Journalism', 664.
60 Beegan, *The Mass Image,* 165.
61 For a discussion of truth values in war illustration during this period, see Wilkinson, *Depictions and Images of War in Edwardian Newspapers, 1899–1914.*
62 Grove, 'Röntgen's Ghosts', 144.
63 Barthes, *Camera Lucida,* 32.
64 Meade and Eustace, 'The Star-Shaped Marks', 664.
65 Ibid., 662.
66 Meade and Halifax, 'The Snake's Eye', 60.
67 Crosthwaite, 'Röntgen's Curse', 472.
68 Ashley, *The Age of the Storytellers,* 258.
69 For an overview of the X-rays in Wells's novella, see Grove, *'Röntgen's Ghosts',* 169.

70 'You May See Them On Bank Holiday'. Pearson's Weekly no. 368 (7 August 1897): 56.
71 Wells, 'The Invisible Man', 31 July 1897, 41.
72 Wells, 'The Invisible Man', 12 June 1897, 777.
73 Wells, 'The Invisible Man', 7 August 1897, 56. My emphases.
74 Wells, *The Invisible Man*, 1897, 278.
75 See Wiener, 'How New Was the New Journalism?', 52.
76 Grove, 'Röntgen's Ghosts', 143.
77 Calhoun, 'Introduction: Habermas and the Public Sphere', 9.
78 Sontag, *On Photography*, 6.
79 Wells, 'The Invisible Man', 24 July 1897, 26.
80 Stead, 'Psychic Pictures without the Camera', 29.
81 *The Photogram* published a special issue called 'The New Light and the New Photography' in February 1896; the term recurs throughout the magazines, including in science publications such as *Nature*.
82 Worth, 'Imperial Transmissions: H. G. Wells, 1897-1901', 69.
83 Mussell, *Science, Time and Space in the Late Nineteenth-Century Periodical Press*, 34.
84 For a thorough discussion of Stead's investigative journalism in this regard, see Boston, 'W. T. Stead and Democracy by Journalism'.
85 Stead, 'The Future of Journalism', 664.
86 Stead, 'Psychic Photography', 317.
87 Stead, 'Government by Journalism', 669.
88 Kern, *The Culture of Time and Space*, 152.
89 Luckhurst, 'W. T. Stead's Occult Economies', 125.
90 Hari, 'My Journalism Is at the Centre of a Storm. This Is What I Have Learned'.
91 O'Neill, 'Johann Hari and the Tyranny of the "Good Lie"'.
92 Sontag, *On Photography*, 59.

Chapter 4

1 Kern, *The Culture of Time and Space*, 164.
2 [Stead], '"How I Shall Start for the North Pole" by Dr. Nansen', 265.
3 Editorial note in Nansen, 'Towards the North Pole', 614.
4 Ibid., 614; 615.
5 Huntford, 'Introduction', xi.
6 Conan Doyle, 'The Adventure of the Final Problem', 570; Nansen, 'Towards the North Pole', 622.
7 Conan Doyle, 'The Adventure of the Final Problem', 567.
8 Conan Doyle, 'The Adventure of the Empty House', 368.
9 Bain, 'A Talk with Dr. Nansen', 695.
10 Nansen, 'Towards the North Pole', 623.
11 Verne, *Twenty Thousand Leagues Under the Seas*, 312.

12 Shelley, *Frankenstein*, 5; 6.
13 Nansen, 'Towards the North Pole', 623; 621.
14 Hill, *White Horizon*, 3.
15 Porter, *The Lion's Share*, 10.
16 Moss, *Scott's Last Biscuit: The Literature of Polar Travel*, 26.
17 Alden, 'Wisdom Let Loose', May 1896, 525–26.
18 Verne, *Twenty Thousand Leagues Under the Seas*, 312.
19 Griffith, 'From Pole to Pole', 533.
20 Le Gallienne, 'Wanderings in Bookland', 404.
21 Latour, *Pandora's Hope*, 61.
22 Munro, 'How I Discovered the North Pole', 483.
23 Ibid., 484.
24 'A full account of the expedition will be given in a book which I am about to publish, including the narrative of our adventures, fac-similies of the photographs, and the scientific observations'. Ibid., 489.
25 Ibid., 486.
26 Ibid., 489.
27 Stam and Stam, 'Bending Time', 302 and 321. See this article in full for an account of the numerous periodical practices taken by polar explorers cut off from the circuit of magazines.
28 Latour, *Pandora's Hope*, 64.
29 Huntford, 'Introduction', viii.
30 For an account of the Andrée expedition, and of ballooning generally, see Rolt, *The Aeronauts*.
31 Story, 'Mr. Andrée's Balloon Voyage to the North Pole', 77.
32 Munro, 'How I Discovered the North Pole', 486.
33 Story, 'Mr. Andrée's Balloon Voyage to the North Pole', 91.
34 For a summary of the Moon Landing "Hoax", see for eg. Plait, *Bad Astronomy*, 155–73.
35 Munro, 'How I Discovered the North Pole', 483.
36 Ibid., 484.
37 Hill, *White Horizon*, 5.
38 Codell, 'Imperial Co-Histories', 16.
39 Bain, 'A Talk with Dr. Nansen', 694.
40 Ibid., 309.
41 Bain, 'The Nansens', 306.
42 Qtd. in Whymper, 'Nansen and the North Pole', 31.
43 Bain, 'The Nansens', 308.
44 Qtd. in Whymper, 'Nansen and the North Pole', 32.
45 See, for instance, Pettitt, *Doctor Livingstone, I Presume?*.
46 Hill, *White Horizon*, 20.
47 'They arrived at Vardö at half-past four in the afternoon of August 13, having got clear of ice in fifty-two hours after leaving Franz Josef Land!' Whymper, 'Nansen and the North Pole', 32.

48 Munro, 'How I Discovered the North Pole', 489.
49 For the Native American in nineteenth-century British popular culture, see Flint, *The Transatlantic Indian, 1776–1930*, 161–66.
50 Bratlinger, *Rule of Darkness*, 39.
51 Hill, *White Horizon*, 3.
52 Ball, 'The Wanderings of the North Pole', 173.
53 Conrad, 'Heart of Darkness'.
54 Alden, 'Very Cold Truth', 252.
55 Ibid., 254.
56 Ibid.
57 Alden, 'Wisdom Let Loose', January 1896, 97.
58 Alden, 'Very Cold Truth', 253.
59 Alden, 'Wisdom Let Loose', January 1896, 97.
60 Alden, 'Very Cold Truth', 256.
61 Ball, 'The Wanderings of the North Pole', 173.
62 Stam and Stam, 'Bending Time', 317.
63 Bain, 'The Nansens', 309–10.
64 Ball, 'The Wanderings of the North Pole', 174.
65 Moss, *Scott's Last Biscuit: The Literature of Polar Travel*, 2.
66 See Kern, *The Culture of Time and Space*, 12.
67 Griffith, 'A Corner in Lightning', 264.
68 Ibid., 266.
69 Ibid., 265.
70 Gleick, 'At the Beginning: More Things in Heaven and Earth', 27.
71 Griffith, 'A Corner in Lightning', 270.
72 Latour, *Pandora's Hope*, 258.
73 Midgley, *Science and Poetry*, 36–37.
74 Luckhurst and McDonagh, 'Encountering Science', 9.
75 Bain, 'A Talk with Dr. Nansen', 694.
76 Harrison, *Fram*, 24.
77 Bain, 'The Nansens', 305.
78 Latour, *Pandora's Hope*, 18. In the original, this whole passage is italicised.
79 Ibid., 16.
80 Ibid., 17.
81 Bain, 'The Nansens', 306–7.
82 Bain, 'Mrs. Nansen', 596.
83 Latour, *Pandora's Hope*, 244.
84 Bain, 'A Talk with Dr. Nansen', 694.
85 Cox, Holmes, and Rosenthal, 'Platforms: Frankenstein's Science'. My transcription.
86 Schulman, 'Cryopolitics', 16.
87 'Canada to Strengthen Arctic Claim'.
88 Moss, *Scott's Last Biscuit: The Literature of Polar Travel*, 238.
89 Drummond, 'A Secret of the South Pole', 613.
90 Ibid., 618.

91 McCorristine, 'The Supernatural Arctic: An Exploration', 52.

92 Drummond, 'A Secret of the South Pole', 619.

93 Ibid., 612.

94 Myers, 'On Board A Cable Hospital', 628.

95 McCorristine, 'The Supernatural Arctic: An Exploration', 51.

96 Conan Doyle, 'The Glamour of the Arctic', 633.

97 'glamour | glamor, n'.. *OED Online*. March 2015. Oxford University Press. www.oed.com/view/Entry/78690 (accessed 8 May 2015).

98 Conan Doyle, 'The Glamour of the Arctic', 632.

99 Ibid., 638.

100 Ibid.

101 Ibid., 632.

102 Conan Doyle, 'Life on a Greenland Whaler', 21.

103 Conan Doyle, 'The Glamour of the Arctic', 626.

104 Ibid.

105 Conan Doyle, 'Life on a Greenland Whaler', 23.

106 Conan Doyle, 'The Glamour of the Arctic', 627.

107 Large, unfathomable alien intelligences are ubiquitous in SF, but even if we limit ourselves merely to "Space Whales" we can see recent examples in the TV show *Farscape* (1999–2003) and the 2010 *Doctor Who* episode 'The Beast Below'. Perhaps the most famous SF whales appear in *Star Trek IV: The Voyage Home* (1986) in which it is revealed that humpbacks are an alien race living on earth.

108 Conan Doyle, 'The Glamour of the Arctic', 629.

109 Conan Doyle, 'Life on a Greenland Whaler', 21.

110 Story, 'Harnessing the Stars', 585.

111 Ibid.

112 Masefield, 'Sea-Fever', 59.

113 Huntford, 'Introduction', vii.

114 Wells, 'The First Men in the Moon', December 1900, 698.

115 Wells, 'The First Men in the Moon', April 1901, 402.

116 Wells, 'The First Men in the Moon', May 1901, 500.

117 Wells, *The First Men in the Moon*, 1901, 223.

118 See McLean, *The Early Fiction of H. G. Wells*, 131–32.

119 Worth, 'Imperial Transmissions: H. G. Wells, 1897–1901', 78.

120 Wells, 'The First Men in the Moon', December 1900, 704.

121 Wells, 'The First Men in the Moon', January 1901, 32.

122 Ibid., 36.

123 See Rieder, *Colonialism and the Emergence of Science Fiction*.

124 Fernandes and al-Ayad, *We See A Different Frontier*, 4.

125 Reed, *The Popular Magazine in Britain and the United States*, 11.

126 Le Gallienne, 'Wanderings in Bookland', 403.

127 Drew, 'The North Pole Up to Date: A Sketch', 740.

128 Bratlinger, *Rule of Darkness*, 43.

129 Jones, 'Deploying the Lunar Roving Vehicle'.

130 Fuchs, *Mimesis and Empire: The New World, Islam, and European Identities*, 18–19.
131 Fayter, 'Strange New Worlds of Space and Time', 258.
132 Jerome, 'Letters to Clorinda', 473.
133 Ibid.
134 Ibid., 474.
135 Le Gallienne, 'Wanderings in Bookland', 405.

Conclusion

1 Ohmann, *Selling Culture*, 233.
2 Arnold, 'Literature and Science', 62. My emphasis.
3 Ibid., 62–63.
4 Parrinder, *Science Fiction: Its Criticism and Teaching*, 134–35.
5 Goldacre, 'Battling Bad Science'. See also Goldacre, *Bad Science*, 317.
6 Goldacre, *Bad Science*, 100.
7 Ibid., 12.
8 'In fact, as you know, I claim no special expertise whatsoever: I hope I can read and critically appraise medical academic literature – something common to all recent medical graduates – and I apply this pedestrian skill to the millionaire businesspeople who drive our culture's understanding of science'. Ibid., 134.
9 Ibid., 116.
10 Arnold, 'Literature and Science', 58.
11 Collini, *What Are Universities For?*, 11.
12 For a recent study that discusses far more fully the role of the humanities in similar terms, see chapter 1 in particular of Small, *The Value of the Humanities*.
13 Jordanova, 'And?: Essay Review', 345.
14 See Goldacre, *Bad Science*, 224–25.

Bibliography

Addison, P. L. 'Is Mars Inhabited?'. *Pall Mall Magazine* 7, no. 31 (November 1895): 442–48.

Alden, W. L. 'Very Cold Truth'. *The Idler* 11, no. 2 (March 1897): 252–58.

'Wisdom Let Loose'. *Pearson's Magazine* 1, no. 1 (January 1896): 97–101.

'Wisdom Let Loose'. *Pearson's Magazine* 1, no. 5 (May 1896): 524–28.

Aldiss, Brian W. *Billion Year Spree*. London: Corgi Books, 1973.

Anderson, Benedict. *Imagined Communities: Reflections on the Origin and Spread of Nationalism*. Rev. ed. London: Verso, 2006.

Arkas, Alfred. 'A Twentieth Century Dinner: Foods of the Future'. *Harmsworth Monthly Pictorial* 2, no. 10 (May 1899): 361–64.

Arnold, Matthew. 'Literature and Science'. In *Philistinism in England and America*, edited by R. H. Super, x: 53–73. *The Complete Prose Works of Matthew Arnold*. Ann Arbor: University of Michigan Press, 1974.

'Up to Easter'. In *Essays, Letters and Reviews by Matthew Arnold*, edited by Fraser Neiman, 338–54. Cambridge, MA: Harvard University Press, 1960.

Ashley, Mike. *The Age of the Storytellers: British Popular Fiction Magazines 1880–1950*. London: The British Library, 2006.

'Science Fiction Magazines: The Crucibles of Change'. In *A Companion to Science Fiction*, edited by David Seed, 60–76. Malden, MA: Blackwell Publishing, 2005.

The Time Machines: The Story of the Science-Fiction Pulp Magazines from the Beginning to 1950. Liverpool: Liverpool University Press, 2000.

Bain, J. Arthur. 'Mrs. Nansen'. *Strand Magazine* 12, no. 71 (November 1896): 593–96.

'The Nansens'. *The Idler* 9, no. 2 (March 1896): 304–13.

'A Talk with Dr. Nansen'. *Strand Magazine* 12, no. 72 (December 1896): 693–702.

Bakhtin, Mikhail. 'Epic and Novel: Toward a Methodology for the Study of the Novel'. In *The Dialogic Imagination*, edited by Michael Holquist, translated by Cary Emerson and Michael Holquist, 3–40. Austin, TX: University of Texas Press, 1981.

'Forms of Time and of the Chronotope in the Novel: Notes Toward a Historical Poetics'. In *The Dialogic Imagination*, edited by Michael Holquist, translated by Cary Emerson and Michael Holquist, 84–258. Austin, TX: University of Texas Press, 1981.

'From the Prehistory of Novelistic Discourse'. In *The Dialogic Imagination*, edited by Michael Holquist, translated by Cary Emerson and Michael Holquist, 41–83. Austin, TX: University of Texas Press, 1981.

Baldick, Chris. *The Oxford Dictionary of Literary Terms*. 3rd ed. Oxford: Oxford University Press, 2008.

Ball, Robert S. 'The Wanderings of the North Pole'. *Fortnightly Review* 54, no. 320 (August 1893): 171–83.

Barthes, Roland. *Camera Lucida*. London: Vintage, 2000.

Beare, Geraldine. *Index to the Strand Magazine, 1891-1950*. Westport, CT: Greenwood Press, 1982.

Beaumont, Matthew. *Utopia Ltd.: Ideologies of Social Dreaming in England, 1870–1900*. Leiden: Brill, 2005.

Beegan, Gerry. *The Mass Image: A Social History of Photomechanical Reproduction in Victorian London*. Basingstoke: Palgrave Macmillan, 2008.

Beer, Gillian. *Darwin's Plots: Evolutionary Narrative in Darwin, George Eliot and Nineteenth-Century Fiction*. 3rd ed. Cambridge: Cambridge University Press, 2009.

Bellamy, Edward. *Looking Backward: 2000–1887*. Boston: Houghton Mifflin, 1889.

Bell, Walter George. 'A Journey Through Space'. *Windsor Magazine* 23, no. 132 (December 1905): 111–15.

Benjamin, Walter. 'A Short History of Photography'. Translated by Stanley Mitchell. *Screen* 13, no. 1 (Spring 1972): 5–26.

Bleiler, Everett F. *Science-Fiction, the Early Years*. Kent, OH: Kent State University Press, 1990.

Boston, Ray. 'W. T. Stead and Democracy by Journalism'. In *Papers for the Millions: The New Journalism in Britain, 1850s to 1914*, edited by Joel H. Wiener, 91–106. Westport, CT: Greenwood Press, 1988.

Bould, Mark, and Sherryl Vint. 'Learning from the Little Engines That Couldn't: Transported by Gernsback, Wells and Latour'. *Science Fiction Studies* 33, no. 1 (March 2006): 129–48.

The Routledge Concise History of Science Fiction. London: Routledge, 2011.

Bowker, Geoffrey C., and Susan Leigh Star. *Sorting Things Out: Classification and Its Consequences*. Cambridge, MA: The MIT Press, 1999.

Brake, Laurel. *Print in Transition, 1850–1910: Studies in Media and Book History*. Basingstoke: Palgrave, 2001.

Subjugated Knowledges: Journalism, Gender and Literature in the Nineteenth Century. Basingstoke: Macmillan, 1994.

Brake, Laurel, and Julie F. Codell. 'Encountering the Press'. In *Encounters in the Victorian Press*, 1–7. Basingstoke: Palgrave Macmillan, 2005.

Bratlinger, Patrick. *Rule of Darkness: British Literature and Imperialism, 1830–1914*. Ithaca, NY: Cornell University Press, 1988.

Broks, Peter. *Media Science before the Great War*. Basingstoke: Macmillan, 1996.

Bull, Charles Livingston. 'An Artist in Bermuda'. *Windsor Magazine* 23, no. 132 (December 1905): 78–83.

Burgin, G. B. 'The Horseless Future'. *The Idler* 9, no. 4 (May 1896): 577–81.

Calhoun, Craig. 'Introduction: Habermas and the Public Sphere'. In *Habermas and the Public Sphere*, edited by Craig Calhoun, 1–48. Cambridge, MA: The MIT Press, 1992.

'Canada to Strengthen Arctic Claim'. *BBC News*, 10 August 2007. http://news .bbc.co.uk/1/hi/world/americas/6941426.stm.

Cantor, Geoffrey, Gowan Dawson, Graeme Gooday, Richard Noakes, Sally Shuttleworth, and Jonathan R. Topham, eds. *Science in the Nineteenth-Century Periodical: Reading the Magazine of Nature*. Cambridge: Cambridge University Press, 2004.

'Carl Sagan'. *Great Lives*. BBC Radio 4, 18 May 2010.

Chappell, Warren, and Robert Bringhurst. *A Short History of the Printed Word*. 2nd ed. Point Roberts, WA: Hartley & Marks, 1999.

Clarke, Arthur C. *Profiles of the Future: An Inquiry into the Limits of the Possible*. London: Victor Gollancz, 1982.

Clute, John. 'Club Story'. *Science Fiction Encyclopedia*, 26 December 2012. http:// sf-encyclopedia.com/entry/club_story.

Clute, John, Henry Wessells, and David Langford. 'Infodump'. *Science Fiction Encyclopedia*, 27 July 2013. http://sf-encyclopedia.com/entry/infodump.

Codell, Julie F. 'Imperial Co-Histories and the British and Colonial Press'. In *Imperial Co-Histories: National Identities and the British and Colonial Press*, 15–26. Madison, WI: Fairleigh Dickinson University Press, 2003.

Collini, Stefan. 'Introduction'. In *The Two Cultures*, by C. P. Snow, vii–lxxi. edited by Stefan Collini. Cambridge: Cambridge University Press, 1998.

What Are Universities For?. London: Penguin, 2012.

Compton, Roy. 'Mr. Frederic Villiers'. *The Idler* 12, no. 2 (September 1897): 238–55.

Conan Doyle, Arthur. 'The Adventure of the Empty House'. *Strand Magazine* 26, no. 154 (October 1903): 363–76.

'The Adventure of the Final Problem'. *Strand Magazine* 6, no. 36 (December 1893): 558–70.

'Life on a Greenland Whaler'. *Strand Magazine* 13, no. 73 (January 1897): 16–25.

'The Glamour of the Arctic'. *The Idler* 1, no. 6 (July 1892): 624–38.

Conrad, Joseph. 'Heart of Darkness'. In *Heart of Darkness and Other Tales*, edited by Cedric Watts, 101–87. Oxford: Oxford University Press, 2002.

Courtney, W. L. Letter to Francis Galton, 2 October 1896. 241/9. The Galton Papers, UCL Library Services, Special Collections.

Letter to Francis Galton, 12 October 1896. 241/9. The Galton Papers, UCL Library Services, Special Collections.

Cox, Brian, and Jeff Forshaw. *Why Does E=mc²?*. Cambridge, MA: Da Capo Press, 2009.

Cox, Brian, Richard Holmes, and Daniel Rosenthal. 'Platforms: Frankenstein's Science'. *National Theatre*, London, 4 March 2011.

Crossley, Robert. *Imagining Mars: A Literary History*. Middletown, CT: Wesleyan University Press, 2011.

Crosthwaite, C. H. T. 'Röntgen's Curse'. *Longman's Magazine* 28, no. 167 (September 1896): 468–85.

Dam, H. J. W. 'A Wizard of To-Day'. *Pearson's Magazine* 1, no. 4 (April 1896): 413–19.

Damstruther, Archibald Mosely, and Barry Pain. 'The Treble-X Rays'. *Pearson's Magazine* 9, no. 54 (June 1900): 677–80.

Dark, Sidney. *The Life of Sir Arthur Pearson*. London: Hodder and Stoughton, 1922.

Dawson, Gowan. 'Literary Megatheriums and Loose Baggy Monsters: Paleontology and the Victorian Novel'. *Victorian Studies* 53, no. 2 (Winter 2011): 203–30.

'Literature and Science under the Microscope'. *Journal of Victorian Culture* 11, no. 2 (2006): 301–15.

Derrida, Jacques. 'The Law of Genre'. Translated by Avital Ronell. *Critical Inquiry* 7, no. 1 (Autumn 1980): 55–81.

Drew, Andrew A. W. 'The North Pole Up to Date: A Sketch'. *English Illustrated Magazine*, no. 118 (July 1893): 735–40.

Dr. Grymm. *1000 Steampunk Creations*. Beverly, MA: Quarry Books, 2011.

Drummond, Hamilton. 'A Secret of the South Pole'. *Windsor Magazine* 15 (April 1902): 612–20.

Fayter, Paul. 'Strange New Worlds of Space and Time: Late Victorian Science and Science Fiction'. In *Victorian Science in Context*, edited by Bernard Lightman, 256–80. Chicago: University of Chicago Press, 1997.

Fernandes, Fabio, and Djibril al-Ayad, eds. *We See A Different Frontier*. Futurefire.net Publishing, 2013.

Fleming, The Rev. Canon. 'The Problem of Inebrity: Is There a Cure?'. *Pearson's Magazine* 15, no. 88 (April 1903): 449–52.

Flint, Kate. *The Transatlantic Indian, 1776–1930*. Princeton: Princeton University Press, 2009.

The Victorians and the Visual Imagination. Cambridge: Cambridge University Press, 2000.

Frow, John. *Genre*. London: Routledge, 2005.

Fuchs, Barbara. *Mimesis and Empire: The New World, Islam, and European Identities*. Cambridge: Cambridge University Press, 2001.

Fyfe, Aileen, and Bernard Lightman, eds. *Science in the Marketplace: Nineteenth-Century Sites and Experiences*. Chicago: University of Chicago Press, 2007.

Fyfe, Herbert C. 'Signalling through Space'. *Pearson's Magazine* 8, no. 43 (July 1899): 114–22.

Galton, Francis. Draft Letter to the *Spectator*, 1892. 177. The Galton Papers, UCL Library Services, Special Collections.

'Intelligible Signals Between Neighbouring Stars'. *Fortnightly Review* 60, no. 359 (November 1896): 657–64.

'The Just-Perceptible Difference', January 1893. 154A. The Galton Papers, UCL Library Services, Special Collections.

Memories of My Life. London: Methuen & Co., 1908.

'Signals'. Notes, January 1893. 154D. The Galton Papers, UCL Library Services, Special Collections.

'Sun Signals to Mars'. *The Times*. 6 August 1892.

Gernsback, Hugo. 'A New Sort of Magazine'. *Amazing Stories* 1, no. 1 (April 1926): 3.

Gleick, James. 'At the Beginning: More Things in Heaven and Earth'. In *Seeing Further: The Story of Science and the Royal Society*, edited by Bill Bryson, 16–35. London: HarperPress, 2010.

Goldacre, Ben. *Bad Science*. 2nd ed. London: Fourth Estate, 2009.

'Battling Bad Science'. *TED.com*, July 2011. www.ted.com/talks/ben_goldacre_battling_bad_science.html.

Griffith, George. 'A Corner in Lightning'. *Pearson's Magazine* 5, no. 27 (March 1898): 264–71.

'From Pole to Pole'. *Windsor Magazine* 20, no. 118 (October 1904): 531–44.

'A Photograph of the Invisible'. *Pearson's Magazine* 1, no. 3 (April 1896): 376–80.

Grove, Allen W. 'Röntgen's Ghosts: Photography, X-Rays, and the Victorian Imagination'. *Literature and Medicine* 16, no. 2 (Fall 1997): 141–73.

Grove, Jack. 'Universities "worse than Bankers"'. *Times Higher Education*, 2 April 2015. www.timeshighereducation.co.uk/news/universities-worse-than-bankers/2019426.article.

Habermas, Jürgen. *The Structural Transformation of the Public Sphere: An Inquiry into a Category of Bourgeois Society*. Translated by Thomas Burger and Frederick Lawrence. [no place]: Polity Press, 1989.

Hari, Johann. 'My Journalism Is at the Centre of a Storm. This Is What I Have Learned.' *The Independent*, 29 June 2011. www.independent.co.uk/opinion/commentators/johann-hari/johann-hari-my-journalism-is-at-the-centre-of-a-storm-this-is-what-i-have-learned-2304199.html.

Harrison, Tony. *Fram*. London: Faber & Faber, 2008.

Hayles, N. Katherine. 'Material Entanglements: Steven Hall's "The Raw Shark Texts" as Slipstream Novel'. *Science Fiction Studies* 38, no. 1 (March 2011): 115–33.

Henniker Heaton, J. 'Postal and Telegraphic Progress under Queen Victoria'. *Fortnightly Review* 61, no. 366 (June 1897): 839–49.

Hill, Jen. *White Horizon: The Arctic in the Nineteenth-Century British Imagination*. Albany: State University of New York Press, 2008.

Holmes, Richard. *The Age of Wonder*. London: Harper Press, 2009.

Holquist, Michael. 'Introduction'. In *The Dialogic Imagination*, by Mikhail Bakhtin, xv–xxxiv. edited by Michael Holquist, translated by Cary Emerson and Michael Holquist. Austin, TX: University of Texas Press, 1981.

Huntford, Roland. 'Introduction'. In *Farthest North*, by Fridtjof Nansen. London: Duckworth, 2000.

Jerome, Jerome K. 'Letters to Clorinda'. *The Idler* 9, no. 3 (April 1896): 470–75.

Jones, Eric M. 'Deploying the Lunar Roving Vehicle'. *NASA - Apollo 15 Lunar Surface Journal*. Accessed 8 May 2015. www.hq.nasa.gov/alsj/a15/a15.lrvdep.html.

Jordanova, Ludmilla. 'And?: Essay Review'. *British Journal for the History of Science* 35 (2002): 341–45.

Kern, Stephen. *The Culture of Time and Space 1880–1918*. Cambridge, MA: Harvard University Press, 1983.

Kincaid, Paul. 'On the Origins of Genre'. *Extrapolation* 44, no. 4 (Winter 2003): 409–19.

Kipling, Rudyard. *Actions and Reactions*. London: Macmillan & Co., 1927.

——— *Something of Myself*. London: Macmillan & Co., 1937.

——— 'With the Night Mail'. *McClure's Magazine* 26 (November 1905): 23–35.

——— 'With the Night Mail'. *Windsor Magazine* 23, no. 132 (December 1905): 52–66.

——— *With the Night Mail: A Story of 2000AD (together with Extracts from the Contemporary Magazine in Which It Appeared)*. New York: Doubleday, Page & Co., 1909.

Latour, Bruno. *Pandora's Hope: Essays on the Reality of Science Studies*. Cambridge, MA: Harvard University Press, 1999.

——— *The Pasteurization of France*. Translated by Alan Sheridan and John Law. Cambridge, MA: Harvard University Press, 1988.

Le Gallienne, Richard. 'Wanderings in Bookland'. *The Idler* 11, no. 3 (April 1897): 403–7.

Legg, Marie-Lou. 'New Review'. Edited by Laurel Brake and Marysa Demoor. *Dictionary of Nineteenth-Century Journalism*. Gent: Academia Press, 2009.

Levine, Caroline. *The Serious Pleasures of Suspense: Victorian Realism and Narrative Doubt*. Charlottesville: University of Virginia Press, 2003.

Levine, George. 'Defining Knowledge: An Introduction'. In *Victorian Science in Context*, edited by Bernard Lightman, 15–23. Chicago: University of Chicago Press, 1997.

——— 'Introduction'. In *Realism, Ethics and Secularism: Essays on Victorian Literature and Science*, 1–21. Cambridge: Cambridge University Press, 2008.

——— 'Why Science Isn't Literature: The Importance of Differences'. In *Realism, Ethics and Secularism: Essays on Victorian Literature and Science*, 165–81. Cambridge: Cambridge University Press, 2008.

Liddle, Dallas. *The Dynamics of Genre: Journalism and the Practice of Literature in Mid-Victorian Britain*. Charlottesville: University of Virginia Press, 2009.

Lightman, Bernard. '"The Voices of Nature": Popularizing Victorian Science'. In *Victorian Science in Context*, 187–211. Chicago: University of Chicago Press, 1997.

Luckhurst, Roger. *Science Fiction*. Cambridge: Polity Press, 2005.

——— 'W. T. Stead's Occult Economies'. In *Culture and Science in the Nineteenth-Century Media*, edited by Lousie Henson, Geoffrey Cantor, Gowan Dawson, Richard Noakes, Sally Shuttleworth, and Jonathan R. Topham, 125–35. Aldershot: Ashgate, 2004.

Luckhurst, Roger, and Josephine McDonagh. 'Encountering Science'. In *Transactions and Encounters: Science and Culture in the Nineteenth Century*, edited by Roger Luckhurst and Josephine McDonagh, 1–15. Manchester: Manchester University Press, 2002.

MacCracken, Elizabeth. 'An Antiphony in Orange and Red'. *Pearson's Magazine* 15, no. 88 (April 1903): 443–48.

Masefield, John. 'Sea-Fever'. In *Salt-Water Ballads*, 59–60. London: Grant Richards, 1902.

McCorristine, Shane. 'The Supernatural Arctic: An Exploration'. *Nordic Journal of English Studies* 9, no. 1 (2010): 47–70.

McLean, Steven. *The Early Fiction of H. G. Wells: Fantasies of Science.* Basingstoke: Palgrave Macmillan, 2009.

Meade, L. T., and Robert Eustace. 'The Star-Shaped Marks'. *Strand Magazine* 15, no. 90 (June 1898): 649–64.

Meade, L. T., and Clifford Halifax. 'The Snake's Eye'. *Strand Magazine* 12, no. 67 (July 1896): 57–68.

Medawar, Peter. 'An Essay on Scians'. In *The Limits of Science*. Oxford: Oxford University Press, 1985.

Menke, Richard. *Telegraphic Realism: Victorian Fiction and Other Information Systems.* Stanford, CA: Stanford University Press, 2008.

Midgley, Mary. *Science and Poetry.* London: Routledge, 2001.

Miller, Carolyn R. 'Genre as Social Action'. *Quarterly Journal of Speech* 70 (1984): 151–67.

Moskowitz, Sam, ed. *Science Fiction by Gaslight: A History and Anthology of Science Fiction in the Popular Magazines, 1891–1911.* Westport, CT: Hyperion Press, 1968.

Moss, Sarah. *Scott's Last Biscuit: The Literature of Polar Travel.* Oxford: Signal Books, 2006.

Munro, J. 'How I Discovered the North Pole'. *Cassell's Magazine* 20, no. 235 (June 1894): 483–89.

Mussell, James. 'New Journalism'. Edited by Laurel Brake and Marysa Demoor. *Dictionary of Nineteenth-Century Journalism.* Ghent: Academia Press, 2009.

——— *The Nineteenth-Century Press in the Digital Age.* Basingstoke: Palgrave Macmillan, 2012.

——— 'Science and the Timeliness of Reproduced Photographs in the Late Nineteenth-Century Periodical Press'. In *The Lure of Illustration in the Nineteenth Century: Picture and Press*, edited by Laurel Brake and Marysa Demoor, 203–19. Basingstoke: Palgrave Macmillan, 2009.

——— *Science, Time and Space in the Late Nineteenth-Century Periodical Press: Movable Types.* Aldershot: Ashgate, 2007.

Myers, A. Wallis. 'On Board a Cable Hospital'. *Windsor Magazine* 15 (April 1902): 621–28.

Nansen, Fridtjof. 'Towards the North Pole'. *Strand Magazine* 6, no. 36 (December 1893): 614–24.

Nicholls, Peter, and David Langford. 'Prediction'. *Science Fiction Encyclopedia*, 3 April 2015. http://sf-encyclopedia.com/entry/prediction.

——— 'Time Machine'. *Science Fiction Encyclopedia*, 12 October 2012. http://sf-encyclopedia.com/entry/time_machine.

Ohmann, Richard. *Selling Culture: Magazines, Markets, and Class at the Turn of the Century.* London: Verso, 1996.

O'Neill, Brendan. 'Johann Hari and the Tyranny of the "Good Lie"'. *The Telegraph Blogs*, 29 June 2011. http://blogs.telegraph.co.uk/news/brendanoneill2/100094506/johann-hari-and-the-tyranny-of-the-good-lie/.

Oswald, F. L. 'Cities of the Future'. *The Idler* 9, no. 3 (April 1896): 421–26.

Parrinder, Patrick. *Science Fiction: Its Criticism and Teaching*. London: Methuen, 1980.

Pearson, C. A. 'The Editorial Mind'. *Pearson's Magazine* 1, no. 3 (March 1896): 352A.

Pearson, Karl. *The Life, Letters and Labours of Francis Galton*. 3 vols. Cambridge: Cambridge University Press, 1914.

Pettitt, Clare. *Doctor Livingstone, I Presume?: Missionaries, Journalists, Explorers, and Empire*. Cambridge, MA: Harvard University Press, 2007.

Plait, Philip. *Bad Astronomy: Misconceptions and Misuses Revealed, from Astrology to the Moon Landing 'Hoax'*. New York: John Wiley & Sons, 2002.

Poe, Edgar Allan. 'The Murders in the Rue Morgue'. In *Selected Tales*, edited by David Van Leer, 92–122. Oxford: Oxford University Press, 1998.

Porter, Alfred W. 'The New Photography'. *Strand Magazine* 12, no. 67 (July 1896): 107–17.

Porter, Bernard. *The Lion's Share: A Short History of British Imperialism*. 4th ed. Harlow: Pearson Longman, 2004.

Price, Katy. 'On the Back of the Light Waves: Novel Possibilities in the "Fourth Dimension".' In *Literature and Science*, edited by Sharon Ruston, 91–110. Cambridge: D. S. Brewer, 2008.

Reed, David. *The Popular Magazine in Britain and the United States 1880–1960*. London: The British Library, 1997.

Rieder, John. *Colonialism and the Emergence of Science Fiction*. Middletown, CT: Wesleyan University Press, 2008.

'On Defining SF, or Not: Genre Theory, SF, and History'. *Science Fiction Studies* 37, no. 2 (July 2010): 191–209.

Robinson, B. Fletcher. 'Chronicles in Cartoon: A Record of Our Own Times'. *Windsor Magazine* 23, no. 132 (December 1905): 35–51.

Rolt, L. T. C. *The Aeronauts: A History of Ballooning 1783–1903*. London: Longmans, 1966.

Röntgen, W. C. 'On a New Kind of Rays'. *Nature* 53, no. 1369 (23 January 1896): 274–76.

Rubery, Matthew. *The Novelty of Newspapers*. Oxford: Oxford University Press, 2009.

Ruston, Sharon. 'Introduction'. In *Literature and Science*, edited by Sharon Ruston, 1–12. Cambridge: D. S. Brewer, 2008.

Saintsbury, George. *A History of Nineteenth Century Literature (1780–1895)*. London: Macmillan, 1896.

Sawyer, Andy. 'Tales of Futures Passed: The Kipling Continuum and Other Lost Worlds of Science Fiction'. In *World Weavers: Globalization, Science Fiction, and the Cybernetic Revolution*, edited by Gary Westfahl and Amy Kit-sze Chan with Wong Kin Yuen, 113–34. Hong Kong: Hong Kong University Press, 2005.

Schmidt, Barbara Quinn. 'Pearson's Magazine'. In *British Literary Magazines*, edited by Alvin Sullivan, 3: 310–13. Westport, CT: Greenwood Press, 1984.

Schulman, Zachary Nathan. 'Cryopolitics: The New Geopolitics of the Northwest Passage and Implications for Canadian Sovereignty'. MA, George Washington University, 2009. http://gradworks.umi.com/14/67/1467471.html.

Sell, Henry, ed. *Sell's Dictionary of the World's Press and Advertisers' Reference Book*. London: Sell's Advertising Agency, 1891.

— ed. *Sell's Dictionary of the World's Press and Advertisers' Reference Book*. London: Sell's Advertising Agency, 1907.

Shelley, Mary. *Frankenstein*. Edited by Marilyn Butler. Oxford: Oxford University Press, 1994.

Sleigh, Charlotte. *Literature and Science*. Basingstoke: Palgrave Macmillan, 2011.

Small, Helen. *The Value of the Humanities*. Oxford: Open University Press, 2013.

Smith, David C. *The Journalism of H. G. Wells: An Annotated Bibliography*. Edited by Patrick Parrinder. Haren, Netherlands: Equilibris, 2012.

Sokal, Alan. *Beyond the Hoax: Science, Philosophy and Culture*. Oxford: Oxford University Press, 2008.

Sontag, Susan. *On Photography*. London: Penguin, 1979.

'Sozodont Advertisement'. *Strand Magazine* 12, no. 67 (July 1896): ix.

Stableford, Brian, John Clute, and Peter Nicholls. 'Definitions of SF'. *Science Fiction Encyclopedia*, 2 April 2015. www.sf-encyclopedia.com/entry/definitions_of_sf.

Stam, David H., and Deirdre C. Stam. 'Bending Time: The Function of Periodicals in Nineteenth-Century Polar Naval Expeditions'. *Victorian Periodicals Review* 41, no. 4 (Winter 2008): 301–22.

Stead, W. T. 'The Future of Journalism'. *Contemporary Review* 50 (November 1886): 663–79.

— 'Government by Journalism'. *Contemporary Review* 49 (May 1886): 653–74.

— 'My System'. *Cassell's Magazine*, August 1906, 292–97.

— 'Preface'. In *Index to the Periodical Literature of the World (Covering the Year 1891)*, 5–6. London: Review of Reviews, 1892.

— ed. 'Miscellaneous'. *Borderland* 4, no. 2 (April 1897): 200–6.

— ed. 'Psychic Photography'. *Borderland* 3, no. 3 (July 1896): 313–21.

— ed. 'Psychic Pictures without the Camera: A Confirmation of the Dorchagraph Discovery'. *Borderland* 4, no. 1 (January 1897): 26–32.

[Stead, W. T.]. '"Borderland", A New Quarterly Review and Index'. *Review of Reviews* 7 (June 1893): 675–78.

— '"How I Shall Start for the North Pole" by Dr. Nansen'. *Review of Reviews* 4, no. 21 (September 1891): 265.

— 'News from Mars'. *Borderland* 4, no. 4 (October 1897): 406–9.

— 'Throughth; Or, on the Eve of the Fourth Dimension'. *Review of Reviews* 7 (April 1893): 426–32.

Story, Alfred T. 'Harnessing the Stars'. *Pearson's Magazine* 2, no. 11 (November 1896): 585–92.

'Mr. Andrée's Balloon Voyage to the North Pole'. *Strand Magazine* 12, no. 67 (July 1896): 77–91.

Suvin, Darko. *Metamorphoses of Science Fiction: On the Poetics and History of a Literary Genre*. New Haven, CT: Yale University Press, 1979.

'The New Patent Sound Discs Advertisement'. *Strand Magazine* 12, no. 67 (July 1896): viii.

Tindal, Marcus. 'Skeleton Leaves'. *Pearson's Magazine* 4, no. 23 (November 1897): 494–98.

Turner, Mark W. 'Periodical Time in the Nineteenth Century'. *Media History* 8, no. 2 (December 2002): 183–96.

'Time, Periodicals, and Literary Studies'. *Victorian Periodicals Review* 39, no. 4 (Winter 2006): 309–16.

'Toward a Cultural Critique of Victorian Periodicals'. *Studies in Newspaper and Periodical History* 3, no. 1–2 (1995): 111–25.

Trollope and the Magazines. Basingstoke: Macmillan, 2000.

Twyman, Michael. *Printing 1770–1970: An Illustrated History of Its Development and Uses in England*. London: The British Library, 1998.

VanderMeer, Jeff, and S. J. Chambers. *The Steampunk Bible: An Illustrated Guide to the World of Imaginary Airships, Corsets and Goggles, Mad Scientists, and Strange Literature*. New York: Abrams, 2011.

Verne, Jules. *Twenty Thousand Leagues Under the Seas*. Translated by William Butcher. Oxford: Oxford University Press, 1998.

[Ward], Mrs. Humphry. 'London in 1930: A Forecast'. *The Idler* 8, no. 6 (January 1896): 572–75.

Weber, Gary. 'Henry Labouchere, "Truth" and the New Journalism of Late Victorian Britain'. *Victorian Periodicals Review* 26, no. 1 (Spring 1993): 36–43.

Wells, H. G. 'Anticipations: An Experiment in Prophecy'. *Fortnightly Review* 69 (April 1901): 747–60.

The First Men in the Moon. London: George Newnes, 1901.

'The First Men in the Moon'. *Strand Magazine* 20, no. 120 (December 1900): 697–705.

'The First Men in the Moon'. *Strand Magazine* 21, nos. 121 & 123–25 (January 1901): 30–41; 279–90; 400–9; 497–507.

'Human Evolution, An Artificial Process'. *Fortnightly Review* 60, no. 358 (October 1896): 590–95.

The Invisible Man: A Grotesque Romance. New York & London: Edward Arnold, 1897.

'The Invisible Man: A Grotesque Romance'. *Pearson's Weekly*, nos. 360 & 366–68 (12 June, 24 July, 31 July, & 7 August 1897): 777–78; 25–6; 41–2; 56.

'Popularising Science'. *Nature* 50, no. 1291 (26 July 1894): 300–1.

'Stories of the Stone Age: The Fight in the Lion's Thicket'. *The Idler* 12, no. 4 (November 1897): 430–7.

'Stories of the Stone Age: The First Horseman'. *The Idler* 11, no. 6 (July 1897): 736–44.

'Stories of the Stone Age: The Reign of Uya the Lion'. *The Idler* 12, no. 1 (August 1897): 4–11.

'Stories of the Stone Age: Ugh-Lomi and the Cave Bear'. *The Idler* 11, no. 5 (June 1897): 586–94.

'Stories of the Stone Age: Ugh-Lomi and Uya'. *The Idler* 11, no. 4 (May 1897): 418–29.

'The Time Machine'. *New Review* 12, nos. 68 & 71–72 (1895): 98–112; 453–72; 577–88.

The Time Machine. Edited by Patrick Parrinder. London: Penguin, 2005.

'The War of the Worlds'. *Pearson's Magazine* 3, nos. 16–17 (April–May 1897): 363–73; 486–96.

Westfahl, Gary, and R. D. Mullen. 'An Exchange: Hugo Gernsback and His Impact on Modern Science Fiction'. *Science Fiction Studies* 21, no. 2 (July 1994): 273–83.

Westfahl, Gary, and George Slusser, eds. *Science Fiction and the Two Cultures: Essays on Bridging the Gap between the Sciences and the Humanities*. Jefferson, NC: McFarland and Company, 2009.

White, Fred M. 'The River of Death'. *Pearson's Magazine* 17, no. 102 (June 1904): 612–25.

Whitworth, Michael. 'Roundtable: Versions of History, Versions of Chronology'. *Journal of Literature and Science* 5, no. 2 (2012): 72–76.

Whymper, Edward. 'Nansen and the North Pole'. *The Leisure Hour*, November 1896, 25–32.

Wiener, Joel H. 'How New Was the New Journalism?'. In *Papers for the Millions: The New Journalism in Britain, 1850s to 1914*, edited by Joel H. Wiener, 47–71. Westport, CT: Greenwood Press, 1988.

'Introduction'. In *Papers for the Millions: The New Journalism in Britain, 1850s to 1914*, edited by Joel H. Wiener, xi–xix. New York: Greenwood Press, 1988.

Wilkinson, Glenn R. *Depictions and Images of War in Edwardian Newspapers, 1899–1914*. Basingstoke: Palgrave Macmillan, 2003.

Willis, Martin. *Literature and Science. Readers' Guides to Essential Criticism*. London: Palgrave, 2015.

Worth, Aaron. 'Imperial Transmissions: H. G. Wells, 1897–1901'. *Victorian Studies* 53, no. 1 (Autumn 2010): 65–89.

Zangwill, I. 'Without Prejudice'. *Pall Mall Magazine* 7, no. 29 (September 1895): 151–60.

Index

Crossley, Robert, 50, 55
Crosthwaite, C. H. T., 122–24

daily life, 75–76, 78
Daily Mirror, 102
Dam, H. J. W., 95, 108–10, 113–14
Darwin, Charles, 13, 29, 43, 46, 58, 107
dateline, 67, 71, 80
democracy, 4, 128–30, 182
Derrida, Jacques, 17
detective fiction, 38
disciplines
    as colonial territory, 25
    as genres, 15, 17, 21
    as historical entities, 3, 53
    effect of segregation on students, 187
    in popular press, 4, 55
dorchagraph. *See* Glendinning, Andrew
Drew, Andrew A. W., 178
Drummond, Hamilton, 164, 166, 168, 176
Du Maurier, George, 50
Dupin, C. Auguste, 37

Einstein, Albert, 73, 96
em dash, 38
empathy, 37
Encyclopedia of Science Fiction, The, 14, 76
English Illustrated Magazine, 116, 178
enrolment, 2, 12–15, 19–20, 23, 27, 62, 74, 183
ether, 95, 123
eugenics, 29, 54, 131
Eustace, Robert, 6
exploration, 25, 162–63, 173, 176, 179

fact
    as distinct from truth, 50
    place in popular press, 97
fact and fiction
    not at odds, 53, 136, 144, 164, 166
favourable opposition (astronomical
    phenomenon), 23, 28, 55
Fayter, Paul, 44, 179
feather-brainedness. *See* New Journalism
Flint, Kate, 99, 101
Fortnightly Review, 23, 31–32, 34–35, 42–47, 50,
    54, 56, 58–59, 63, 69, 153
fourth dimension, 82, 94, 96
Fram, 132, 135, 143, 148, 150–51, 178, 181
Fram Crater (Mars), 179
Framjee, 143
Franklin, John, 136, 156
Franz Joseph Land, 150
Frow, John, 9, 15–17
Fuchs, Barbara, 179
Future Fire, The, 176
Fyfe, Herbert C., 56

Galton, Francis, 23–24, 28, 31–35, 37, 39–49,
    52–61, 69, 88
    as communicator of science, 42, 44, 55
    as imaginative writer, 33, 38, 43
    as serious scientist, 33, 41
    biography of, 29
    early version of signals idea, 54, 57
    relationship to Darwin, 43
    relationship to Wells, 45–48
    struggle against own narrative. *See* narrative
        eddies
    travels in Africa, 30, 48, 54
    universal communication. *See* intrinsic
        intelligibility
    wide-ranging enthusiasm of. *See* wide-ranging
        enthusiasm
Gazette des Tribunaux, 37
general interest, 8–9, 23, 55, 60, 126
genre
    and biological taxonomy, 17
    as signalling system, 42, 60
    composed rather than essential, 13, 23, 27, 108,
        155
    conversations between, 9–10, 14, 16, 19, 31, 98,
        111, 138, 185
    economies of, 16
    individual authors considered as, 26
    of illustration, 117
    political element, 25, 59
    varying uses of the term, 2, 15–17
Gernsback, Hugo, 10–13, 19
Glendinning, Andrew, 106, 127
Goble, Warwick, 50
Goldacre, Ben, 4, 184–88
Graham's Magazine, 37
Greenland, 132, 149, 169–71
Grieg, Edvard, 162
Griffith, George, 110–11, 113–14, 123, 140, 157, 160,
    162–63, 166, 173, 176
Grove, Allen W., 96–97, 120, 126

Habermas, Jürgen, 4, 14, 53, 60–61, 126, 182
halftone, 101, 116
Harmsworth London Magazine. *See* Harmsworth
    Monthly Pictorial
Harmsworth Magazine. *See* Harmsworth
    Monthly Pictorial
Harmsworth Monthly Pictorial, 5, 72, 76
Hayles, N. Katherine, 189
Heinlein, Robert A., 13
heliostat, 30, 48
Henley, W. E., 81
Henniker Heaton, J., 56
heteroglossia, 8, 27, 90–91, 93, 108, 182
hieroglyphics, 57
Hill, Jen, 137, 149, 151–52, 156

CAMBRIDGE STUDIES IN NINETEENTH-CENTURY LITERATURE AND CULTURE

General Editor
GILLIAN BEER, *University of Cambridge*